国家双高“铁道机车专业群”系列　多语种教材
——动车组检修技术专业

Operation and Management of High-speed Railway EMUs
高速铁路动车组运用与管理

（中英对照版）

主　编　宋慧娟　张龙华　时　蕾
副主编　宋振刚
主　审　石高山

西南交通大学出版社
·成　都·

图书在版编目（CIP）数据

高速铁路动车组运用与管理：中英对照版/宋慧娟，张龙华，时蕾主编. —成都：西南交通大学出版社，2022.6
ISBN 978-7-5643-8745-7

Ⅰ. ①高… Ⅱ. ①宋… ②张… ③时… Ⅲ. ①高速动车－高等职业教育－教材－汉、英 Ⅳ. ①U266

中国版本图书馆 CIP 数据核字（2022）第 103534 号

Operation and Management of High-speed Railway EMUs

高速铁路动车组运用与管理

（中英对照版）

主　编　宋慧娟　张龙华　时　蕾

责任编辑　张文越
封面设计　何东琳设计工作室

出版发行　西南交通大学出版社
（四川省成都市金牛区二环路北一段 111 号
西南交通大学创新大厦 21 楼）
邮政编码　610031
发行部电话　028-87600564　028-87600533
网址　http://www.xnjdcbs.com
印刷　四川森林印务有限责任公司

成品尺寸　185 mm × 260 mm
印张　17
字数　458 千
版次　2022 年 6 月第 1 版
印次　2022 年 6 月第 1 次
定价　58.00 元
书号　ISBN 978-7-5643-8745-7

课件咨询电话：028-81435775
图书如有印装质量问题　本社负责退换

PREFACE

Under the initiative of the Chinese government on the "one road and one belt", the international railway market has shown an obvious revival trend. Developed countries such as Europe, America, Japan and Russia have made great efforts to develop high-speed railway network. More and more developing countries such as central and Eastern Europe, Asia, Africa and Latin America have also given priority to railway development. With the increasingly frequent technical exchanges at home and abroad, it is very necessary for technicians engaged in EMU operation and management to master professional English knowledge to promote international exchanges and cooperation and understand the latest trends. On the basis of digesting and absorbing the technical data related to EMU management and operation provided by the EMU Depot of various railway bureaus, meeting the needs of English teaching, and proceeding from the actual needs, we have compiled the book *Operation and Management of High-speed Railway EMUs*. This book is prepared to conscientiously implement the relevant requirements of the post access system for the main types of running work of high-speed railway, ensure that a solid and reliable talent guarantee is provided for the operation, safety, sustainability and stability of high-speed railway at home and abroad, and quickly improve the professional level of students' practical application and maintenance.

This textbook mainly covers many disciplines, such as train operation organization, railway signal, EMU turnover, crew system, operation safety, train accident rescue, etc.. And there are also the basic knowledge that the machinist should master, the post responsibilities of the on-board machinist, and the emergency fault handling processes and methods in this book according to the post responsibilities of the on-board machinist of the railway corporation described. In terms of maintenance, it introduces the maintenance mode, characteristics, operation and maintenance process, operation steps, series standards, special operations, maintenance system and management of high-speed railway EMUs. In view of the type changes of high-speed railway running vehicles at present, this paper mainly introduces the relevant maintenance contents of CRH380A and CRH380B multiple units.

Huijuan Song, Longhua Zhang and Lei Shi of Zhengzhou Railway Vocational and Technical College are the editors of the book, Zhengang Song of CRCC Rail Transit Operation Ltd. is the associate editor, and Gaoshan Shi of EMUs Section of Zhengzhou Railway Bureau is the chief reviewer. The division of work is as follows: Lei Shi and Zhengang Song prepares Project 1(Chinese part); Huijuan Song prepares Project 1 (English part), Project 2 (Chinese and English part) and Project 3 (Chinese and English part); Longhua Zhang prepared Project 4 (Chinese and English part) and Project 5 (Chinese and English part).

Due to the rapid development of high-speed railway and the limited level of editors, it is inevitable that there are omissions and inadequacies in the book. Please criticize and correct them.

Editor
March 2022

前　言

在中国政府“一带一路”的倡议下，国际铁路市场呈现明显的复兴态势。欧美发达国家、日本、俄罗斯等大力发展高速铁路网，中东欧、亚、非、拉美等地区的越来越多的发展中国家也把铁路作为优先发展领域。随着国内外技术交流的日益频繁，对于从事动车组运用管理相关工作的技术人员来说，熟练掌握专业的英语知识对于促进国际交流与合作、了解国内外最新动态，是十分必要的。为了认真贯彻落实高速铁路主要行车工种岗位准入制度的相关要求，确保为国内外高铁运营及安全持续稳定提供坚实可靠的人才保障，快速提升学生的实际运用和检修的专业水平，在消化吸收各铁路局动车段提供的动车组管理及运行相关技术资料的基础上，满足英语教学需求，从实际需要出发，我们编写了《高速铁路动车组运用与管理》一书。

本教材主要涉及行车组织、铁路信号、动车组周转、乘务员乘务制度、运用安全、行车事故救援等多个专业，并且根据中国国家铁路集团有限公司（简称：国铁集团）随车机械师岗位职责讲述了机械师应掌握的基础知识、包括随车机械师岗位职责以及应急故障处理流程和方法。维修方面介绍了高速铁路动车组维修模式、特点、动车组运用及检修流程、作业步骤、系列标准、专项作业及动车组检修体系和管理方面的内容。针对目前高速铁路运行车辆的类型变化，着重介绍了 CRH380A、CRH380B 型动车组的相关检修内容。

全书由郑州铁路职业技术学院宋慧娟、张龙华、时蕾任主编，中铁建轨道运营有限公司宋振刚任副主编，郑州铁路局动车段段长石高山任主审。编写分工如下：时蕾、宋振刚编写项目一（中文部分）；宋慧娟编写项目一（英文部分）、项目二（中英文部分）、项目三（中英文部分）；张龙华编写项目四（中英文部分）、项目五（中英文部分）。

由于高速铁路发展较快，且编者水平所限，书中难免有遗漏和不妥之处，恳请读者批评指正。

编　者

2022 年 3 月

CONTENTS

目　录

Project 1

Overview of Motor Train Unit (EMU) Application and Maintenance

[Ideological and Political Classroom]

Fuxing EMU runs on the vast land of the motherland

"Fuxing EMU runs on the vast land of the motherland." The cordial speech of President Xi Jinping in the 2018 New Year's greetings is the encouragement and encouragement to the railway work, and is highly affirmed for the past few years, especially since the 18th National Congress of the Communist Party of China achievements in railway work.

In the past few years, the travel experience and happiness index of passengers have become higher and higher. The railway department continues to innovate service forms. From the basic requirements in the past to a series of new service measures such as high-speed rail WiFi, motor car takeout, wechat payment and face brushing in the station, it has increasingly met people's needs to go fast and well. The seemingly change in transportation demand is actually a higher requirement for railway transportation supply and enterprise development quality. Only when we always keep the people-centered development thought in mind can we do so.

Looking forward to the future, the development of China's railway is expected. With the high-speed railway, continue to expand the coverage of high-speed railway and make the transition of eight horizontal and eight vertical, which will further narrow people's "life circle" and enable more and more people to enjoy the fast and convenient high-speed railway. "Going out" is no longer a difficult problem, and tired trip has passed by. China Railway will start a new journey, and the continuously powerful independent innovation Fuxing EMU will lead the "made in China"; The continuous improvement of high-speed railway network will make the connection between large and medium-sized cities closer; The continuously open Chinese railway will contribute to China's strength in sharing; The continuously strengthened responsibility mission of "traffic power and railway first" will witness the historical responsibility of China's railway.

I have seen that the "Fuxing" carrying the Chinese dream of the great rejuvenation of the Chinese nation and the new yearning of the Chinese people for a better life is heading for another spring of the new era with full confidence and speed.

[Project Description]

At the end of this project, students are expected to understand the basic situation and characteristics of EMU application at home and abroad; understand the basic tasks of EMU application and maintenance. Through the analysis of the application and maintenance organization of EMU, students can recognize the responsibilities and management contents of organizations at all levels.

Task 1 Overview and Basic Task of EMU Operation

[Task Description]

1. Understand the Basic Situation and Characteristics of EMU Operation.

2. Clarify the Basic Tasks of EMU application and maintenance.

Ⅰ. *Basic Situation and Characteristics of EMU Operation*

1. Basic situation and characteristics of EMU operation abroad

The application of EMU varies greatly due to different national conditions. There are 4 types of high-speed railway construction management modes abroad. The first one is the newly-built high-speed railway special line which is used to transport passengers rapidly. For example, Japan's Shinkansen and France's high-speed railway are passenger special lines, which are operated during the day and maintained at night. Second, the newly-built high-speed railway double line which implements passenger and freight co-line operation, such as the Rome—Florence high-speed railway has a passenger speed of 225 km/h and freight speed of 120 km/h. Third, part of newly-built high-speed railway and part of the existing line mixed operation, such as the Berlin—Hannover line, which undertakes the task of transporting passengers and goods. Fourth, swing trains are used on existing lines, which is common in European countries. In the United States, the speed of swing trains on the "Northeast Corridor" also reaches 240 km/h. Different construction management modes make EMU operation management modes are not the same.

(1) Japan Shinkansen EMU operation.

Japan Shinkansen railway started operation in 1964, and after many years of practice, the Shinkansen Railway has gradually summed up and developed a set of train operation organization methods with Japanese characteristics. The basic process of the organizational method is as follows. Firstly, the train operation plan that reasonably and accurately reflects the transportation demand is formulated, and then various means are used to ensure the implementation of the train operation plan. When the train operation fluctuates, the necessary methods are used to restore the stable operation of the train as quickly as possible. As shown in Fig. 1-1, the operation, maintenance and standby of the Shinkansen line are reasonably coordinated with the operation diagram, and the skills of avoiding and crossing are skillfully used.

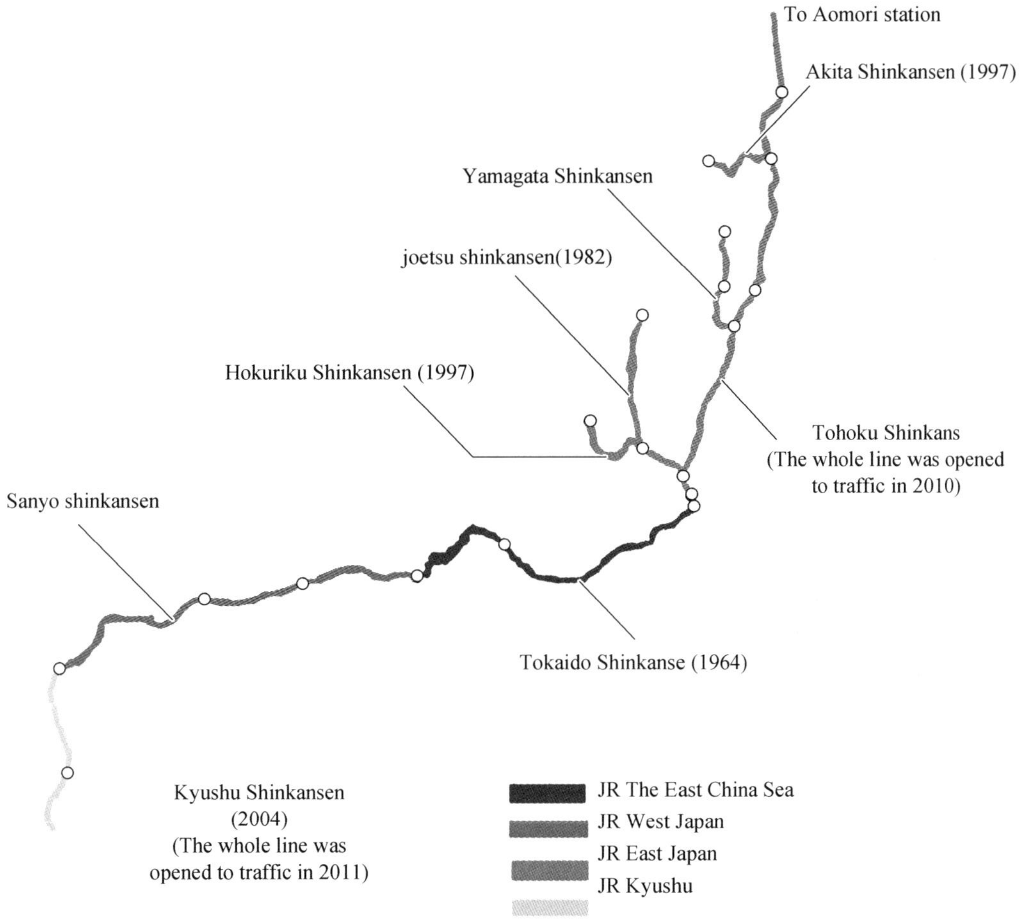

Fig. 1-1 Map of Shinkansen EMU in Japan

(2) German ICE EMU operation.

Since the 1970s, Germany has gradually formed an inter-city express train system (IC system) in all directions that connects more than 30 important cities and transportation centers (As shown in Fig. 1-2). Some sections of German high-speed railway are transformed from existing lines, and all high-speed lines are operated by passenger and freight trains. The basic organization model of German high-speed railway is the mixed operation of passenger trains with different speeds during the day and mixed operation of passenger trains and freight trains at night. The reason why Germany adopted this model is mainly that Germany has a relatively rich interval transit capacity, and the technical level of existing railway trains and high-speed trains are not very different.

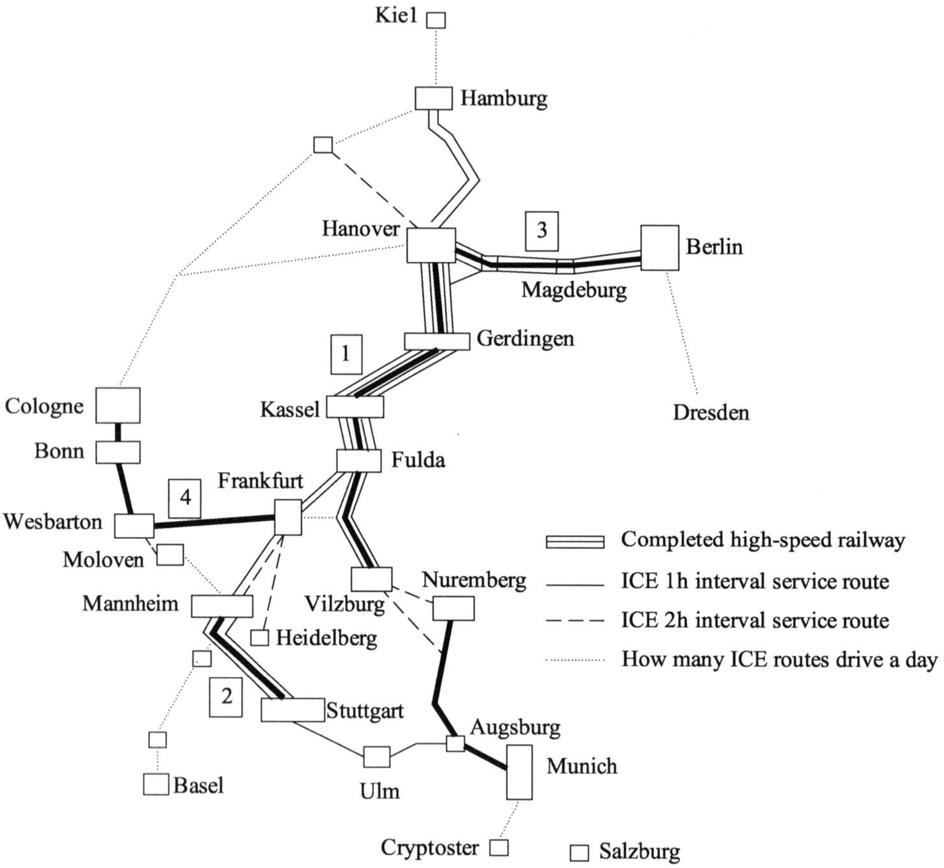

Fig. 1-2 Map of high speed railway in Germany

(3) France TGV EMU operation.

In terms of construction mode, French high-speed railway adopts the mode of partially constructing new lines and partially transforming old lines, radiating in all directions from the center of Paris, and is a special railway for passenger trains. Each high-speed line only runs the same type of high-speed trains, so train operation organization is relatively simple. The train operation line is parallel, and the train only stops at different stations and times. The whole train diagram is parallel. To meet the needs of passenger flow, high-speed trains running on high-speed lines can go down to existing lines.

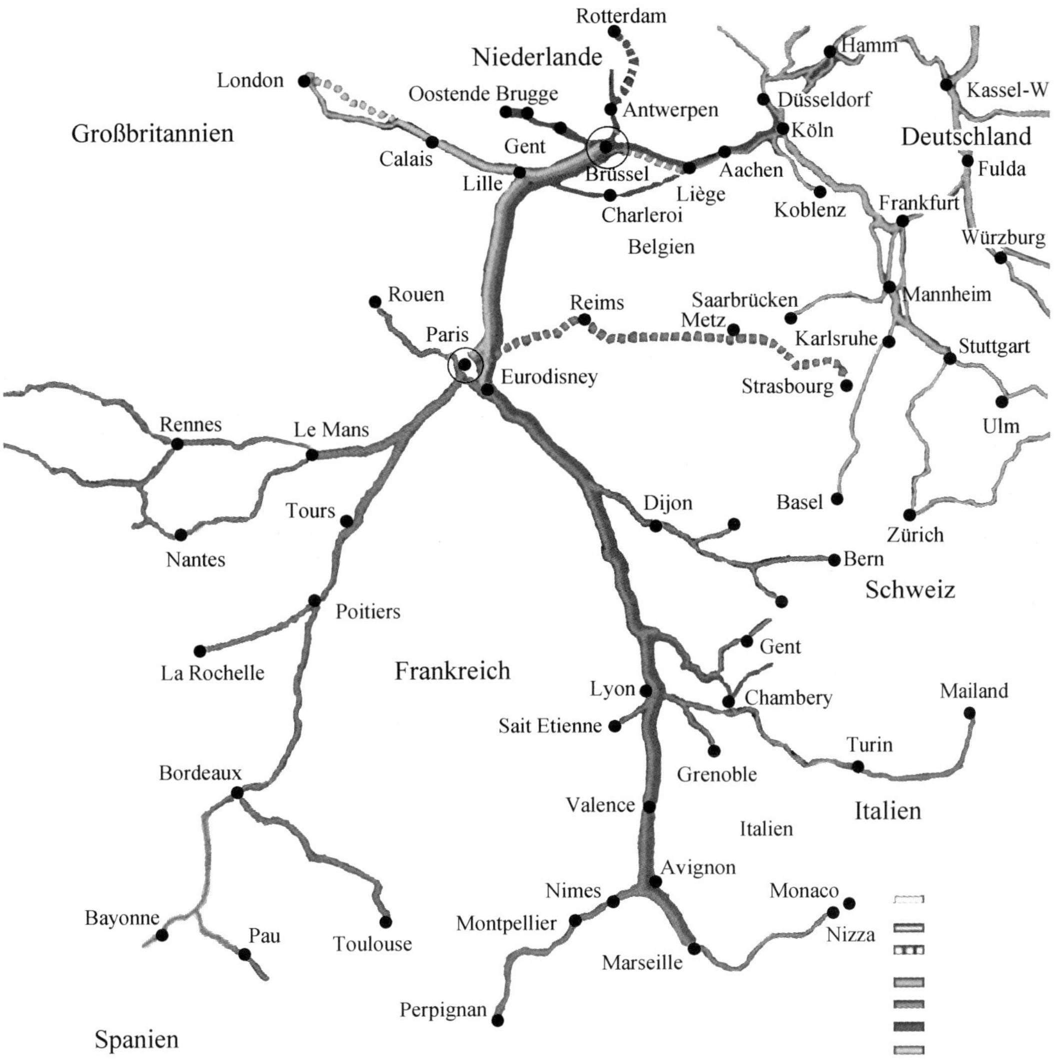

Fig. 1-3 Map of high speed railway in France

2. Basic situation and characteristics of EMU operation in China

(1) Basic situation of high speed railway lines in china.

China' s high-speed railway has entered a stage of rapid development since Beijing—Tianjin Intercity which is the first 350 km/h high-speed railway put into operation on August 1st, 2008. On December 26th, 2009, the Wuhan—Guangzhou section of Beijing—Hong Kong high-speed railway with the longest operating distance and the most complex project type in the world was put into operation. By the end of 2020, the operating length of high-speed railway and passenger special line in China has reached 39,000 km, accounting for more than 70% of the global high-speed railway operating distance. In 2020, the objectives required in the medium and long-term railway network planning issued on July

13rd, 2016 have been completed ahead of schedule. It is required in the document that "the scale of railway network will reach 150000 km, including 30,000 km of high-speed railway, covering more than 80% of large cities; by 2025, the scale of railway network will reach 175,000 km, including about 38,000 km of high-speed railway". According to the plan, by 2030, it will basically realize internal and external interconnection, smooth inter-regional multi-channel, provincial capital high-speed rail connection, rapid access to prefectures and cities, and basic coverage of the county.

(2) Basic characteristics of EMU operation in China.

So far, many passenger special lines have been built and completed in China, with a total investment of hundreds of EMUs, forming a beautiful scenery in railway transportation. China's EMU has many characteristics in operation:

① High operation speed: In the trial operation of the Beijing—Shanghai line, China's high-speed railway EMUs ran the world's highest operating speed (486.1 km/h), the highest operating speed on the Wuhan—Guangzhou high-speed railway is 394 km/h, and the continuous operating speed of EMUs on the Beijing—Tianjin Intercity and Beijing—Shanghai railway can also reach more than 350 km/h.

② Huge traffic volume: Affected by China's national conditions, under the existing railway conditions, China's high-speed railway multiple units reduce the train tracking interval as much as possible, increase the train passenger capacity as much as possible, and realize the shortest train tracking interval of 3 minutes.

③ High operational reliability: The critical instability speed of CRH series EMUs in China exceeds 550 km/h, which has excellent dynamic performance and excellent stability. In addition, CRH series EMUs are also equipped with new operation monitoring devices, which can realize real-time detection and control of their own parameters and performance changes. Moreover, the EMU also has the function of fault-oriented safety, and the train operation safety has a reliable guarantee.

④ Intelligent control: China's high-speed railway EMUs are connected into a system through a complete network. The highly intelligent computer control technology realizes the real-time control of the operation system and auxiliary system, so that the ground monitoring system can collect all aspects of information to judge the vehicle operation and status.

⑤ All-weather operation: When the wind speed is below grade 8, China's high-speed railway can operate continuously at the established speed of 350 km/h. It is also suitable for all kinds of bad weather such as wind, sand, rain and snow to achieve all-weather operation in the real sense.

Ⅱ *Basic Tasks of EMU Operation Management*

EMU is significant equipment to complete the production task of passenger transportation. The operation of EMU is an important part of railway transportation. The operation management of EMU adopts modern management means, establishes and improves accurate and rapid response communication network, information acquisition and data processing system, implements network management, and realizes orderly and controllable. Therefore, China National Railway Group Co., Ltd. has prepared the rules which are short for " Transport Regulations " for the operation and maintenance of Railway Multiple Units, which puts forward overall requirements for the operation and management of multiple units, and requires the operation personnel of multiple units at all levels to have a high sense of responsibility and realistic spirit and love their own work. Transport Regulations require EMU operators to work to achieve high standards and strict requirements as well as keep improving technology. It also requires EMU operators to take the overall situation into account, joint labor cooperation, obey orders and deep into practice to do a solid job.

The basic requirements of EMU operation management are :

① To manage and make good use of EMU, to complete transportation and production tasks with high quality and efficiency;

② To ensure traffic and personal safety by strengthening safety management ;

③ Strengthen the construction of the staff team, and constantly improve the political quality, technical quality and cultural knowledge level of workers

④ Adhere to the reform and opening up, promote advanced experience, follow the economic law, promote asset returns, and constantly improve the efficiency of EMU use.

Adhering to the principle of quality first and service for transportation, carrying out the policy of paying equal attention to repair and maintenance, giving priority to prevention, continuously strengthening basic work, perfecting the management system of operation and maintenance, and providing good quality EMU are the basic tasks of EMU operation and maintenance.

[Task Detection]

1. Summarize the characteristics of EMU operation.

2. Analyze and compare the operation and management modes of EMUs in Japan, Germany and France according to the operation and management of EMUs abroad.

3. What are the basic tasks of EMU Operation Management?

Task 2 Organization and Content of EMU Operation Management

[Task Description]

1. Clarify EMU Operation Organization and management content.

2. Know the usage and management classification of EMUs.

Ⅰ. *System and Responsibilities of EMU Operation Management Department*

The characteristics of railway operation management in China are as follows : ①To carry out the principle of ' unified command and hierarchical management ' so as to give full play to the function of operation management organizations at all levels; ②To implement of the responsibility system for safe production. Implement the requirements of ' Party and government responsibility, one post and two responsibilities, joint management, negligence responsibility' and 'leadership responsibility, professional responsibility, division of labor responsibility, post responsibility'. Use management organization as shown in Fig. 1-4.

EMUs implement the three-level professional management of China National Railway Group Co., Ltd., railway bureau and EMU (passenger train)depot.

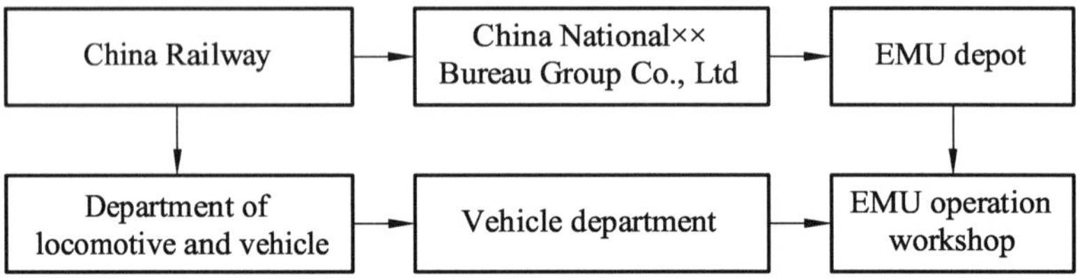

Fig. 1-4 Organizations of EMU operation management

1. China National Railway Group Co., Ltd.

China National Railway Corporation Limited which is short for "China Railway" is responsible for clarifying the management interface of EMU related disciplines; According to the transportation needs, the layout of operation and maintenance capacity of EMUs on the whole road shall be planned, and the allocation of transportation capacity resources shall be coordinated. China Railway formulates top-level management regulations on operation and maintenance of multiple units, supervise the implementation, and guide the transportation enterprises affiliated to the head office to carry out operation and maintenance.

2. China Railway ×× Bureau Group Co., Ltd.

Bureau Group Co., Ltd. is the liability subject of the professional management of EMUs. It is responsible for formulating the professional management measures of EMUs, clarifying the management functions of transportation-related professional departments, and assuming the safety and quality responsibilities for the operation and maintenance of its EMUs. According to the relevant management regulations such as maintenance rules and EMU technical manuals, they formulate relevant management measures and technical standards and organize the implementation.

3. Multiple unit train depot

Multiple unit train (passenger car)depot (hereinafter, all passenger car depots and Multiple unit train depots managed with motor car units are referred to as Multiple unit train depot, which is no longer distinguished)is the liability subject of the operation and maintenance of EMUs. Multiple unit train depot shall standardize the staffing and management of various departments in the depot, optimize the production organization and process, and coordinate the joint labor unit to jointly do a good job in the operation and maintenance of EMUs.

Ⅱ. *Management of EMU*

1. Technical management of EMU

Adopt the maintenance technology management system and organization of the head office, Railway Bureau and Multiple unit train depots, and clarify the division of responsibilities. The head office is responsible for organizing the formulation of EMU Operation and maintenance rules and other relevant management regulations; The railway administration is responsible for organizing the formulation of operation and maintenance methods for EMUs, and clarifying the maintenance items, maintenance cycle, maintenance contents, technical requirements and maintenance process; The motor car depot is responsible for organizing the preparation of operation instructions for the operation and maintenance of motor car units, and clarifying the operation contents, operation steps, operation standards, tooling and equipment, safety matters, etc.

The Railway Bureau shall allocate and strengthen professional and technical personnel according to the actual operation and maintenance of EMUs. The vehicle department shall be equipped with the director in charge of EMU and full-time management personnel such as operation, maintenance, safety, regulations, equipment and training. The technical responsibility system of the chief engineer shall be implemented in the multiple unit train depot, and full-time (Part-time)management personnel such as EMU operation, maintenance, machinery, axle, electrical, network, traction, braking, air conditioning, safety, regulations, equipment, training and informatization shall be equipped. Managers at all levels should strive to improve their technical literacy and abide by technical discipline.

The technical regulations for the operation and maintenance of EMUs shall be subject to hierarchical management. China National Railway Group Co., Ltd. is responsible for organizing the formulation of EMU Operation and maintenance standards and publishing them in the EMU management information system; The railway Bureau is responsible for organizing the formulation of operation and maintenance measures for EMUs, which shall be issued in the form of bureau documents; The multiple unit train depot is responsible for organizing the preparation of operation instructions for operation and maintenance of motor train units, which shall be issued in the form of deporting documents.

The use of maintenance methods must be combined with the actual optimization of maintenance projects, content and period. When the project, content is deleted, and the period is extended, it is reported for approval according to regulations.

The operation instructions shall specify the operation contents, operation steps, operation standards, tooling equipment, testing instruments, safety matters, etc. It shall require concise words and strong operability, and timely repair, build, supplement and scrap according to the actual situation and issue them regularly. When the maintenance parts, equipment and facilities change, multiple unit train depot shall organize the verification of the operation instructions.

The railway Bureau shall standardize the management of outsourced maintenance, formulate and apply the management measures for outsourced maintenance, and clarify the requirements for handling process, qualification review, quality card control, etc.

2. Repair system of EMU

The EMU implements a planned preventive maintenance system based on the running kilometer cycle (the running kilometer is subject to the EMU management information system)and supplemented by the time cycle. It is divided into five levels of repair. Level Ⅰ and Level Ⅱ maintenance is operation maintenance, which is carried out in the motor train station. Level Ⅲ、Level Ⅳ and level Ⅴ maintenance are high level maintenance, which shall be carried out in the maintenance unit with corresponding vehicle maintenance qualification.

3. Allocation management of EMU

EMUs are uniformly managed and allocated by China Railway, and the allocation system is implemented. The so-called allocation system refers to the system that China

Railway allocates EMUs to each Railway Bureau and EMU Depot for use and storage according to the needs of transportation tasks and transportation equipment conditions, so as to complete transportation and production tasks.

4. Road EMU

Road EMUs include EMUs for special purposes such as inspection, maintenance, test and official business, which shall be allocated by the China Railway.

The road EMUs allocated to non Railway Bureau units shall be entrusted to the Railway Bureau for custody and the custody agreement shall be signed.

The maintenance of road EMU vehicles and on-board electrical equipment shall be the responsibility of the allocated (Escrow)Railway Bureau, and the maintenance of professional equipment and facilities such as detection, maintenance and test shall be the responsibility of the property right unit.

Before the road EMU performs the tasks of road network inspection, maintenance and test, the user unit must communicate with the allocated (Escrow)Railway Bureau to formulate level Ⅰ and level Ⅱ maintenance plans to ensure that the maintenance does not exceed the time limit. The Railway Bureau designated by the inspection plan shall be responsible for the level Ⅰ maintenance and servicing operations; The assigned (Escrow)railway bureau is responsible for the level Ⅱ maintenance.

The Special Transportation Office of the China Railway is responsible for the operation, maintenance and repair of the official EMU. When the operating EMU is changed to road EMU, it must be reported to the China Railway for approval.

5. EMU retirement

When EMUs are identified to have one of the following conditions, they can complete the whole or part of the vehicle scrap procedures.

(1) The operation of the whole EMU exceeds the design life and cannot continue to be used after technical appraisal. (As shown in Tab. 1-1)

Tab. 1-1 Design Life List of EMUs

Number	EMU Model	Design Life(year)
1	CRH1A/1B/1E	25
2	CRH1A-A CRH1E(1229-1233)	20
3	CRH2A/2B/2E/2G/2C	20
4	CRH3C	30
5	CRH5A	20
6	CRH5G	20

Continue

7	CRH380A(L)	20
8	CRH380B(L)	20
9	CRH380CL	20
10	CRH380D	20
11	CRH6A/F	20
12	CRH3A	20
13	CR400AF/BF	30

(2) The repair cost exceeds 70% of its replacement price in case of an accident or accidental disaster of the whole or part of the EMU; Or the car body structure is deformed and damaged seriously and cannot be repaired.

Retirement procedure:

① The scrapping identification of EMUs shall be organized by the allocation Bureau. In case of scrapping at the place of accident, the allocation bureau can entrust the local railway bureau. In case of manufacturing and repair enterprises, the allocation bureau shall entrust the manufacturing and repair enterprises to organize appraisal, and the allocation bureau shall send personnel to participate.

② If the appraisal committee has identified that it meets the conditions for scrapping, the property right unit shall follow the prescribed procedures and report it to the China Railway for approval.

③ The scrapped EMUs approved by the China Railway are not allowed to rent, sell or transfer the whole or part of the vehicles.

Ⅲ *EMU Inspection and Repair*

1. EMU maintenance plan

The operation and maintenance plan of EMU shall be prepared monthly, weekly and daily, and the high-level maintenance plan shall be prepared annually and monthly. The < EMU buckle repair list >shall be filled in before EMU is sent for high-level maintenance. The EMU level Ⅱ maintenance monthly plan shall be prepared by the EMU Depot and reported to the Railway Bureau for filing. The level Ⅱ maintenance weekly plan and operation maintenance daily plan shall be prepared and organized by the motor train station. The one level maintenance time of EMU in the inspection shed shall not be less than 4 hours. EMU depot shall strengthen the management of EMU maintenance plan and strive to improve the fulfillment rate of EMU maintenance plan. The group items that are not fulfilled as planned shall be adjusted in time and shall not be out of repair.

2. One-level maintenance of EMUs

Level Ⅰ maintenance refers to the maintenance operation of rapid routine inspection, test and fault treatment for the roof, bottom, sides, inner and driver's cab of EMU in operation, which must be inspected and implemented in the depot of the EMU. The number of operation teams shall be reasonably determined in combination with the intensive entry (exit)of EMUs and the workload of each shift. EMUs staying for more than 48 hours must undergo level Ⅰ maintenance before going online. In principle, one level maintenance of EMU shall be carried out in this substation, except for the following cases.

(1) EMU diagram designated outside maintenance. The allocation section must sign the entrusted maintenance agreement with the maintenance section to clarify the quality, safety responsibility, maintenance cost and other relevant contents.

(2) In case of bad weather and other special conditions, one level maintenance of EMU may be overdue, and it is necessary to enter the foreign EMU station for maintenance. The responsible bureau shall timely submit an application for maintenance to the local railway bureau. The local railway bureau shall actively organize and arrange, and the responsible bureau shall cooperate well.

When the EMU enters the external station for maintenance, the allocation section must sign the entrusted maintenance agreement with the maintenance section to clarify the quality, safety responsibility, maintenance cost and other relevant contents. After level Ⅰ maintenance, the completion form shall be filled in <EMU level Ⅰ maintenance completion list>.

3. Two-level maintenance of EMUs

Level Ⅱ maintenance refers to the periodic maintenance, inspection and test of all systems and parts of EMU, without omission or overdue. When detaining the train for centralized maintenance, <EMU buckle repair list>must be filled in, and < EMU buckle repair completion list > must be filled in after the repair. The multiple unit train depot shall reasonably combine the maintenance items of "the same cycle, close parts and similar nature", evenly arrange the maintenance plan and optimize the production organization. Level Ⅱ maintenance can be carried out by detaining maintenance or combined with level Ⅰ maintenance.

4. EMU temporary repair

When the EMU needs to be detained for temporary repair due to failure, <EMU buckle repair list>must be filled in, and < EMU buckle repair completion list > must be filled in after repair.

5. Installation and transformation of EMU

The structural change, parameter adjustment and software upgrading of EMU shall be approved according to relevant regulations. The installation and transformation can be carried out in EMU manufacturing and repair enterprises or multiple unit train depot and motor train station with transformation conditions.

6. Information management of EMU

EMU management information system which is short for information system bellow shall be designed, constructed and used synchronously with multiple unit train depot and motor train station to form a comprehensive and highly integrated information platform to realize modern management and scientific decision-making.

The information system shall comply with relevant national and railway information security regulations. The information system shall meet the four-level management and production requirements of the China Railway, Railway Bureau, multiple unit train depot and motor train station. The automation equipment and other relevant systems of multiple unit train depot and motor train station shall realize information interaction with the information system. The railway Bureau shall formulate management measures for the use and maintenance of information systems and actively promote the construction, use and maintenance of information systems; Relying on the information system, through the accumulation and analysis of application and maintenance data, constantly standardize the business process, improve the maintenance process and optimize the maintenance system.

7. Technical diversion of EMU

Technical changes such as EMU structure change, performance parameter adjustment, software optimization and upgrading shall be approved in accordance with relevant regulations. Technical changes can be carried out in EMU manufacturing and repair enterprises or multiple unit train depot and motor train station with implementation conditions.

Ⅳ. *EMU Operation*

1. EMU train diagram

The train diagram of multiple units is the main basis for the operation of multiple units. To ensure the normal implementation of the train diagram, the EMU type, quantity, main technical parameters, maintenance operation standards, maintenance, storage, service capacity and other factors of the EMU shall be fully considered when compiling the diagram. The number and location of hot standby EMUs shall be relatively fixed, which shall be determined by the Railway Bureau. The railway bureau's vehicle department should actively participate in the demonstration of EMU train operation scheme and the outline of train bottom routing and strictly implement EMU technical operation standards to ensure safety moreover optimize EMU Operation and Improve Efficiency. The multiple unit train depot shall scientifically prepare the EMU operation plan according to the EMU Operation Diagram, the maintenance, storage, servicing capacity and maintenance standards of the motor train station, and improve the on-line rate, reasonably use the EMU, and minimize the intensive maintenance of high level maintenance. The multiple unit train depot shall scientifically arrange the crew plan of the on-board machinist of the EMU, reasonably arrange the on-duty routing, and overwork is strictly prohibited. Each railway bureau shall draw the trial operation route of EMU according to the actual situation, and the trial operation can be carried out by using the comprehensive inspection, weekend, peak and other operation lines according to the test items when conditions permit.

2. EMU marshalling

Single-row EMU is a fixed formation, and its operation state cannot be disassembled. Two identical short train units (8 units) can be coupled. The reconnection and unmarshalling of multiple train units shall be carried out in accordance with the <measures for reconnection and unmarshalling of multiple train units>. It is forbidden to add various types of locomotives and vehicles to the EMU (Shunting machine or dual-purpose vehicle of highway and railway when there is no power shunting, locomotive and return transition vehicle when there is rescue or no power return). EMU shall not be incorporated into other trains.

3. Pick-up and drop EMU

When locomotive shunting operation is adopted, the on-board mechanic or competent personnel of multiple unit train depot shall be responsible for the connection and disassembly of transition coupler, special air duct and electrical connecting line, and open the door. The shunting personnel shall be responsible for the connection and disassembly of coupler and hose.

4. EMU running

It is strictly prohibited to put on-line operation of overdue EMUs.

Passenger train inspection is not arranged for EMU at departure, arrival and passing stations for technical operation. Railway Bureau shall actively promote the use of dynamic image detection system for EMU operation faults, aiming to effectively improve the operation safety prevention ability of EMU.

The infrared hotbox detection system must detect the axle temperature of the operating

EMU. When the system detecting the axle and alarming, Infrared ray attendant should alarm the train dispatching but should not stop the train. The train dispatching shall immediately notify the driver of the EMU, and the driver of the EMU shall immediately notify the on-board machinist of the EMU. The on-board machinist of the EMU shall determine whether the EMU continues to run according to the detection situation of the on-board axle temperature detection system. The driver of the EMU shall give feedback on handling situation to the train dispatching, and the train dispatching shall give feedback to the infrared duty officer.

In case of fault during the operation of EMU train, the EMU driver shall handle it in time according to the prompts of on-board information monitoring device; When it needs to be handled by the on-board mechanic of EMU, the on-board mechanic of EMU shall be notified. When it is confirmed that it cannot operate normally after disposal, the driver of the EMU shall select the mode of maintaining operation or stopping according to the prompt of the on-board information monitoring device and the requirements of the on-board mechanic of the EMU, and report to the train dispatcher.

After discovering or receiving the notice of vehicle equipment fault, the on-board mechanic of EMU shall timely identify the fault, correctly handle it according to the EMU emergency fault handling manual, and report the fault information as required. The responsible person shall input the fault information into the EMU management information system within 1 hour after the fault occurs.

Before the on-board mechanic of EMU gets off the train to check and deal with the fault, he shall apply for the speed limit of the adjacent line according to relevant regulations.

EMU and locomotive can be used for rescue, and EMU rescue is preferred. The specific implementation shall be in accordance with the measures for mutual rescue of multiple units.

CRH2C and CRH380A EMUs are not allowed to be overcrowded, and the overcrowding rate of other EMUs shall not exceed 15%. Evacuation shall be carried out when personnel are too concentrated during operation.

5. EMU shunting

In principle, EMU shunting adopts the power mode. The locomotive department shall set EMU ground service drivers in multiple unit train depot and EMU station to be responsible for shunting operation.

When locomotive shunting operation is adopted, the on-board machinist of EMU or competent personnel of multiple unit train depot (station)are responsible for the connection and disassembly of transition coupler, special air duct and electrical connecting line, and opening the door. Shunting personnel are responsible for the connection and disassembly of coupler and hose.

The speed limit of EMU through maintenance and detection equipment shall be implemented according to the specific equipment technical conditions. The speed limit of main equipment is as follows:

Tread diagnosis equipment: passing speed limit: 30 km/h; The detection speed limit is 8–12 km/h.

Non-wheel dropping lathe, bogie replacement and wheel dropping equipment: the speed limit is 5 km/h.

Car washing machine: the speed limit is 3–5 km/h during self-running; The speed limit of tractor traction is 1.5–3 km/h.

Track bridge: speed limit 10 km/h.

6. EMU return

The EMU shall be returned when required by new allocation, allocation, rental, maintenance, etc. The return of EMU is generally carried out by special train. According to the usable state of EMU power, it can be divided into powered return and unpowered return, also known as live return and unpowered return. The return specification of EMU is quite different from that of locomotives and vehicles on existing lines. See relevant contents of project III for details.

The return of EMU shall be handled as per passenger train, and the powered return controlled by ATP shall be adopted in principle. When the high-speed railway line is parallel to the existing line, the return of high-speed railway line shall be arranged as far as possible. Two short marshaling (8-car marshaling)EMUs of the same type can be reconnected and sent back. When there is no power return, the maximum speed limit is 120 km/h. During return, emergency braking shall be avoided as far as possible; In case of emergency braking, the driver of the EMU shall notify the on-board mechanic of the EMU to get off the train and confirm that the transition coupler is in good condition before driving. When it is necessary to attach a return transition vehicle, the transition vehicle shall be determined through consultation between the user unit and the host enterprise, and personnel shall be sent to escort to ensure the safety of return.

7. EMU delivery-receiving

When the EMU is newly manufactured, advanced maintenance, transferred and leased, it is necessary to handle the handover of technical status, onboard tools and spare parts, technical resume, technical data (only newly manufactured and delivered), maintenance records (the latest level Ⅱ maintenance records), etc. The vehicle department shall take the lead in organizing the pick-up and delivery of EMUs. When newly manufactured, transferred and leased between bureaus, the access bureau shall establish a receiving team composed of locomotive, electrical and vehicle disciplines; During advanced maintenance, the allocation bureau shall establish a receiving (sending)train group composed of locomotive, electrical and vehicle disciplines.

8. EMU commissioning

In case of the following circumstances, EMU trial operation shall be arranged

Simulation and special commissioning shall be organized and arranged by the head office. Newly built, advanced maintenance, temporary repair and trial operation shall be organized by the Railway Bureau. The order shall be requested by the multiple unit train depot and arranged by the dispatching office. In case of inter Bureau trial operation, the dispatching office of Railway Bureau shall apply to the head office for dispatching order according to the application of vehicle department. Before trial operation, the multiple unit train depot shall organize relevant departments to carry out maintenance and servicing of motor car units to ensure that they are in good technical condition. In case of the following circumstances, EMU trial operation shall be arranged.

(1) Simulation test run (before the new EMU is officially put into operation or when the new line is opened).

(2) After the newly manufactured EMU leaves the factory and the advanced maintenance is completed.

(3) After temporary repair and replacement of bogie, wheel set, universal shaft, main transformer and traction motor.

(4) Special commissioning.

[Task Detection]

1. Briefly describe the system and responsibilities of EMU Operation Management Department.

2. What is the allocation principle of EMU?

3. What are the classifications of EMU management?

Project 2

Organization Management of EMU Operation

[Ideological and Political Classroom]

In the early 1990s, the construction plan of high-speed railway has been put forward. However, the construction method has aroused controversy and demonstration for more than ten years. The dispute between "maglev faction" and "wheel rail faction" is a significant symbol in the history of laying the foundation of China's high-speed rail technology theory. At that time, maglev faction believed that maglev train represented the development trend of high-speed rail technology in the future, while wheel rail faction believed that building wheel rail high-speed rail was the top priority both technically and in terms of project cost. The 18 year debate can be regarded as an ideological enlightenment on high-speed railway. During this period, the repeated discussion and exploration on how to build high-speed railway and what standards to build high-speed railway have just laid a solid technical and theoretical foundation. Finally, considering the compatibility with China's existing wheel rail technology and cost, the wheel rail technology is selected.

In early 2004, China prepared to popularize high-speed rail throughout the country, but it was unable to design and manufacture it by itself. So the Chinese railway department held an international bidding. Many international bidders such as Japan's Kawasaki, Germany's Siemens, Canada's Bombardier and France's Alstom participated. Instead of selecting a bidder, China's railway authorities require each enterprise to design and produce its own type of high-speed train. The condition is that China's signal standards must be accepted. In this way, China's high-speed rail network runs various trains of brand enterprises in different countries. At this stage, China has basically mastered the manufacturing technology of high-speed trains with speeds of 200–250 km/h through introduction, digestion and absorption.

Next, China put forward new requirements for trains, that is, up to 380 km/h. In order to overcome technical barriers, China has established a special team since the end of 2008. The role of this team is to solve key technical problems. The team consists of Qingdao SiFang, CRRC, CRRC Tangshan, 25 universities in China, 56 key laboratories and 500 original equipment manufacturers. It includes more than 500 researchers and about 10,000 engineers. With the efforts of everyone, in 2010, China successfully designed its own vehicle integration, aerodynamics, topology, load-bearing system, dynamic transmission, braking system, train control and operation system, traction power supply and key material components. The first independently designed Chinese high-speed train 380-A was officially launched.

Up to now, China has mastered the complete set technology of designing and manufacturing high-speed EMU trains with different speed levels to meet various operation needs, and has a strong independent innovation ability of system integration, adaptation modification, comprehensive solution and localization. Finally, China Railway has formed its own technical standards and design, and completed the transformation from "made in China" to "created in China".

At present, China's high-speed rail technology has been at the forefront of the world, and has begun to compete in the global high-speed rail market. It has undertaken 60% of the world's high-speed rail network, mainly involving the following countries: Indonesia, Pakistan, Laos, Thailand, Russia, Ethiopia, etc. China's high-speed railway is striding towards the world.

The development of EMUs in China is the road of independent innovation, and only independent innovation can be in the forefront of high-speed railways in the world.

[Project Description]

At the end of this project, students are expected to understand the main job responsibilities of each discipline of EMU and be familiar with the management regulations of EMU professional interface. Students should be familiar with the safety management regulations of EMU and the emergency response plan for fire and explosion accidents and master the train operation organization rules of EMU. Students should be familiar with the requirements of EMU receiving, dispatching and operation and be familiar with the provisions of various emergency plans. Understand the anti-freezing management measures for EMU parking.

Task 1 Regulations on Professional Management of EMUs

[Task Description]

1. Understand the main job responsibilities of each discipline of EMU.
2. Get familiar with the interface management regulations of EMU discipline.

Ⅰ. *Professional Staffing and Affiliation of All Disciplines of EMU*

(1) The leading driver and ground service driver of EMU are under the management of locomotive depot.

(2) The on-board mechanic, the vehicle dispatcher at the storage point and the ground service mechanic are under the management of the multiple unit train depot.

(3) Passenger crew (train conductor and train attendant)are under the management of passenger depot.

(4) The staffing and affiliation relationship of EMU are shown in Fig. 2-1.

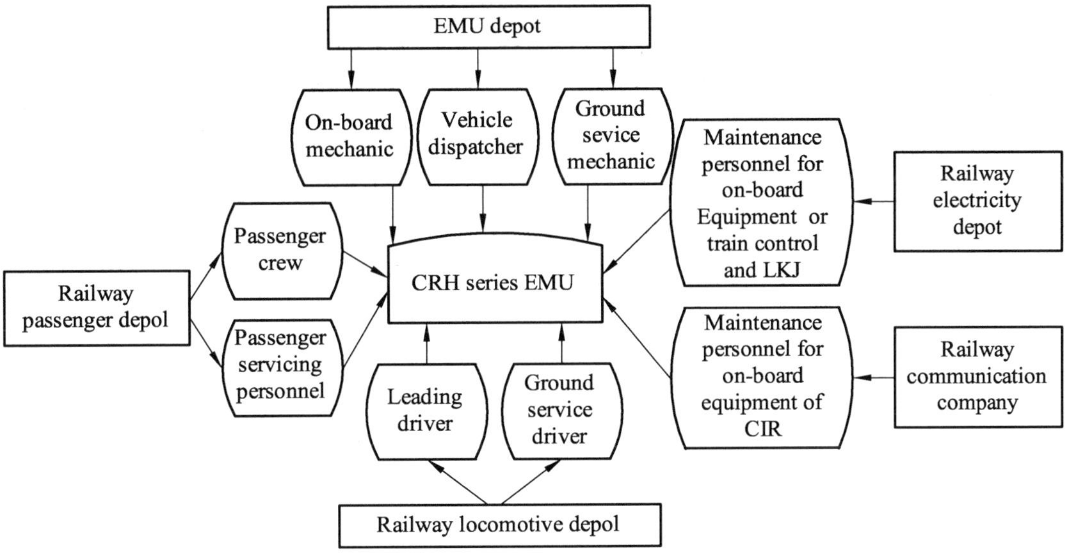

Fig. 2-1 The staffing and affiliation relationship of EMU

Ⅱ. *Main Job Responsibilities*

1. Leading driver

(1) Earnestly implement rules and regulations, obey orders, obey commands, and earnestly perform specified duties.

(2) When the EMU is forced to stop in the section, the leading driver shall be responsible for commanding the on-board machinist and passenger crew to deal with relevant accident rescue and other matters.

(3) After leaving the station, the leading driver shall be responsible for the door centralized control switch of EMU. At the station, leading driver shall be responsible for stopping the train at the specified position and opening the door; Also closing the door according to the notice of the passenger crew before driving.

(4) In case of failure during the operation of EMU, it shall be handled in time according to steps according to the prompt of on-board information monitoring device; Inform the on-board machinist when it needs to be handled with the cooperation of the on-board machinist.

(5) Be responsible for handing over the technical status of EMU driving, train control on-board equipment, LKJ, CIR equipment and braking system, master control key, cab door key and train control on-board equipment cabinet key with the ground driver in the cab at the operation end of EMU in the operation station (or storage point).

2. Ground service driver

(1) Earnestly implement rules and regulations, obey orders, obey commands, and earnestly perform specified duties.

(2) When the EMU enters and exits the operation post (storage point), it shall be responsible for handing over the technical status of EMU driving, train control on-board equipment, LKJ, CIR equipment and braking system, master control key, cab door key and train control on-board equipment cabinet key with the service driver.

(3) When the EMU leaves the depot, it shall be responsible for confirming the technical status of train safety equipment and handling the handover of train safety equipment certificate with relevant train safety equipment maintenance units; Be responsible for handing over the technical status of driving equipment with the quality inspector of EMU station.

(4) Be responsible for shunting operation of EMU.

(5) Be responsible for the setting and removal of anti-slip of EMUs parked outside the inspection and repair shed.

3. On-board mechanic

(1) Earnestly implement rules and regulations, obey orders, obey commands, and earnestly perform specified duties.

(2) Be responsible for monitoring the technical status of EMU during operation, timely notifying the driver of relevant information in case of fault, and taking measures to deal with it properly.

(3) When the EMU enters and exits the station, it shall be responsible for handling the technical handover with the operation station (quality inspector); Handle the key handover of door centralized control switch with the dispatcher or ground service mechanic.

(4) Handle accident rescue and other matters under the command of the driver.

(5) In case of faults endangering driving safety or other emergencies, use the emergency brake valve to stop or notify the driver to take stopping measures.

4. Passenger crew

(1) Earnestly implement rules and regulations, obey orders, obey commands, and earnestly perform specified duties.

(2) In case of an emergency endangering the safety of driving and passengers, use the emergency brake valve to stop or notify the driver to take measures; When it is necessary to organize passengers to evacuate the train, the driver shall be notified, and the driver shall report to the train dispatcher or notify the attendant of the nearest station; Handle accident rescue and other matters under the command of the driver.

5. Vehicle dispatcher at EMU storage point

(1) Organize and coordinate the operation of each discipline according to the operation plan, convey orders and register before and after operation.

(2) Be responsible for the on-board mechanic's check-in and check-out, and the management of EMU master control key, cab door key, door centralized control switch key and train control on-board equipment cabinet key.

(3) Be responsible for organizing, coordinating and handling matters related to EMU and reporting in time.

6. Ground service mechanic of EMU storage site

(1) Responsible for the use and management of EMU equipment.

(2) Be responsible for coordinating the shunting, passenger servicing, cleaning and sewage suction operations at the storage point, and checking the quality of sewage suction operations.

(3) Be responsible for anti-freezing of EMU.

(4) Handle handover with the on-board mechanic of EMU at the storage point.

Ⅲ. *Professional Interface Management of EMU*

(1) EMU operation management.

The multiple unit train depot shall complete the operation and maintenance of the EMU according to the specified repair process and system so as to ensure that the technical state of the EMU meets the standard requirements when it leaves the depot. The locomotive depot shall set shift dispatching room and waiting room in the EMU operation station, and arrange the driver of the locomotive to go on duty as planned.

(2) On-board equipment management of EMU.

The signaling depot is responsible for train control on-board equipment and LKJ equipment, Tietong is responsible for cir equipment, and the depot is responsible for the maintenance of on-board broadcasting equipment. Maintenance points for the above equipment shall be set in the operation station to be responsible for the inspection, inspection and maintenance of relevant access stations.

(3) Use and management of in vehicle equipment.

The power distribution panel of EMU, air conditioning, lighting and passenger information system equipment in the vehicle shall be operated by the onboard mechanic. The passenger transport depot is responsible for recording the broadcast content of the automatic broadcasting device according to the specified requirements, and the rolling stock depot is responsible for inputting the automatic broadcasting device. In case of equipment failure, the passenger steward shall notify the onboard mechanic to deal with it in time. In case of equipment damage during operation, the onboard machinist and the conductor shall jointly confirm and fill in the damage record of upper facilities, which shall be signed by both parties.

(4) Servicing and cleaning management of EMU.

The passenger transport department shall be responsible for the passenger servicing and interior cleaning of the EMU, and the vehicle department shall be responsible for the skin cleaning and sewage absorption of the EMU.

(5) The EMU shall be taken care of by the department designated by the railway bureau.

(6) EMU operation management.

The maintenance, passenger servicing and cleaning of on-board driving safety equipment (train control on-board equipment, CIR equipment and LKJ equipment)must be uniformly included in the operation and maintenance plan of EMU and managed by the operation office. Before operation, ground service drivers, ground service mechanics, passenger servicing personnel, sewage suction operators, caretakers and other relevant operators shall report to the dispatcher of the operation station and accept the order; After the completion of each professional operation, register with the dispatcher and fill in the maintenance completion form.

(7) EMU shunting management.

The operation of EMU access post (storage point)shall be determined by each railway bureau according to the specific situation; The ground handling driver shall be responsible for the operation of EMU transfer and shunting in the depot (or storage point)according to the arrangement of the EMU. Each railway bureau shall formulate detailed shunting operation methods according to specific conditions.

(8) EMU storage point management.

① The EMU storage point set by the railway bureau must meet the storage conditions of EMUs and report to the Ministry for approval.

Each bureau shall set dispatchers, ground service mechanics and ground service drivers at the EMU storage point, and establish operation registration system, key handover management system and check-in and check-out system. According to the opinions of the former Ministry of Railways on the sixth large-scale railway speed increase and adjustment map on the labor organization, staff training and salary distribution of EMUs (TLW [2007] No. 67), the dispatchers and ground service mechanics required for the storage point of EMUs shall be adjusted and solved by the Railway Bureau.

② Operation management of storage point.

For the parked EMUs without maintenance, the railway bureau of the parking place shall designate relevant units to be responsible for the pollution absorption, antifreeze, passenger servicing, cleaning and other operations and custody of the EMUs, and arrange the waiting, rest and pick-up conditions for the crew; The management of the EMU that does not carry out maintenance operation shall be carried out by reference to the external EMU.

(9) Handover management of EMU.

① When the EMU enters the operation station or storage point, the service driver and the ground handling driver shall handle the status handover of driving equipment and driving safety equipment and the handover of master control key, cab door key and train control on-board equipment cabinet key, and submit the EMU Operation Status handover form.

The ground handling driver shall hand over the master control key, cab door key and train control on-board equipment cabinet key with the dispatcher, and hand over the operation technical status of train control on-board equipment and LKJ and cir with the personnel of the train safety equipment maintenance unit. When the EMU enters the EMU Depot, the onboard machinist and the dispatcher shall handle the handover of the technical status of the EMU and the key of the door centralized control switch, and fill in the handover record. When the EMU enters the storage point, the onboard machinist and the ground machinist shall handle the handover of the technical status of the EMU and the key of the door centralized control switch, and fill in the handover record; The on-board mechanic shall sign in at the dispatcher with the handover record; The ground mechanic and the dispatcher shall handle the key handover of the door centralized control switch.

② Before the EMU leaves the operation station, the quality inspector of the EMU shall organize the ground handling driver, passenger transport personnel, on-board machinist, train control on-board equipment, LKJ and cir maintenance unit to carry out ex warehouse joint inspection, and fill in the ex warehouse joint inspection record sheet.

The passenger transport personnel shall be responsible for checking and confirming the integrity of service facilities in the carriage and handling handover with the quality inspector; The on-board mechanic is responsible for the inspection and confirmation of the technical status of the EMU and handling the handover with the quality inspector; The train safety equipment maintenance unit is responsible for checking and confirming the train control on-board equipment, LKJ and cir equipment out of the warehouse, filling in the train safety equipment certificate, the ground handling driver confirming the technical status of the train safety equipment, and handling the certificate handover with the maintenance unit; The service driver and the ground handling driver shall handle the handover of driving safety equipment certificate and technical status of driving equipment.

③ Before the EMU leaves the storage point, the ground service mechanic, on-board mechanic and ground service driver shall sign in at the dispatcher.

The ground handling driver shall obtain the master control key, cab door key and train control on-board equipment cabinet key from the dispatcher, and be responsible for confirming the technical status of driving safety equipment; The ground service driver removes the anti-slip, and the service driver signs the anti-slip removal record; Both parties shall handle the handover of master control key, cab door key and train control on-board equipment cabinet key in the cab at the control end. The driver of this service is responsible for confirming the technical status of driving equipment and filling in the handover record. The ground handling machinist shall obtain the key of door centralized control switch from the dispatcher, handle the technical status and key handover of EMU with the onboard machinist, and fill in the handover record. The ground handling driver and ground handling mechanic shall hand over the handover record to the dispatcher.

④ The following ride of EMU shall be handed over by the driver of this service and the accompanying mechanic according to the regulations.

⑤ Key handover management of train control on-board equipment cabinet. When the train control on-board equipment and LKJ access station are tested, the equipment testing unit and the operation station shall handle the key handover.

(10)The service driver of EMU shall carefully fill in the handover form of EMU operation technical status.

According to the professional management regulations of EMU, the safe operation of EMU requires the cooperative operation between various departments of the railway system. The interface management relationship between the designed departments can be summarized as shown in Fig. 2-2.

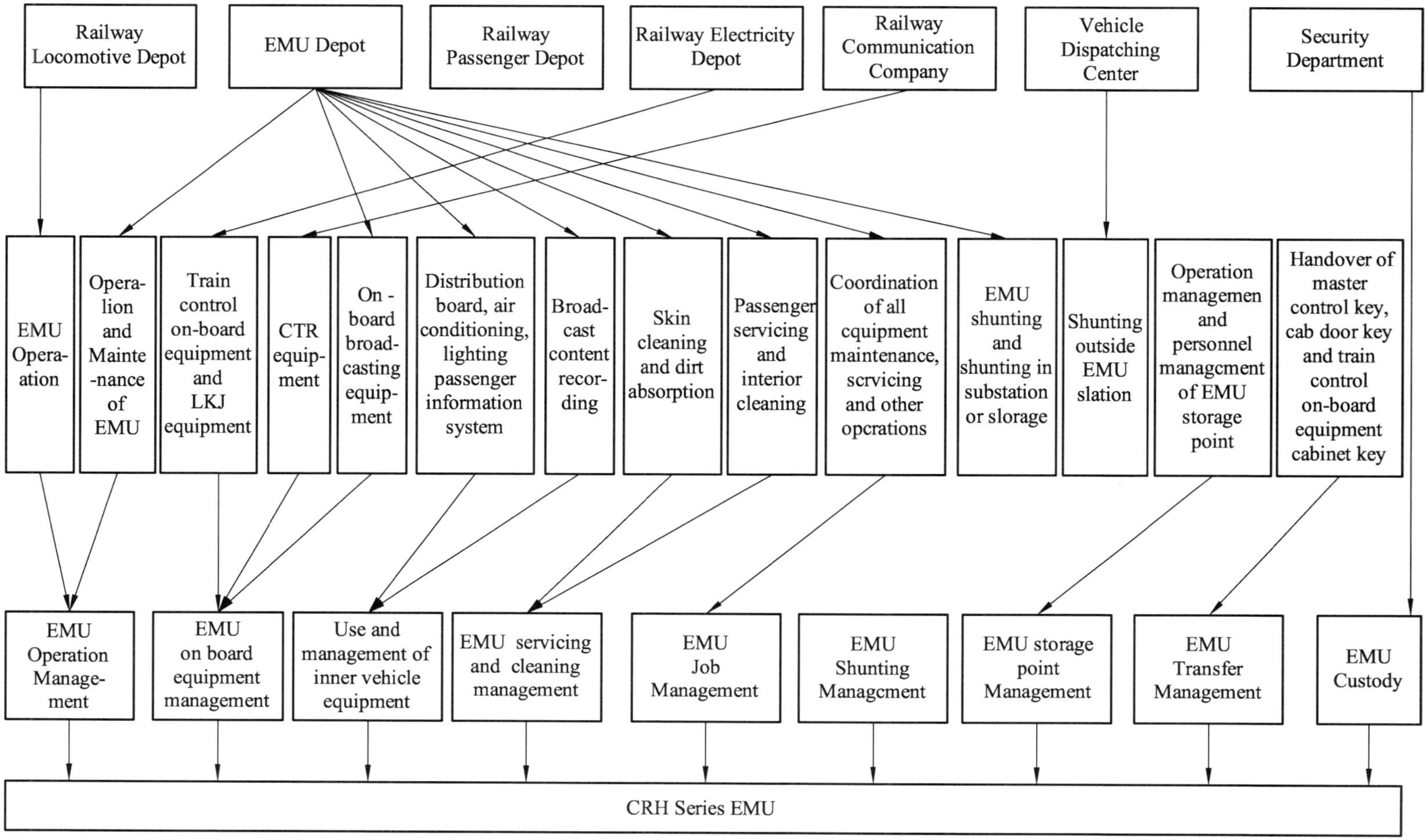

Fig. 2-2 Interface management relationship between operation and maintenance departments of EMU

[Task Detection]

1. Give an example to illustrate the numbering rules of EMU.
2. What are the responsibilities of the main driver of EMU?
3. What are the responsibilities of EMU ground service driver?
4. What are the regulations on handover management of EMU?

Task 2 Regulations on Operation Safety Management of Multiple Units

[Task Description]

(1) Get familiar with the safety management measures of EMU.

(2) Recognize the allocation, use and management classification of EMUs.

Ⅰ. *Safety Rules*

(1) The crew members of the train (conductor, cleaner, caterer, waiter, vehicle mechanic and traffic policeman)shall accept the unified leadership of the conductor, take their own responsibilities and perform their own duties, and complete their own work in good quality under the condition of ensuring the safety of passengers. Under special circumstances, the crew members shall also obey the unified command of the driver according to the regulations.

(2) Before taking the post, the passenger crew must pass the training of the railway administration. After passing the labor safety examination of the section, the railway administration can take the post after uniformly issuing the post certificate.

(3) The train conductor and train attendant are mainly responsible for serving passengers, checking tickets, handling ticketing, card control of dangerous goods, emergency handling, etc. In case of any problem affecting the safety of passengers, the passenger crew shall immediately take effective measures to protect the safety of passengers' lives and property.

(4) Passenger boarding and landing shall be carried out according to the division of "Get off at the front door and get on at the back door". Under special circumstances, the specific change organization scheme of the station can be notified.

Before arriving at the intermediate station, the passenger crew organize passengers to wait for getting off at the front door in the running direction of each carriage through the train broadcast. Stop check-in 5min in advance before the station starts, check-in and release passengers 20 min in advance at the departure station, and the conductor notifies the driver and the driver notifies the mechanic to open the door 20 min in advance (10 min at the turn back station).

When the arrival station is a low platform, the conductor shall organize to open the door flap in advance before arrival, and remind nearby passengers of safety precautions. After driving, the flap shall be leveled and locked in time; When the arrival station is a high platform, the door flap shall not be opened. Before departure, the conductor shall notify the driver to close the door after confirming that passengers have boarded and landed (the departure station is 2 min before departure), and the term is "motor train" ×× Driver, please close the door after boarding and landing, and the driver answered "motor car" ×× The driver understands. In case of failure of the automatic door opening and closing device, the driver shall notify the on-board machinist and conductor. The conductor is responsible for organizing the manual opening and closing of the door, and the on-board machinist is responsible for handling relevant failures. After the EMU arrives at the station and stops stably, the driver is responsible for opening the door. If the button is not on the driver's console, the driver shall notify the mechanic to open and close the door. When the EMU is reconnected, the two train leaders shall confirm that the boarding and landing of passengers are completed at the same time, and the two train leaders and one train leader echo that the boarding and landing are completed. The term is“ ×× The conductor of the first group of the front conductor shall be responsible for confirming the boarding and landing of passengers and notifying the driver. The call language is the same as that of the departure call.

(5) The train crew shall be equipped with wireless interphone to timely report all kinds of information, but shall not use the walkie interphone to engage in things unrelated to work.

The EMU train is equipped with two hooks with length of 1.5m and pole handle as insulating material, which are positioned and placed to assist passengers in picking up luggage falling under the platform in time.

(6) The crew room of EMU train can only be used to place team data and office supplies, and shall not be stored or used for other purposes.

(7) Smoking is prohibited in all carriages except the designated smoking place. Train attendants shall strengthen publicity and explain and guide smoking passengers.

(8) The food and drinks sold by the train must be national famous and high-quality products, and unified procurement, purchase price and sales price shall be implemented. The purchase channels of food and drinks shall be strictly controlled to prevent passengers from food poisoning.

(9) Train attendants shall pay attention to the management of train safety equipment during train operation, and prevent passengers from moving, touching safety equipment and other unsafe behaviors. No one is allowed to open the airtight window during train

operation. Unless the work requires the permission of the conductor or the staff designated by the conductor to enter the cab, other personnel shall not enter the cab.

(10) On the electrified line, the connecting parts of each conductor of the catenary usually have high voltage, and it is forbidden to contact the above equipment directly or indirectly (through any object such as bar, conductor and water flow).

To ensure personal safety, except that professionals operate according to regulations, the articles carried by any person (including long rods, wires, etc.)must be kept more than two meters away from the live part of catenary equipment. When the EMU needs skin washing, it must be carried out in the power-off area of overhead contact line equipment. It is strictly forbidden for cleaning personnel to wash the roof pantograph and high-voltage cable head connector with water. The above parts shall be cleaned with wet rag. At the same time, safety protection measures shall be taken for climbing operation. It is forbidden to wash the floor, wallboard and vehicle connection with water.

(11) The opening and closing of all train doors are controlled by the driver.

After the train door is closed, the train crew shall not open the door at will; When the door must be opened under special circumstances, the conductor must first confirm that the train is not started and the door can be opened only with the consent of the driver; After the door closed again, the conductor shall confirm the door status one by one, inform the driver that the door has been closed, and the motor car can be started only after the driver confirms the door status. In case of door failure during train operation, which endangers personal safety, the personnel found on site shall immediately take temporary safety protection measures and notify the mechanic for treatment. If the door fails when the train stops, the train crew can manually open and close the door.

(12) In case of affecting the normal operation of the train during train operation, the conductor shall ask the driver for the reasons and explain the situation to the passengers according to the relevant regulations on late disposal, then do a good job in safety publicity and stabilize the passengers' mood. Prevent passengers from opening the door without authorization.

(13) When the train stops or interrupts on the way due to temporary power failure of overhead contact line equipment or train failure, the conductor shall organize the train crew to start the emergency response plan for train interruption of EMU. The crew at each post shall stick to their posts, strengthen the inspection in the train, take good care of key passengers, and make publicity and explanation to passengers. They shall not open the door without authorization to prevent accidents.

(14) When a passenger has to stop temporarily for rescue due to injury or illness during train operation, the conductor shall report the situation to the train dispatcher of the Railwany Bureau through the driver and request temporary stop.

The conductor shall organize the train crew to start the emergency response plan for personal injury or emergency events of EMU passengers, timely prepare passenger transport records and prepare for handover. The conductor shall timely report the on-site situation to the section dispatching room and the person in charge of the team. Train attendants shall not get off the train to participate in handling.

(15) In case of fire and explosion during train operation, the conductor shall organize the train crew to start the emergency response plan for fire and explosion accident of EMU. The train crew shall immediately press the alarm button and emergency stop button to evacuate passengers to the safe carriage. If there is a fire partition door, the fire partition door shall be closed, the situation shall be reported to the driver and conductor in time, and the on-site situation shall be reported to the depot dispatching room in time.

(16) Safety of train operation and operation on the way:

① During the operation of the bus, the staff are strictly prohibited from throwing and sweeping garbage under the bus; Passengers are forbidden to throw things or sundries under the train during train operation; The protective fence of the dining car must be firmly locked in the slot; The train direction sign must be firmly locked in the slot; The dining table, tea table and empty wine and beverage bottles must be cleaned in time; Peel plates and other garbage must be cleaned in time.

② The train direction plate running in the speed-up section must have a locking device. Before hanging the direction plate, the safety state inspection should be carried out. The failure of the locking device is strictly prohibited. After hanging the direction plate, it must be confirmed that it is in a locked state.

③ Management of train waste treatment. If the staff in the operation of the bus to the car to throw, sweep the garbage (did not cause serious consequences), the responsible person transfer training for 6 months, direct responsibility team leader dismissal and transfer training for 6 months, leading the responsibility team leader transfer training for 3 months, the direct responsibility of cadres, leading the responsibility of cadres to warn.

Ⅱ. *EMU Emergency Disposal and Organizational Responsibilities*

1. Organizations and responsibilities

The responsibilities of the emergency response leadership group are:

(1) According to the conditions of line and bridge equipment, geology, topography, meteorology and hydrology along the railway, emergency response leadership group determine the types of possible disasters, strengthen the monitoring of hazard sources, summarize the important information that may cause accidents, and formulat corresponding guidelines, policies, systems and methods for emergency disposal.

(2) Strengthen the contact with local water conservancy, meteorology, earthquake, land and resources and other relevant departments, establish an emergency contact mechanism and do a good job in disaster prevention.

(3) Command, guide and supervise the emergency response command group to start the emergency plan and fully master the implementation of the emergency plan.

(4) Listen to the report of the emergency response command group and put forward guidance on the work of the emergency response command group.

(5) Other major matters that need to be solved and coordinated by the emergency response leading group.

The responsibilities of the emergency response command group are:

(1) In case of fire, explosion, disaster or accident endangering the life and property safety of passengers and employees, emergency response command group should organize to start and implement the emergency response plan for passenger train safety.

(2) Be responsible for formulating emergency response plan for passenger train safety and organizing its implementation.

(3) Command the site to start the safety emergency plan, and put forward guiding opinions on the problems in the implementation of the safety plan.

(4) Other problems that need to be solved and coordinated by the emergency response command group of safety emergencies.

The responsibilities of the crew organization emergency response command group are:

(1) In case of food poisoning, personal injury, acute illness, death and other emergencies on the passenger train, organize and start the passenger train crew to organize the emergency response plan.

(2) Be responsible for formulating and implementing the emergency response plan of passenger train crew organization.

(3) Put forward guiding opinions on the problems in the implementation of the plan.

(4) Other problems that need to be solved and coordinated by the crew emergency command group.

The responsibilities of the on-site emergency response group are:

(1) The on-site emergency response group leader is responsible for the initiation, ...g, organization, command and implementation of all emergency plans.

...der the unified command of the conductor, each deputy team leader shall lead ... response team to organize and implement the plan according to the division ... in the emergency response plan.

... the emergency response team shall implement the plan according to ...cific groups of the plan.

2. Emergency disposal principle

Rapid response and correct disposal; Put out the fire first and give unified command; Coordination between stations and trains to ensure train safety; Rely on science and reduce losses.

3. Emergency disposal requirements

Establish an on-site disposal team; Rapid on-site response, accurate information transmission and proper aftermath handling; Clear division of labor, consistent step and unified command; Strengthen training and improve treatment skills.

Ⅲ. *EMU Emergency Response Plan*

1. Emergency response plan for initial electrical fire of EMU

(1) In case of smoke and fire of electrical equipment in EMU, the crew members who first find and arrive at the site shall immediately turn off the power supply and use fire extinguishers to extinguish the fire. At the same time, the alarm button and emergency stop button shall be pressed immediately, and the conductor and all stewards shall be informed immediately by wireless interphone. The conductor shall immediately organize all crew members to participate in the fire fighting.

(2) After receiving the notice, all crew members, under the unified command of the conductor and the traffic police, take their own responsibilities, perform their own duties, go all out to put out the fire, and the motor car driver sticks to his post and handles it together.

(3) Start the emergency response plan for fire and explosion accidents of EMU according to the fire situation. After all stewards arrive at the scene, under the unified command of the conductor and the traffic police, gather all the fire-fighting equipment of the train, take effective fire-fighting schemes and measures to put out the fire according to the actual situation of the fire scene, control the fire and put out the fire source.

(4) The vehicle mechanic requires the driver to turn off the power completely according to the fire. The motor car driver shall immediately stop ventilation to the vehicle.

2. Emergency response plan for fire and explosion accident of EMU

(1) Disposal during operation:

① In case of fire and explosion accident of EMU, the crew members who first find and arrive at the site shall immediately press the alarm button and emergency stop button, quickly report the situation to the driver and conductor, and use fire extinguishers or items that can extinguish the fire quickly. After receiving the notice, the train conductor shall immediately use the wireless walkie-talkie to inform all crew members to participate in the fire fighting. The motor car driver shall stick to his post, immediately stop ventilation to the vehicle and deal with it together.

② Under the unified command of the conductor and the train police, personnel, fire-fighting equipment and other items that can put out the fire shall be organized in an orderly manner in accordance with the principle of personnel first and property later. Effective fire-fighting schemes and measures shall be taken according to the division of labor according to the plan and the actual situation of the fire site, so as to quickly carry out fire fighting, control the fire and put out the fire.

③ In case of burning of clothes, cotton wadding and sundries on the floor, water or local materials shall be used first, and windows shall not be opened for ventilation. If fire extinguishers are needed, they shall be used decisively to avoid delaying the time of fire fighting; In case of smoke at the branch line of the power supply, first turn off the power supply or disconnect the fuse, and use a fire extinguisher to spray smoke or burning parts.

④ When organizing fire fighting before turning off the power supply, the distance between the burning object and overhead contact line equipment shall be confirmed in advance. When the fire on the upper part of the carriage is less than 4m away from the overhead contact line equipment, water shall not be used to extinguish the fire. The position of the fire extinguisher shall be 2m away from the overhead contact line equipment. Water and general fire extinguishers must be powered off to extinguish the fire.

⑤ As required, the EMU driver shall notify the nearest station to ask the power dispatcher to cut off the power supply of the overhead contact line equipment.

⑥ While putting out the fire, the crew shall quickly and orderly command the passengers to evacuate under the train and adjacent safe carriages to rescue the besieged passengers. Passengers who have been evacuated are strictly prohibited from returning to the accident carriage.

⑦ Rescue shall be carried out in a planned way according to the degree of passenger injury and whether it is life-threatening. Passengers still in danger shall be rescued first to get them out of danger. Organize and mobilize passengers with medical experience to participate in the rescue of the wounded. Initial on-site rescue measures such as hemostasis, simple fixation and bandage shall be taken for the wounded according to the specific conditions to create conditions for hospital treatment.

⑧ Publicity should be strengthened to maintain order in the car and prevent passengers from jumping and chaos. After the fire is handled, special personnel shall be assigned to monitor to prevent re-ignition.

⑨ The conductor and locomotive driver shall report the situation to the passenger traffic personnel and traffic dispatcher of the railway bureau where the accident occurs in the shortest time, and put forward the requirements for rescue from the station, local fire department, local government and garrison according to the fire situation. The report shall be concise, mainly including train number, time, interval and accident summary. The fire situation shall be reported clearly.

(2) Disposal after parking:

① After the train stops, the EMU driver immediately opens the side door or the mechanic and crew start the side door emergency opening device to open the side door and evacuate passengers to the ground safety zone. In case of dense smoke in the vehicle endangering the life safety of personnel, the safety hammer shall be used to break the side window glass immediately. If necessary, the side window can be used as an emergency exit to evacuate passengers to the ground.

② When the train stops in the section, the EMU driver shall immediately use the train wireless dispatching telephone to inform the stations at both ends, track the train and the train dispatcher, and do a good job in train protection as required. When evacuating passengers to the ground in the section, the EMU driver shall also notify passing trains.

③ When the train needs to be disassembled, the driver and vehicle mechanic shall cooperate closely. For example, when using the multiple train set, they shall communicate and cooperate closely with the multiple train driver and mechanic in time, and decompose and separate the train set according to the method of first detaching the behind train and then detaching the front train, that is, first separate the train from the rear train set, and transfer the train to the flat place of the line as far as possible, Then separate the front train from the front train to cut off the fire source and prevent the fire from spreading.

④ When the train is disassembled, the waist door of the rear carriage shall be locked to prevent accidents. After the train is separated, the EMU driver shall quickly protect the train (including the vehicles left in the section after the train is decomposed).

⑤ The train police conductor shall take measures to maintain the on-site order and prevent confusion, set up a warning area according to the situation, prohibit personnel other than rescue from entering the site, and shall not move any items on the site without authorization. Effective measures shall be taken to properly protect the traces, physical evidence and relevant evidence materials on the accident site. While putting out the fire, the train crew shall cooperate with the passenger police, pay attention to the protection of the fire site, take various forms to do a good job in publicity, stabilize passengers' mood and jointly maintain order to avoid confusion. If possible, the passenger ticket and address shall be registered as far as possible for verification.

⑥ After the Rescue Department arrives, the train conductor shall introduce the cause of fire and explosion, fire situation, casualties and evacuation in detail, and assist the Rescue Department to put out the fire.

(3) Aftermath disposal:

① The train conductor should seriously understand the number and extent of injuries, and register the name, gender, age, unit, address, ticket, ID number, other documents and carry-on items. The detailed records will be provided to prepare the station for the aftermath.

② The train police shall timely investigate and collect evidence, and the evidence materials shall be objective and detailed, so as to create favorable conditions for on-site investigation and identification of the cause of the fire. The train crew shall actively help the public security personnel understand the situation and provide clues. At the same time, we should actively assist the public security organs in investigating the accident.

③ The train conductor shall hand over the casualties, passenger property losses and relevant records to the station in time, so that the station can deal with the aftermath as soon as possible.

3. Emergency response plan for food poisoning in EMU

(1) In case of suspected food poisoning of passengers in EMU, the conductor and train police shall rush to the scene immediately, timely understand the main symptoms of poisoned passengers, master the number of poisoned passengers, onset time, etc., accurately judge the source of poison or determine the food suspected to cause food poisoning, and judge the basic situation of the patient.

(2) The conductor shall report to the front parking station, the front health and epidemic prevention department and the depot production dispatching room. The depot production dispatching room shall immediately report to the competent department of health and passenger transport of the railway administration and the railway disease prevention and control center at the location of the train and the region. If food poisoning is suspected, it shall also be reported to the local railway public security organ. The contents of the report include: date, train number, operation section, time and place of onset, main symptoms of patients, number of patients (including critically ill and dead), food that may cause poisoning, etc., and the measures required to be taken by the station organization.

(3) Using the medical aid kit provided by the train, the train rescuers take emergency treatment measures, such as vomiting and drainage, and emergency treatment measures to carry out preliminary treatment, actively organize the rescue of poisoned passengers, and find doctors to help rescue and treat through broadcasting, so as to control the further development of the disease. According to the instructions of the superior, handle the

handover with relevant stations. If the poisoning is serious and life-threatening and requires immediate stop for first aid, the conductor shall immediately report to the passenger dispatching department of the local railway bureau or immediately contact the dispatcher with the operating conductor's radio station, stop at the nearest parking station with rescue conditions, and organize first-aid personnel to make preparations for handover with the midway station, Assist the station to send the patients to the nearest hospital as soon as possible.

(4) When more than 3 people have suspected food poisoning symptoms, in addition to the treatment according to the above requirements, the conductor shall immediately report to the front parking station and report to the affiliated units. When it is suspected that food poisoning is caused by poisoning, he shall also report to the railway public security organ at the same time. Relevant records shall be made and handled in accordance with the relevant provisions of the measures for the handling of railway passenger personal injury and loss of their own luggage (Order No. 12 of the Ministry of Railways of the people's Republic of China). When necessary, passenger transport records shall be prepared and submitted to the front parking station for handling. Make preparations for station handover. If necessary, the conductor shall contact the train operation dispatching and stop at the large station ahead for rescue.

(5) The train conductor and the train police conductor shall timely investigate the cause of the disease, collect evidence materials, understand the symptoms and eating history of passengers, and make records to form first-hand data. Register the basic information of poisoning patients, so as to assist the health and epidemic prevention departments in the final investigation and determination of diagnosis.

(6) The train conductor and the train police shall organize relevant personnel to do a good job in stabilizing passengers' mood to prevent confusion, recover the sold suspicious food, seal the suspicious food and raw materials at low temperature, retain the packaging and utensils that cause food poisoning or may cause food poisoning, collect vomit and excreta samples, close the contaminated toilet and wait for the inspection of health and quarantine personnel. If it cannot be ruled out that the food poisoning is caused by the food supplied by the station train, the food supply shall be stopped immediately to prevent the further consumption of suspicious food from expanding the poisoning situation.

4. Emergency response plan for train interruption of EMU

(1) In case of train interruption of EMU for some reason, the conductor shall contact the driver or the station where the train stops and the dispatching of Railway Bureau to master the situation and know it well. Explain to passengers in time and apologize to

passengers through radio.

(2) When the EMU cannot continue to operate, the train conductor shall timely contact the driver or the station and dispatcher where the train stops to master the delay situation at any time. When necessary, the train conductor shall use special digital communication equipment to contact the passenger dispatching department of the Railway Bureau by unified telephone to master the delay time, reason, estimated arrival time and so on. According to the situation, timely deploy the key work that should be done well in the next step. The train crew shall timely explain to the passengers, truthfully explain the time and reasons for the delay, and apologize to the passengers through the radio.

(3) "Passengers, this is ×× train conductor, this train is late for ×× reason. It's about late for ×× hours ×× minutes. On behalf of the railway department, I sincerely apologize to you for the inconvenience caused by the train delay." The causes of delay or line interruption shall be described according to the following contents: natural disasters (rainstorm, fog, snow, landslide, debris flow...), accident impact and equipment failure.

(4) When the line is interrupted and the train cannot continue to run, the conductor and the train police shall appease the passengers, strengthen the inspection of the carriage, explain and serve the passengers at any time, stabilize the order in the train and ensure good public order in the train.

(5) Under the unified command of the conductor, the train crew shall take their own responsibilities and do a good job in safety, service and other work. The train attendants must be aware of the delay of the passenger train, and timely inform the passengers of the expected delay time and adjust the train operation scheme. In case of passengers' inquiries, they shall answer patiently and carefully, and shall not use irresponsible language such as "don't know" and "no point" or show impatience, so as not to cause passengers' dissatisfaction and intensify contradictions.

(6) If the train stays for a long time, try not to let passengers get off. When passengers get off at the station, they should be organized to a safe area to ensure the safety of passengers. The conductor shall organize the service, drinking water and food supply for passengers, and try his best to provide convenience for passengers and ensure their living needs. If the drinking water is insufficient, contact the station to supply water or supplement drinking water in time. If the food is insufficient, contact the station or the local government in time to organize procurement. The station shall help the train solve the problems of food, meal materials and drinking water, ensure the needs of passengers or contact the superior, and organize the supply and catering.

(7) When the train stops and brings inconvenience to passengers' life or causes passengers' uneasiness, the train crew shall take the initiative to understand the visiting

passengers, try their best to provide convenience for passengers on the premise of ensuring passengers' safety, especially strengthen the service for key passengers, try to reduce many inconveniences in life caused by delay, and maintain the reputation of railway transportation enterprises.

(8) When the train must stop halfway, try to stop the passenger train at the station where the passenger transport is large or the station where the town is located, so as to facilitate the catering and emergency treatment of passengers. The train shall take various measures to ensure the safety of life and property of stranded passengers.

(9) The train conductor shall actively contact the passenger dispatching department of the Railway Bureau, and report the situation in the train and resume operation as soon as possible. At the same time, the train conductor shall understand and master the continuous stay time, report the passengers, order, supply, safety and other conditions in the train to the dispatching and the emergency leading group of the unit at any time, and ask for assistance to solve the problems, so that the dispatching can master the situation in the train at any time. The conductor shall actively put forward suggestions on train detour and turnaround operation according to the situation.

(10) For the passenger train of EMU that is withdrawal and turnaround for some reason, for the passengers who get off the train and ask for ticket refund, transfer, extension of validity period, detour and return, the train conductor shall indicate the date, train number, reason and return station on the back of the ticket and affix his seal as the certificate for passengers to return, handle ticket refund, transfer or extension of validity period free of charge.

5. Emergency response plan for passenger personal injury or emergency

(1) Investigate the site, understand the injury and condition, organize rescue, check tickets and collect testimony.

① In case of personal injury or emergency illness of passengers on the passenger train, the conductor shall investigate the scene together with the passenger police, check the degree of injury and incidence of passengers, collect circumstantial evidence and physical evidence, investigate the cause of the accident, and actively take rescue measures according to the specific conditions of injured and sick passengers. At the same time, check the ticket type, ticket number, departure and arrival station, train number, validity period and additional cutting of the ticket held by the passenger; Collect at least two copies of testimony and relevant evidence of peers or witnesses, and protect the evidence materials.

② When collecting witness testimony, the name, gender, age, address, contact method, ID number and so on shall be recorded. The testimony and evidence shall be accurate and true, and can prove the process and cause of the accident (the Railway Bureau added that the testimony of witnesses shall be made by non-railway staff with the most legal effect). In addition, after the accident, the evidence shall be obtained at the first time. If there is no witness, the self-report materials shall be collected as much as possible. After collecting the testimony materials, if conditions permit, the testimony can be copied or copied, one for reference, and the other must be handed over to the processing station within three days.

③ When a passenger is seriously ill on the train, the train attendant on duty shall immediately report to the train conductor. The conductor shall rush to the scene at the first time and notify the announcer to use the train broadcast to find the medical staff. When the medical staff do not arrive at the scene or there are no medical staff on the train, the train ambulance shall rush to the scene immediately to inquire about the passenger's medical history, Take measures and do a good job in emergency rescue according to the illness of passengers.

④ In the process of emergency rescue, the train staff shall evacuate other passengers to other seats, maintain the order in the car, and ensure that the location of sick passengers is ventilated and in good condition.

(2) Prepare passenger transport records or passenger casualty accident records and handle handover.

① When the injured and emergency passengers on the train need to be handed over to the station for treatment, if necessary, the station shall be notified in advance to make rescue preparations, and the injured and emergency passengers shall be handed over to the third-class or above station (the nearest station when parking in the section for treatment), and the station shall not refuse to accept it. In case of an accident with a large number of casualties, the train shall request the local government to assist in organizing rescue when it deems necessary. When the train handles the handover procedures to the station, the passenger transport record shall be prepared in duplicate (one for storage and one for station and train handover), which shall be handed over together with the ticket, passenger carry on list and evidence materials. If the passenger personal injury accident is caused by public security or criminal cases such as fighting, the train police shall sign on the passenger transport record.

② If there is no time to prepare records due to special circumstances, the conductor must assign a special person to get off and handle the handover with the station, and must hand over relevant materials to the accident handling station within three days.

③ If the injured person is seriously injured and needs to get off the train for treatment immediately, the conductor shall immediately report to the passenger dispatching department of the local railway bureau for instructions, prepare for parking and handover at non scheduled parking stations, make preparations for handover quickly, and report to the production dispatching room of the depot at the same time.

(3) Reporting procedure.

① In case of personal injury or emergency illness of passengers, an accident express report shall be sent at the first time, which shall be mainly sent to the responsible unit or the unit (normal accidental injury shall be mainly sent to the accident treatment station and section), copied to the passenger transport marketing department of the Railway Bureau, and copied to the safety supervision office of the Railway Bureau in case of casualties without tickets. The contents of accident quick report include: a. type of accident; b. Date, time and train number of occurrence; c. Location, station and section mileage (line type, station name, section, kilometer and meter); d. Name, gender, occupation, nationality, age, occupation, unit, address, type of ticket, arrival and departure, ticket number and ID number; e. Brief description of accidents and casualties (describe visual injury and incidence degree).

② If conditions permit, the accident overview shall be reported to the section production dispatching room by telephone.

6. Emergency response plan in case of major epidemic on EMU trains

(1) When the EMU train found suspicious cases like new crown, plague, cholera and other major epidemic cases, or received the notification of suspected cases on the EMU train, the train conductor should report to the driver and the higher authorities immediately. The driver reported to the dispatcher of the train, the dispatcher immediately reported to the operator, and the Duty Officer immediately reported to the railway disease control department.

(2) The train dispatcher shall arrange the EMU to stop at the designated place according to the disposal scheme determined by relevant departments of the Railway Bureau. After receiving the driver's notice to stop at the designated station, the conductor shall make preparations for the disease control personnel to get on the train and the delivery of suspected cases to the station, and the station and railway disease control department shall make preparations for emergency handling.

(3) The conductor shall organize isolation of infectious patients, suspected patients and close contacts, emergency evacuation of other passengers, and register relevant personnel.

(4) The conductor shall organize to block the polluted or possibly polluted area, and prepare for the delivery of the isolated personnel.

(5) The conductor shall hand over infectious patients, suspected patients, close contacts and other passengers requiring follow-up observation and relevant data to the station and railway disease control department at the designated parking station.

(6) The train police shall maintain the order in the vehicle and ensure the normal

operation of regional blockade, passenger isolation, station vehicle handover, etc.

(7) The railway disease control department shall disinfect the polluted or possibly polluted areas on the train. The regional blockade can be lifted only after the railway disease control department confirms the disposal.

(8) The station and the train shall actively cooperate with the on-site medical and disease control departments.

7. Emergency response plan for transfer to hot standby EMU in station in case of EMU train failure

(1) In case of any change in train number, the station shall take back the original ticket, issue a new ticket and refund the fare difference. When the passenger holds an electronic ticket, he or she shall change the ticket first. If the time is tight and it is impossible to exchange a new ticket, the passenger can get on the train directly with the original ticket, and the station and the train shall do a good job in handover. When the passenger holds an electronic ticket, the station shall check and confirm with the ticket sales information provided by the ticket system.

(2) When the fault train stops at the platform, the transfer shall be arranged on two sides of the same platform as far as possible. If the transfer cannot be carried out on two sides of the same platform, the station shall organize passengers to transfer through over-bridge, underground path or other channels, and transfer across station tracks is strictly prohibited; When the failed train does not stop at the platform in the station, the transfer handling procedure shall be handled in accordance with the handling procedure of section transfer to hot standby EMU.

(3) When the fixed number of hot standby EMUs is less than the actual number of failed EMUs, if possible, other EMUs with the fixed number of passengers can be used to organize passenger transfer. In case of vehicle type change, the ticket management office of the railway bureau shall adjust and control the ticket amount. The station shall strengthen the contact with the passenger ticket management office of the Railway Bureau, timely grasp the seat sale, formulate the adjustment scheme, cooperate with the train, and do a good job in passenger seat adjustment, publicity and interpretation.

(4) In case of class difference in seat adjustment and seat classification difference, the conductor shall prepare passenger transport records and refund the fare difference after arriving at the station.

(5) Stations and trains shall strengthen cooperation to jointly do a good job in passenger publicity and guidance, seat arrangement and service, so as to meet the reasonable needs of passengers as far as possible.

(6) During transfer, the station shall carefully organize ticket inspection, and

passengers holding tickets of other train numbers are strictly prohibited to get on the train.

8. Emergency response plan in case of air conditioning failure of EMU train

(1) When the air conditioning of the whole train of EMU fails for more than 20 minutes and cannot be recovered, but the train can operate normally, the conductor can notify the driver to request the train dispatcher to stop at the nearest passenger station in front, and the train dispatcher will arrange the train to stop at the nearest passenger station in front. After the train has installed the protective net at the parking station and opened some doors, the train dispatcher shall issue the dispatching command of opening the door with a speed limit of 60 km/h (40 km/h when passing the line adjacent to the high platform)to the driver (including the rescue driver during rescue)and all stations along the way according to the driver's report.

(2) When the train stops for some reason and cannot maintain operation and the air conditioner fails for more than 20min and cannot be recovered, the conductor shall timely communicate with the driver and on-board mechanic, make a decision to open the door according to the situation, and notify the driver to report to the train dispatcher.

(3) The installation of protective net and opening of train door shall be organized by the conductor and carried out by the train attendants, with the cooperation of the driver and on-board machinist. The protective net shall be installed when the train is stopped, and the installation position is at the door on the left side (non passing side)of the running direction. After the protective net is installed, the conductor confirms that the protective net is firmly installed. After opening the door, the conductor shall organize the train staff to protect until the door is closed.

(4) When it is necessary to organize passengers to get off or transfer to other trains, it shall be carried out at the station platform. When passengers must be organized to get off or transfer in the line or section in the station that is not adjacent to the platform, it shall be approved by the deputy director in charge of transportation (chief dispatcher)of the Railway Bureau.

[Task Detection]

1. To ensure safety, what are the regulations for opening and closing the doors of multiple units?
2. What are the safety requirements for EMU Operation and operation on the way?
3. Briefly describe the responsibilities of EMU emergency response organization.
4. What are the emergency disposal principles of EMU?
5. Briefly describe the emergency response plan for initial electrical fire of EMU.
6. Briefly describe the emergency response plan for fire and explosion accidents of

EMU.

7. Briefly describe the emergency response plan for food poisoning in EMU.

8. Briefly describe the emergency response plan for train interruption of multiple units.

9. Briefly describe the emergency response plan for passenger personal injury or emergency illness of EMU.

10. Briefly describe the emergency response plan in case of major epidemic on EMU trains.

11. Briefly describe the emergency response plan for transferring to hot standby EMU in the fault section of EMU.

12. Briefly describe the emergency response plan in case of air conditioning failure of EMU train.

Task 3 EMU Train Operation Organization

[Task Description]

1. Get familiar with the management measures for EMU reception and departure.
2. Master the provisions of various driving emergency plans.

Ⅰ. *EMU Reception and Departure*

1. "Five fixations " for EMU reception and departure

To ensure the safe operation of EMU trains, orderly passenger boarding and landing, and improve the operation organization and passenger service level of EMU, the "five fixations" must be adhered to when receiving and sending EMU trains.

(1) "Five fixations" contents:

① Fixed route: The reception and departure of EMU trains must be fixed on the basic route

② Fixed arrival and departure track: EMU reception and departure must be handled on the fixed arrival and departure track. When the EMU runs in train control on-board equipment mode, it is prohibited to receive the EMU on the arrival and departure track and route without CTCS-2 information.

③ Fixed platform: the EMU trains receiving and dispatching passenger transport business must stop at the fixed platform.

④ Fixed parking position: the station shall set EMU parking position signs respectively according to different models and marshaling of EMU to fix the parking position of EMU. The driver stopped against the standard.

⑤ Fixed reception and departure personnel: the reception and departure personnel of EMU must be the personnel who have specially trained and passed the examination on the relevant knowledge of EMU, and receive and send EMU trains at a fixed position.

(2) The relevant contents of "five fixations" of receiving and dispatching EMUs shall be included in the detailed rules for station operation. The fixed route, fixed arrival departure track and changed route of EMU shall be listed and placed in relevant train dispatching console and signal building (train room).

(3) In the centralized dispatching section, under the condition that the equipment is qualified, the fixed arrival departure track of receiving and departure EMUs at each station shall be included in the basic train diagram data.

(4) If the EMU reception and departure cannot be handled at the basic route, it shall be approved by the on duty director of the dispatching office of the Railway Bureau and issue the dispatching order. When the EMU handling passenger transport business changes the receiving and departure track, in addition to the permission of the on duty director of the dispatching office of the Railway Bureau and Issuing the dispatching order, the driving personnel shall notify the relevant passenger transport personnel in advance and make preparations for receiving the train. When the receiving and departure personnel need to change shifts temporarily, competent personnel who have passed the examination shall be assigned to handle the receiving and departure of EMUs.

2. Operation method for EMU reception and departure

(1) Before the departure of EMU, the train conductor shall notify the driver to close the door after confirming that the passengers are getting on and off; After the EMU arrives at the station and stops stably, the driver opens the door. If the button is not on the driver's console, the conductor shall notify the on-board mechanic to close the door after confirming that the passengers are getting on and off; After the EMU arrives at the station and stops stably, the on-board mechanic shall open the door. If the automatic door opening and closing device fails, the driver shall notify the train staff to open and close the door manually.

(2) The driver of the EMU can start the train after confirming that the departure (route)annunciator display or the operation certificate of the occupied section is correct and the door has been closed. If it is necessary to cancel the departure route after the departure signal is opened or the operation certificate of the occupied section has been delivered, the station attendant shall confirm that the train has not started, notify the driver, and cancel the departure route after taking back the operation certificate.

(3) When recepting and departing EMUs, the station assistant attendant shall stand at the specified place to pick up and send the train.

(4) When the EMU arrives at the station, within the braking distance outside the annunciator, if the arrival direction is a downhill of more than 6 ‰ and there is no separation equipment at the end of the receiving line, it is prohibited to handle simultaneous receiving in the opposite direction and simultaneous sending and receiving of trains in the same direction (except for the section where EMU trains are only running).

(5) When the train cannot be received at the same time in the opposite direction of the EMU route, the train not suitable for parking outside the station, the train with difficulty in starting after parking or the train with continuous train behind shall be received first. If two trains cannot be received and dispatched at the same time, they shall be received and dispatched according to the train operation plan in principle.

(6) Where the EMU does not meet the 5 min train tracking interval, it is allowed to pass the EMU by the station when the yellow light is displayed on the departure signal with the approval of China Railway Corporation.

(7) When the EMU passes through the station, the station must stop the operation on the passing route and the operation affecting the train operation safety in advance. The advance time shall be stipulated by the Railway Bureau.

3. Regulations on shunting operation of EMU

(1) In principle, the shunting operation of EMU adopts self running mode and operates according to the display of ground signal.

(2) It is forbidden to pass hump, slip shunting, hand push shunting, coupling other locomotive shunting (except for rescue, attached return transition vehicle, shunting machine and road rail tractor when EMU shunting is not powered)and track outbound shunting. It is forbidden to slip shunting and hand push shunting to the stay line of EMU.

(3) During shunting operation, the driver must operate at the front end of the running direction of the EMU. When it is necessary to operate at the rear end of the running direction of the EMU under unavoidable circumstances, the on-board mechanic or other competent personnel shall be assigned to stand at the front end of the running direction of the EMU to command. When it is found that the driving or personal safety is endangered, the emergency stop button (emergency braking device)shall be used immediately or the driver shall be notified to stop. The motor car depot (motor car operation post)is equipped with ground service drivers of motor car units, who are responsible for shunting, trial operation and other mobile train units in the motor car depot (motor car operation post).

(4) When locomotive shunting is adopted, the personnel of the motor car depot (motor car operation station)are responsible for the connection and disassembly of the transition coupler, special air duct and electrical connecting line, and opening the door. The shunting personnel are responsible for the decoupling of the coupler and the decoupling of the hose.

(5)Regulations on speed limit of maintenance and detection equipment during maintenance of EMU: through tread diagnosis equipment, the speed limit is 45 km/h, and the detection speed limit is 8–12 km/h; When passing through the car washing machine, the speed limit is 3–5 km/h; When the tractor pulls the EMU, the speed limit is 1.5–3 km/h; When passing the track bridge, the speed limit is 10 km/h; When passing through the non falling wheel lathe, bogie replacement and wheel dropping equipment, the speed limit is 5 km/h.

Ⅱ. *EMU Operation*

1. Basic requirements

(1) The EMU is equipped with driver, on-board mechanic and passenger crew without operation conductor.

(2) Single EMU is a fixed marshaling, and shall not be ungrouped under operation; Two EMUs of the same type can be reconnected for operation. When two EMUs are reconnected, one pantograph shall be raised for operation, but the mode of raising rear pantograph by front vehicle and raising front pantograph by rear vehicle shall not be adopted. When the mode of raising front pantograph by both front and rear vehicles or raising rear pantograph by both front and rear vehicles is adopted, the working pantograph spacing is 200–215 m. It is forbidden to add various types of locomotives and vehicles to the EMU; EMU shall not be mixed with other trains. EMUs exceeding the period of inspection and repair shall not be put into operation.

(3) Before the EMU is put into operation, it must reach the operation state and meet the requirements of EMU operation technical standards. Passenger train inspection is not carried out during operation. When the EMU equipment fails and cannot continue to operate, it shall not be disassembled or dumped.

(4) When two EMUs are reconnected or disconnected, the on-board mechanic of the EMU shall be responsible for guiding and the driver shall confirm. For multiple units after reconnection or disconnection, the on-board mechanic shall cooperate with the driver to conduct relevant tests. During the uncoupling operation, the active train set must move more than 5 m at a time before stopping.

(5) During the normal operation of EMU, it is strictly prohibited to open the air tight window.

(6) In case of equipment failure affecting train operation (except train equipment failure)during EMU operation, in principle, the failure shall be handled first and then train operation shall be organized. When the equipment fault cannot be repaired temporarily, if it is really necessary to organize the driving, the driving shall be organized according to the

relevant driving restrictions.

(7) When the EMU without power stops at the station, the station shall carry out anti-slip; When the EMU without parking brake device stops without power in the section, the driver of the EMU shall notify the on-board mechanic to prevent sliding. The anti-slip shall be firmly fixed with a wheel stopper. When stopping at the station line, the Turnouts at both ends of the line shall be pulled to the position where the line cannot be entered.

(8) The EMU shall not pass through a curve with a radius of less than 180 m, and shall not pass laterally through less than No. 9 single turnout and No. 6 symmetrical double curve turnout.

(9) When the EMU passes through a high platform with a height of 1,100mm and above, the speed shall not exceed 70 km/h.

(10) The EMU shall be able to be coupled by the rescue locomotive and brake, and the train pipe pressure shall be 600 kPa.

(11) When the EMU is operating in CTCS-2 section, it is prohibited to meet the out of gauge freight train in the section.

2. Section operation

(1) When the EMU is running in the section and the train control on-board equipment displays the stop signal, the train must stop immediately, and the driver shall use the train wireless dispatching communication equipment to notify the on-board mechanic. When the train stops and waits for 2 min, and the train control on-board equipment still does not receive the signal allowing operation, the driver will turn the train control on-board equipment into the visual driving mode, and the train will continue to operate at the speed that can stop at any time in case of obstacles, with the maximum speed not exceeding 20 km/h, until the train control on-board equipment receives the signal allowing operation and operates according to the display of the train control on-board equipment. While parking and waiting, you must contact the train dispatcher and station attendant. If you confirm that there are trains in the front block section, you are not allowed to enter.

(2) In case of failure of train control on-board equipment during the operation of EMU and resulting in train stop, the driver shall use the train wireless dispatching communication equipment to report to the train dispatcher or station attendant, and notify the on-board mechanic to power off the system for 30s and restart it. If the equipment returns to normal, continue to operate; If the equipment still cannot return to normal, turn the train control on-board equipment into isolation mode according to the dispatching command.

(3) When the EMU must return to the rear station after being forced to stop in the section, the train dispatcher must confirm that the EMU to the rear station is free before issuing the dispatching order. The driver turns the train control on-board equipment into

isolation mode and manually controls the return of EMU at a speed not exceeding 20 km/h according to the dispatching command. When the train has to retreat, the train dispatcher shall confirm that the rear section is free. The on-board mechanic or the designated competent personnel shall stand in the cab at the rear of the train and watch the front of the train. If it is found that it endangers the driving or personal safety, the train dispatcher shall immediately notify the driver by using the train wireless modulation communication equipment to stop the train. The reverse speed of the train shall not exceed 15 km/h.

(4) Brake test shall be conducted for EMU during rescue, unpowered return coupling locomotive or return transition vehicle.

3. EMU return requirements

(1) The EMU return shall be handled by passenger train, and the self-running mode shall be adopted in principle. When there is no power return, a return transition vehicle can be added according to the return technical conditions, and the passenger locomotive can be used for traction. When the high-speed railway line is parallel to the existing railway, the return of high-speed railway line shall be arranged as far as possible. Two short EMUs of the same type can be reconnected and sent back.

(2) During the return operation of EMU, the EMU driver and onboard mechanic shall be arranged to be on duty. The on-board mechanic is assumed by the allocation Bureau, the EMU driver is arranged by the locomotive department, and the allocation bureau is responsible for updating LKJ data. In case of self-propelled return, the non-responsible section shall assign a road driver.

(3) No passenger train inspection shall be conducted for the return of EMU. The uncoupling and hose uncoupling of EMU (return transition train)and the locomotive of this service shall be handled in accordance with the relevant provisions of railway technical management regulations. The connection and disassembly of transition coupler, special air duct and electrical connecting line shall be in the charge of the on-board Machinist with the cooperation of EMU driver.

(4) When the EMU is installed with transition coupler return, it shall operate at a speed limit of 120 km/h and avoid emergency braking as much as possible. In case of emergency braking, the driver of this service must notify the on-board machinist, and can continue to operate only after the on-board machinist checks that the transition coupler is in good condition.

(5) When the EMU needs to attach a return transition vehicle, the return transition vehicle shall be determined by the user unit of the EMU and the host enterprise through negotiation. Personnel must be sent to escort the return process to ensure the safety of the return.

During the return of EMU, the train dispatcher shall issue relevant dispatching orders according to the speed limit, return mode (with or without power), whether it can run at a corner and other precautions proposed by the relevant EMU Depot (EMU Operation Station).

4. Coupling and uncoupling of multiple units

(1) Fixed marshaling shall be implemented for single EMU, and marshaling shall not be conducted during operation.

(2) Two EMUs with the same model code can be coupled for operation, and the coupling and uncoupling operation shall be in the charge of the EMU driver and the on-board engineer.

(3) The coupling of two trains shall be carried out in the station yard (on a straight road as far as possible). When operations need to be carried out on the line, safety protection shall be carried out according to the regulations. During the operation, the anti-sliding protection of EMU shall be done according to the regulations.

(4) The requirements for EMU coupling operation are as follows:

① The station handles the route and opens the signal according to the regulations; After confirming that the signal is normal, the driver starts coupling operation.

② The move EMU stops at 10 m away from the coupled trailer unit, the on-board pilot gets off the train, confirms that the connecting device is in good condition, and displays the coupling signal to the driver.

③ During connection, the driver operates in the cab at the coupling end according to the specified procedures, and the coupling speed is 3–5 km/h.

④ After coupling, the on-board pilot shall notify the driver after confirming that the coupling under the vehicle is in good condition. The driver shall confirm that the on-board information display is normal and carry out detection according to the specified procedures.

⑤ After confirming the completion of EMU coupling operation, the driver shall change the cab, enter the front cab in the operation direction, detect the on-board information, and report to the station after confirming that the display is normal.

(5) The requirements of EMU stripping operation are as follows:

① The station handles the route and opens the signal according to the regulations; After confirming that the signal is normal, the driver starts the decoding operation.

② Before uncoupling, the on-board pilot gets off the train to check the status of the connecting device, and displays the uncoupling signal to the driver after confirming that it can be uncoupling.

③ During uncoupling, the driver shall operate according to the specified procedures in the cab at the coupling end to move one EMU, and the other EMU is in braking state.

The moving speed of the EMU shall not exceed 5 km/h, move to a place 10 m away from the parking EMU and stop.

④ After parking, the on-board vehicle mechanic shall confirm that the connecting device is reset normally and notify the driver.

⑤ After receiving the notice, the driver shall switch the cab according to the specified procedures, detect the on-board information, confirm that the display is normal, and report to the station in time.

5. Connection and remove of locomotive and EMU

(1)The coupling of locomotive and EMU shall be operated according to the following requirements:

① Before coupling, the vehicle mechanics shall install intermediate transition coupler, air duct and connecting line at the coupling end of EMU; The driver of the EMU shall operate in the cab at the coupling end according to the specified procedures, make preparations before the connection of the EMU, and notify the locomotive driver.

② After confirming that the coupling conditions are met, the locomotive driver coupling can be carried out.

③ During coupling, the speed limit of locomotive is 5 km/h.

④ After coupling, the crew of the EMU shall operate according to the specified procedures, and the locomotive driver shall organize the air test and power supply status inspection. The EMU driver shall confirm that the on-board information is normal in the cab and report to the locomotive driver.

⑤ The locomotive driver shall confirm that the coupling operation is completed and report to the station.

(2) The uncoupling of locomotive and EMU shall be carried out according to the following requirements:

① Before disconnection, the EMU is in braking state, and the locomotive stops DC 110 V power supply. The Vehicle mechanic of the EMU shall confirm the braking and power failure of the EMU, remove the air duct, connecting line and coupler between the locomotive and the EMU, and notify the driver.

② The locomotive driver can start the stripping operation only after confirming that the stripping conditions are met.

③ When disconnecting, the locomotive speed limit is 5 km/h.

6. EMU rescue

(1) When the EMU is forced to stop in the section and cannot continue to operate, the driver shall immediately use the train wireless dispatching communication equipment to notify the stations at both ends, train dispatchers and on-board mechanics, report the

parking reason and parking position, and quickly request rescue. The driver shall implement parking braking, and the EMU without parking braking shall assign the on-board mechanic to do anti-slip work.

(2) After receiving the rescue request that the EMU is forced to stop in the section, the train dispatcher shall issue the dispatching order to block the section according to the regulations, immediately report to the duty director of the dispatching office, organize the rescue locomotive according to the principle of nearest and fastest, carry out the rescue work, and immediately notify the station duty officer and EMU driver of the rescue scheme.

(3) The EMU that has requested rescue shall not be moved again. The driver of the EMU shall know the direction of the rescue train. The accompanying driver of the EMU (if there is no accompanying driver, the conductor shall designate personnel)shall assist the accompanying mechanic to install transition coupler and special air duct at one end of the rescue train. If the conditions for pantograph lifting are met, the driver must keep in touch with the rescue locomotive before pantograph lifting to prevent pantograph catenary accidents. After the EMU is rescued, the driver's vigilance device can be turned off during operation.

(4) If power failure operation is required, power failure and power inspection procedures must be handled according to regulations.

(5) After installing the transition coupler and special air duct, the on-board machinist shall set protection at not less than 300 m at the incoming end of the rescue locomotive, command the rescue locomotive for coupling operation, confirm that the rescue locomotive is connected with the EMU and the EMU is in the normal state, and notify the rescue locomotive driver of the rescue operation conditions.

(6) During the rescue operation, the rescue locomotive driver shall strictly abide by the relevant regulations such as speed limit and keep in touch with the EMU driver. During rescue operation, the speed shall not exceed 120 km/h, and emergency braking shall be avoided as far as possible.

(7) The EMU shall return to the rear station from the locomotive rescue and switch to the isolation mode. After the locomotive rescue is cancelled, it shall exit the isolation mode and be switched by the EMU driver.

(8) When the EMU continues to operate under the traction of the locomotive, the train dispatcher shall issue the dispatching command with a speed limit of 120 km/h to the rescue locomotive driver.

(9) When the fault EMU can continue to operate after treatment, the train dispatcher shall issue the dispatching command to cancel the EMU rescue according to the request of the EMU driver.

(10) When the EMU is forced to stop in the phase separation and no power area of the

catenary, and the pantograph cannot receive current normally, the diesel locomotive shall be organized as far as possible to take the rescue in the forward direction of the train.

When the electric locomotive is used for rescue, the driver of the EMU shall find out the length of the dead zone in front of the EMU (the length of the dead zone in front of the EMU is determined by subtracting 30 m from the distance between the front end of the EMU and the "closing" beacon). When the front distance can meet the conditions for pantograph raising and current collection of the electric locomotive performing rescue tasks in front of the train, the driver of the EMU shall report to the station attendant or train dispatcher "Electric locomotive can be rescued from the front", otherwise "electric locomotive can only be rescued from the rear" In case of rescue from the rear, the train dispatcher shall issue the train rescue dispatching order, and the driver of the EMU shall be in the cab at the rear of the EMU and keep in touch with the driver of the rescue vehicle. After the EMU is pulled out of the dead zone, it shall stop at a distance of not less than 800 m from the split phase power-off sign and remove the rescue vehicle. The driver of the EMU shall raise the pantograph and collect the current to resume normal operation. The train is forced to stop at the electric split phase of the catenary The driver of the EMU shall immediately report to the station attendant or train dispatcher, handle according to their instructions, and assign the on-board mechanic to do anti slip and protection work according to the regulations.

[Task detection]

1. What are the regulations for reception and departure EMUs?
2. What are the regulations for shunting operation of EMU?
3. What are the basic requirements for EMU Operation?
4. How is the temporary speed limit of EMU?

Task 4 Management Measures for Freezing Prevention of EMU Parking

[Task Description]

(1) Master the management measures for freezing prevention of EMU parking.

(2) Get familiar with anti freezing and drainage operation methods of EMU.

Ⅰ. *Management Measures for Freezing Prevention of EMU Parking*

When the EMU is parked at a temperature lower than 0 °C, these measures are formulated to prevent damage to some equipment (focusing on high-pressure traction, air conditioning and heating, air supply and braking piping, vehicle body sealing, water supply and drainage sanitation and other facilities)due to water storage and freezing, and ensure the integrity of the EMU.

(1) When the temperature is lower than 0 °C, the EMU shall be parked in a place with anti freezing and thermal insulation function, and the parking place shall meet one of the following conditions:

① Power supply by overhead contact line equipment.

② External single-phase AC 400 V ground power supply .

③ Warm library.

(2) Antifreeze under power supply conditions:

① After confirming that the EMU has pantograph raising or ground power supply conditions, the personnel on duty shall carry out power supply operation.

② The personnel on duty shall set the air conditioner of EMU under heating condition through Mon, and confirm that the air conditioner, electric heating in cab and electric heat tracing device of equipment work normally.

③ Interval power supply is allowed. The power can be cut off only when the indoor temperature reaches 18–20 °C and remains for 1 hour. The time interval of power supply shall be determined by the railway bureau according to the specific conditions of each region.

(3) The anti-freezing and drainage operation methods of various EMUs shall be implemented for anti-freezing under non-power supply conditions.

(4) The vehicle department shall be responsible for the anti-freezing work of EMU, and an anti-freezing duty team shall be established.

(5) The EMU must be emptied before entering the advanced maintenance, and the construction and repair unit shall be responsible for the anti-freezing work of the EMU during the advanced maintenance.

(6) Before parking, the EMU shall be drained and absorbed according to the drainage operation procedures, and records shall be made. When the power supply condition is maintained or the warm depot is parked, the EMU can not be drained.

(7) When the power supply is parked, the personnel on duty shall master the power supply status at any time and shall not leave the post without authorization; Handle the handover of EMU keys and equipment spare parts during shift handover, and carefully fill in the handover records.

(8) During power supply, the personnel on duty shall patrol and inspect the operation of power supply equipment and temperature in the EMU every hour and make records. If problems are found, they shall be handled and reported in time.

(9) It is forbidden to use sitting toilet and squatting toilet facilities for parked EMUs.

(10) The vehicle department shall strengthen the leadership of anti-freezing work, appoint special personnel to be responsible for it, regularly carry out anti-freezing drills, and actively explore the law of anti-freezing work of EMUs.

Ⅱ. *Measures for Anti–Freezing and Drainage of EMU*

When the external ambient temperature is lower than 0 °C, the EMU shall be powered for anti-freezing. When the EMU Depot does not have cold and antifreeze conditions, the EMU shall be emptied. China Railway Corporation has promulgated the anti-freezing and drainage operation measures for various types of EMUs, which specifies the operation procedures and operation steps for waterproof operation of various types of EMUs in detail. The following is the anti-freezing and drainage operation measures for crh380a EMUs:

1. Requirements

When the speed class of 350 km/h (CRH380A Series)EMU is parked in the environment where the temperature is lower than zero and under non-power supply conditions, in order to prevent equipment damage caused by water storage and icing of the vehicle, the anti-freezing and drainage operation of the EMU shall be carried out in advance.

2. Technological process

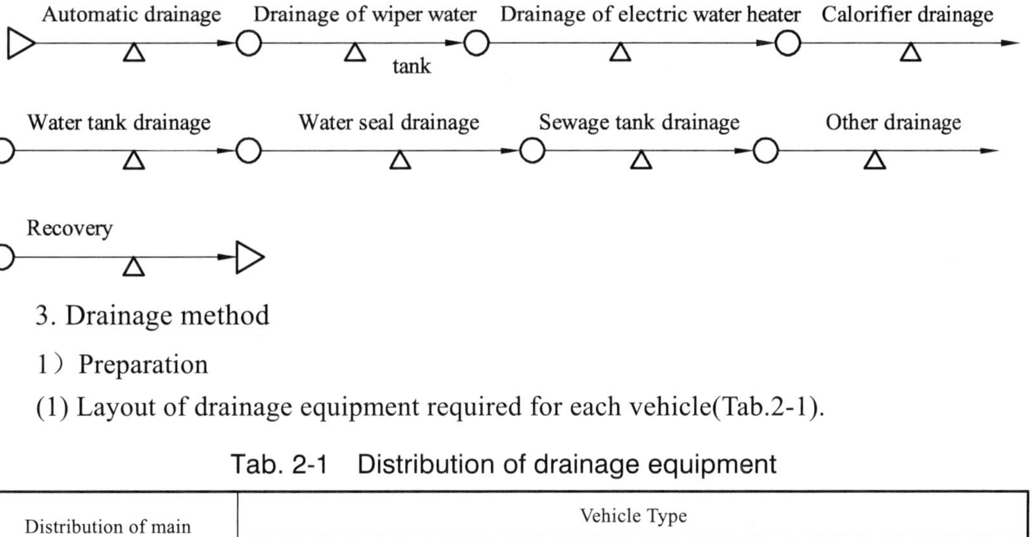

3. Drainage method

1) Preparation

(1) Layout of drainage equipment required for each vehicle(Tab.2-1).

Tab. 2-1 Distribution of drainage equipment

Distribution of main equipment	Vehicle Type							
	T1	M1	M2	M3	M4	M5	M6	T2
Distribution and Capacity of water tank	700 L	Onboard 400 L	700 L	Onboard 400 L	700 L	Onboard 4700 L	700 L	700 L
Toilet Distribution (sitting and squatting)	1 sitting	1 stiting 1 squatting	1 sitting 1 squatting	1 sitting 1 squatting	—	1 sitting 1 squatting	1 sitting 1 squatting	1 squatting
Distnbution and capaciry of sewage tank	450 L	450 L	450 L	450 L	—	450 L	450 L	450 L

Continue

Distnibution of electric water boiler	1	1	1	1	1	1	1	1
Washroom		Have	Have	—	—	Have	Have	—
Water seal	2	2	2	2	1	1	1	1
Wiper tank	1(Under the vehicle)	—	—	—	—	—	—	1(Under the vehicle)

(2) Drainage standard

Open the drain valve. When there is no water dripping at the drain port within 1 minute, it is considered that the water storage of the equipment is drained, and the recovery of each valve can be carried out only after the water storage of each equipment is drained.

2）Automatic drainage

(1) Automatic drainage conditions: the water supply facilities of the vehicle shall be prepared to a normal working state, and the vehicle shall be powered on with high voltage.

(2) Drainage range: it is equipped with main water supply pipeline, water pump, water booster and auxiliary pipeline, toilet, sewage pipeline and transfer box of toilet car; Water pump and water supply pipeline of boiling water boiler and dining car.

(3) Automatic drainage mode: it can be divided into centralized control anti-freezing emptying and single vehicle anti-freezing emptying. Just select one to operate.

(4) Centralized control anti freezing emptying function:

Under the condition of low-voltage power supply (DC 100 V)of EMU, the [toilet control] (dining car is [water supply control])and [water pump power supply] NFB of warm water and dirt distribution board are set to on (As shown in Fig. 2-3 and Fig. 2-4), and the total air pressure is not less than 600 kPa, turn on the [parking] switch in the cab or turn on the [anti freezing emptying] button of DTC one by one (dining car is [anti freezing drainage] button), start the anti freezing emptying function (As shown in Fig. 2-5 and Fig. 2-6).

Fig. 2-3　Warm water dirt distribution board

Fig. 2-4　Distribution board of warm water and dirt in dining car

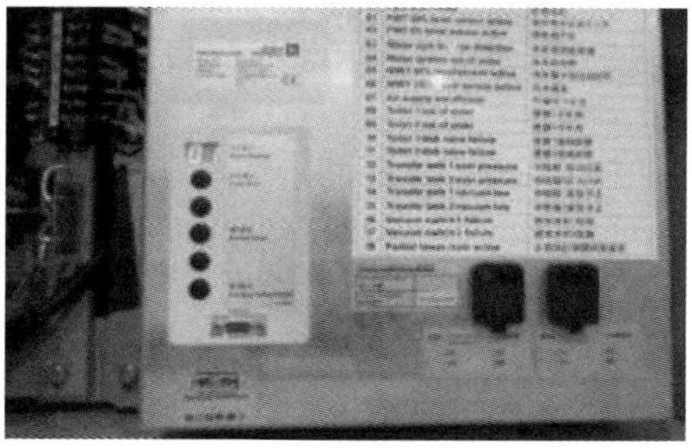

Fig. 2-5　DTC

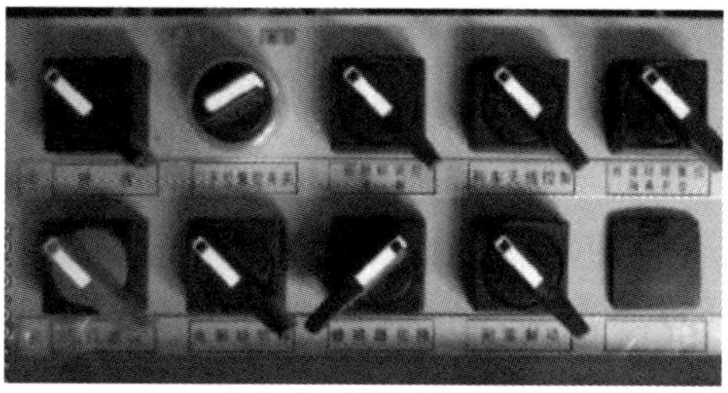

Fig. 2-6　[Parking] Switch

The anti-freezing emptying action process is as follows:

a. the water inlet solenoid valve of the water supply system is powered off and closed, and the water pump stops running;

b. open the drain solenoid valve of the water supply system after power failure to drain the water stored in the water supply pipeline;

c. after the water supply pipeline of the water supply system is drained for 15 minutes, the transfer box will be emptied automatically once, the toilet will be flushed automatically three times, and the transfer box will be emptied automatically three times to drain the water stored in the toilet, water pressurization unit, auxiliary pipeline and transfer box;

d. when the water supply and sanitation system stops working, the toilet is disabled.

After the anti-freezing emptying action is completed, manually open the solenoid valve of the water pressurization unit to confirm that the stored water has been drained.

（5）Anti-freezing emptying function of single vehicle.

Press the [anti-freezing emptying] switch of each vehicle equipped with toilet to empty the main water supply pipeline, water pump, water booster and auxiliary pipeline, toilet, sewage pipeline and transfer tank according to the set procedure. The emptying procedure is the same as that of centralized control anti-freezing emptying.

After drainage, use the [parking] switch for centralized control anti-freezing emptying or the [anti-freezing emptying] switch for single vehicle anti-freezing emptying.

3) Drainage of on-board equipment

(1) Electric boiler drainage.

Open the inspection valve of the electric water boiler, open all the drain cocks of the water production tank, water storage tank and water purifier of the electric water boiler (the cock is open parallel to the pipeline)for drainage, and close all drain valves after the water is drained (see Fig. 2-7).

Fig. 2-7 drain valve of water storage tank and production tank of electric water boiler

(2) Warm water tank drainage.

Open the drain valve of the warm water tank, remove the screw plug at the hot water outlet and water inlet, manually pull out the expansion water safety valve, restore the screw plug after the water is drained, and close the drain valve. Since there is no water tray and floor drain under E28 water heater, dry rags should be placed at the lower end of the two screw plug drainage outlets during the drainage of water heater to prevent drainage from leaking on the floor. At the same time, the water traces on the floor should be wiped dry after drainage (see Fig. 2-8 and Fig. 2-9).

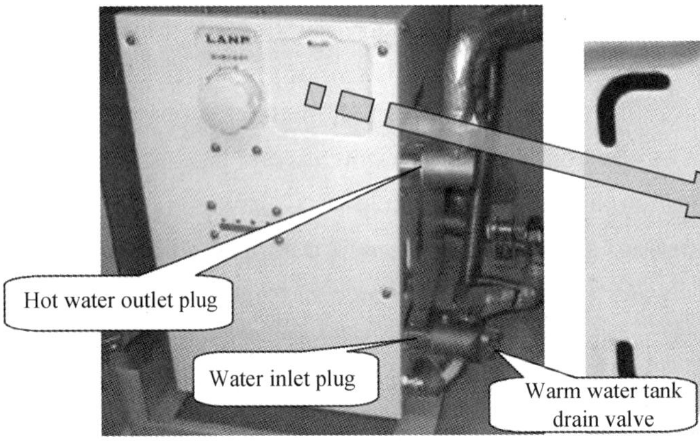

Fig. 2-8 Water supply pipeline of warm water tank

Fig. 2-9 Expansion water safety valve of warm water tank

(3) Faucet and soap dispenser drainage.

Press the faucet and soap dispenser repeatedly until the stored water is drained (see Fig. 2-10).

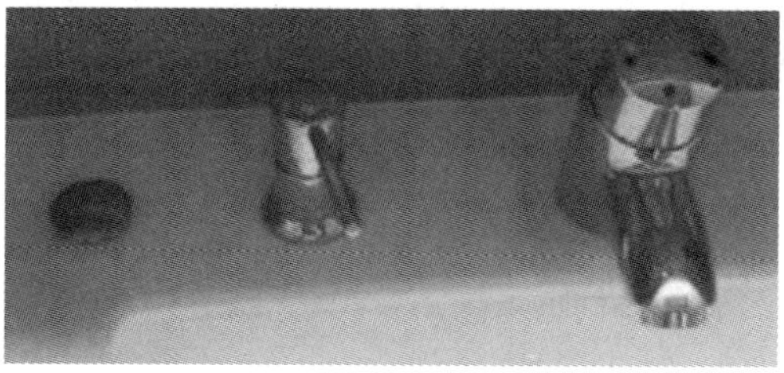

Fig. 2-10 Faucet and soap dispenser

(4) On board water tank drainage.

Open the inspection door of the on-board water tank, open the drain valve of the on-board water tank and water pump (the cock is parallel to the pipeline), and drain the on-board water tank and water pump. See Fig. 2-11 for the valve position.

Fig. 2-11 On board water tank drainage

(5) Other drainage on the vehicle.

Rotate the black handle to drain the water in the wash basin through the drain valve (see Fig. 2-12). Meanwhile, open the two red valves at the lower end of the wash basin for drainage (see Fig. 2-13).

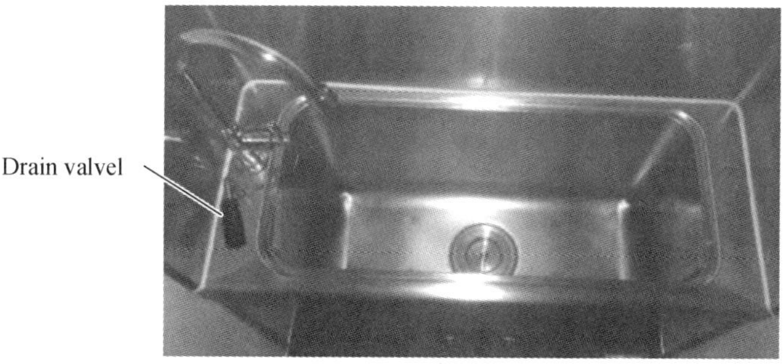

Fig. 2-12 Drainage of car wash basin

Fig. 2-13　Red drain valve at the lower end of car wash basin

4) Drainage of equipment under the vehicle (without power).

(1) Wiper tank drain.

Open the water outlet of the wiper water tank under the vehicle (see the red circle in Fig. 2-14)to drain the wiper water tank until the liquid level of the wiper water tank is at the lowest level. To prevent water storage in the water spray pipeline of the wiper, the wiper drainage action shall be carried out under the power-on state. Until no water is sprayed from the wiper.

Fig. 2-14　Wiper tank

② Under vehicle water tank drainage.

Open the drain valve and water pump emptying valve outside the under vehicle water tank to drain the under vehicle water tank and water pump, as shown in Fig. 2-15.

Fig. 2-15　Drain valve of under vehicle water tank

③ Sewage tank drainage.

Open the blowdown valve of the sewage tank to drain the water stored in the sewage tank (see Fig. 2-16). If necessary, the sewage suction truck can be used for emptying.

Fig. 2-16 Sewage tank blowdown valve

④ Water seal drainage.

Remove the drain plug of the water seal and restore the plug after draining the water (see Fig. 2-17).

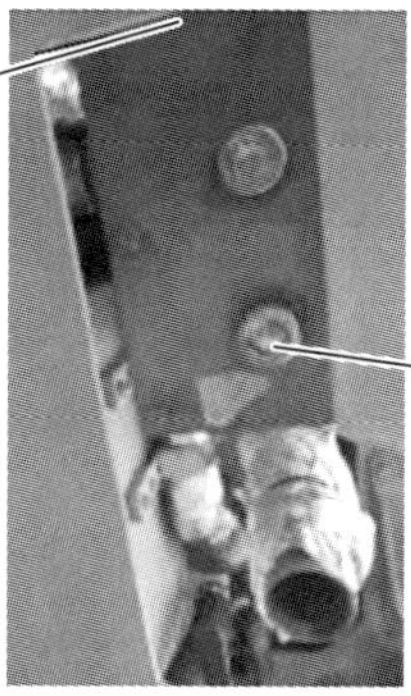

Fig. 2-17 Water seal drain plug

5) Storage of braking system in winter

(1) Auxiliary air compressor drain.

After power failure, open the drain valve of the oil-water separator of the auxiliary air compressor and the drain valve of the auxiliary air compressor to drain the stored water (see Fig. 2-18 and Fig. 2-19).

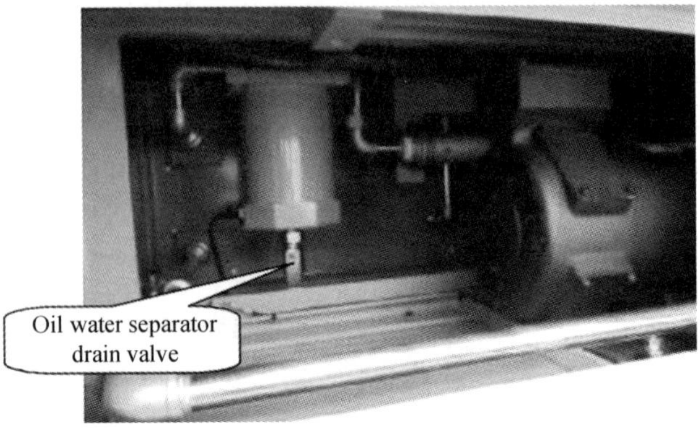

Fig. 2-18 Water separator drain valve

Fig. 2-19 Auxiliary air compressor drain valve

(2) Brake control drain.

After power failure, open the drain cock of three air cylinders (main air cylinder, supply air cylinder and control air cylinder)to drain water (see Fig. 2-20).

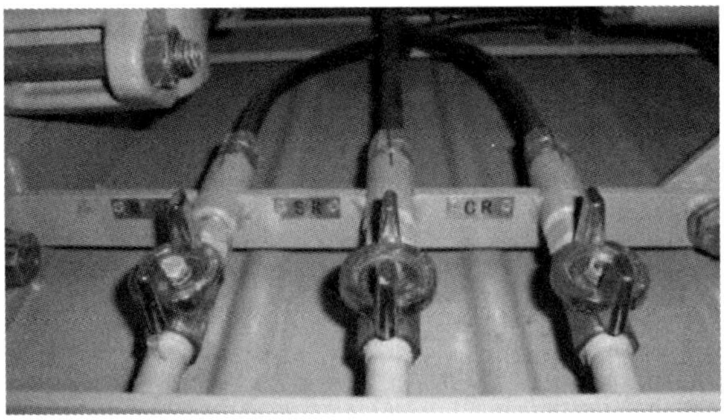

Fig. 2-20 MR、SR、CR valves

6) Restore

After all equipment is drained, restore all water valves, switches, blowdown valves, etc. item by item in order, and restore all equipment inspection doors and covers.

Precautions: after drainage, the fasteners shall be painted with anti loosening marks to confirm that all parts are well sealed.

[Task Detection]

1. What conditions should the parking space of EMU meet when the temperature is lower than 0 °C?

2. How to prevent freezing under power supply condition of EMU?

3. What is the operation process of anti freezing and drainage of EMU?

Project 3

Abnormal Operation Organization of EMU

[Ideological and Political Classroom]

Her mobile phone number is the "110" of the motor car driver–Wang Xiaoxia

China's high-speed railway is not only famous at home and abroad for its high speed and high appearance, but also makes people's travel better with its high safety and high punctuality. Behind the safe and rapid operation of high-speed rail, many people are fighting selflessly for the cause of high-speed rail. Wang Xiaoxia, Secretary of the Party branch and engineer of China Railway Taiyuan Bureau Group Co., Ltd., motor car on-board equipment workshop of Taiyuan electric service section, is such a railway science and technology worker struggling at the forefront.

The motor car on-board equipment workshop where Wang Xiaoxia is located undertakes the tasks of daily maintenance and data analysis of 54 sets of motor car train control on-board equipment (ATP)belonging to Taiyuan Bureau Group Company. Wang Xiaoxia's mobile phone number is the "110 service hotline" of the motor car driver. Over the years, she has been used to quickly switching from anything and any state to ATP fault handling state of EMU, even when sleeping and eating.

"The so-called fault is actually an early warning issued by a module in the ATP system, just like the body reminds us of possible health problems through fever or pain." Wang Xiaoxia explained, "the vast majority of faults are 'small colds' that do not endanger driving safety. The earlier they are found, diagnosed and handled, the smaller the impact on driving safety.

Early detection, accurate judgment and scientific disposal... All Wang Xiaoxia's efforts are to prevent the "small cold" from evolving into a "big problem". Over the past nine years, she has handled more than 300 unexpected problems under her remote guidance. The "zero error" of remote disposal has won Wang Xiaoxia trust and reputation.

On November 13, 2017, the D2508 train from Xi'an north to Taiyuan South failed to deal with the routine alarm during operation. Whether to continue operation or replace the standby train, the train dispatcher and motor train driver were nervously waiting for Wang Xiaoxia's final decision. Wang Xiaoxia quickly and carefully deduced the vehicle condition information in her brain. After determining that even in the worst case, it would not endanger the safety of passengers and trains, she resolutely decided to let the train continue to run according to the diagram. The driver continuously observed and fed back the train status and made emergency preparations at any time. Subsequently, the train drove into Taiyuan South Station on time.

In October 2015, two sample vehicles of China's standard multiple units conducted type test and operation assessment in the comprehensive test section of Yuanping Taiyuan high speed railway. Wang Xiaoxia participated in the test on ATP. During the two years of participating in the test task of Fuxing EMU, she put forward a number of optimization suggestions according to the test content, which contributed to the successful completion of the established test task.

The "Wang Xiaoxia Innovation Studio" established in 2015 is a new platform for her and her innovation team to tackle key technical problems. Under her leadership, the studio has completed the simulation test system of train control on-board equipment of 200C, 200H and 300S, realized the on-line simulation of EMU fault, and filled the gap of the whole road.

[Project description]

At the end of this project, students are expected to master the train operation organization methods under abnormal conditions, master the train operation methods of EMU in disastrous weather, and learn the emergency treatment of EMU emergencies.

Task 1 Train Operation under Abnormal Conditions

[Task Description]

(1) Get familiar with the requirements for EMU drivers under abnormal driving conditions.

(2) Master the relevant regulations of abnormal traffic organization.

Ⅰ. *Basic Requirements for EMU Drivers under Abnormal Driving Conditions*

In case of abnormal driving, the EMU driver must be calm and observe carefully. After an abnormal situation occurs, tension and quick drawing are the big taboos. Any abnormal situation must have its final correct handling procedures and methods. Once it is too nervous and blindly fast, there may be omissions or errors in the first observation of the phenomenon, which will have a devastating effect on the later judgment and handling. If the handling of abnormal driving is divided into three steps, the "observation" in the first step is very important. It directly affects the "judgment" and the final "handling" in the second step. As long as the observation is wrong, the judgment and handling must be wrong.

Ⅱ. *Abnormal Traffic Organization*

1. Double tock section reverse running of EMU

(1) When the train is in double track section, it shall run in one direction on the left; Only when the train is running, the train can run in the opposite direction. If it is a passenger train, it can only run in the opposite direction with the permission of the on-duty Director (deputy director on duty)of the dispatching office under special circumstances such as line blocking in the positive direction section, natural disasters, interruption of train operation due to accidents, failure of equipment in the positive direction seriously affecting the train operation order and good automatic inter station blocking equipment in the opposite direction.

(2) When the train runs in the opposite direction, the train dispatcher shall issue the dispatching command. The train dispatcher (station attendant in case of station control)shall issue corresponding dispatching command after confirming that the section in the opposite direction is free.

(3) When the EMU train runs in the opposite direction in CTCS-3 section, the maximum allowable speed is 300 km/h; When CTCS-2 operates in the opposite direction, the maximum allowable speed is 250 km/h; Among them, in CTCS-2 section, the maximum allowable speed on 250 km/h line is 200 km/h, and the maximum allowable speed on 200 km/h line is 160 km/h.

2. Treatment after the train is forced to stop

(1) When the train is forced to stop in the section and cannot continue to run, the driver shall immediately use the train wireless dispatching communication equipment to notify the train dispatcher (stations at both ends) and on-board Mechanics (train attendants), report the parking reason and parking position, and quickly request rescue as needed.

① The on-board machinist (vehicle steward)and passenger crew shall obey the command of the driver and deal with matters related to driving, train protection and accident rescue.

② After receiving the driver's notice, the train dispatcher (station attendant)shall inform the driver of the train operation in the section, and immediately notify the subsequent trains in the section to stop by using the train wireless dispatching communication equipment. The train shall not be released to the section until the parking causes are eliminated.

③ The train that has requested rescue shall not move again, and the train shall be protected according to the regulations.

④ After the train is forced to stop in the section, local braking shall be ensured to prevent the train from slipping away. In case of automatic brake failure, the driver of passenger train other than EMU shall notify the train crew to immediately organize the train crew to tighten the manual brake of the whole train; Other train drivers shall take safety measures immediately and report to the train dispatcher.

⑤ When protection is required, the driver shall be responsible for the front of the train and the on-board mechanic (vehicle steward)shall be responsible for the rear of the train. The train equipped with train protection alarm device shall first use the train protection alarm device for protection.

(2) When the train is forced to stop and may hinder the adjacent line, the driver shall immediately notify the train running on the adjacent line and the train dispatcher (stations at both ends)using the train wireless dispatching communication equipment, and short circuit the track circuit from the incoming train side of the adjacent line with the on-board mechanic (vehicle steward)near the head or tail of the train. The train equipped with train protection alarm device shall first use the train protection alarm device for protection.

When the train is forced to stop in the section, the driver shall personally or assign personnel to inspect the train along one side of the adjacent line. If it is found that the adjacent line is obstructed, it shall immediately report to the train dispatcher (stations at both ends). If a train from an adjacent line is found, the emergency stop signal shall be sounded. After receiving the notice that the forced parking of the train may hinder the adjacent line, the train dispatcher (station attendant)shall immediately notify the relevant trains of the adjacent line to stop, and shall not release the train to the adjacent line until the parking reasons are eliminated.

(3) After the train is forced to stop in the section, it shall be protected according to the regulations.

① When the train has requested rescue, place the sound pier protection at a distance of not less than 300 m from the train from the direction of the rescue train (in case of unknown, from the front and rear directions of the train); On the line only running EMU trains, when the train has requested rescue after being forced to stop in the section, the on-board machinist shall manually protect the direction of the rescue train at a distance of not less than 300 m from the train, and no sound pier protection shall be placed.

② When the train operates in sections and the locomotive enters the section to pick up the remaining vehicles, the sound pier shall be placed at a distance of not less than 300 m in front of the train.

③ After the shutdown reason is eliminated, the sound pier set by the protection personnel shall be removed by the protection personnel.

3. The train retreats and returns in the section

(1) When the train must retreat in the section under special circumstances, the train dispatcher shall stop the subsequent train and allow the train to retreat after confirming that the block section within the retreat distance is free. The on-board mechanic (vehicle steward)or the designated competent personnel shall stand at the rear of the train and watch the front of the train. If they find that it endangers the driving or personal safety, they shall immediately use the emergency braking device (emergency braking valve) or notify the driver to stop the train. The reverse speed of the train shall not exceed 15 km/h.

(2) If the train needs to retreat to the station, the train dispatcher shall also confirm that the train to the rear station is free. The train dispatcher (station attendant in case of station control) can open the inbound signal or connect the train to the station according to the guidance method according to the line occupation. If the EMU train needs to retreat to the station, the train dispatcher shall issue the dispatching order.

(3) When the EMU train retreats, it retreats according to the isolation mode.

(4) Under fog, storm, snow and other adverse conditions, the train is not allowed to retreat when it is difficult to identify the signal.

(5) When the EMU train must return to the rear station after being forced to stop in the section, the train dispatcher must confirm that the EMU train to the rear station is free before issuing the dispatching command. The driver operates at the front end of the train operation direction (turn back)of the EMU according to the dispatching command, and the train returns according to the isolation mode, and the operation speed shall not exceed 40 km/h.

(6) When the train has to run separately under the condition of necessity, the driver shall report to the train dispatcher (station attendant), and organize the anti-slip and protection of the remaining vehicles, and the station attendant shall report to the train dispatcher immediately. After recording the number of vehicles left and the parking position, the driver can pull the front vehicle to the front station, and still operate according to the signal display during operation. The train dispatcher shall block the section, and the section can be opened only after pulling the remaining vehicles back to the station and confirming that the section is free.

(7) When the train is running separately, the driver must check the penetration status of the brake main pipe of the test train and start the train only after confirming that the driving

conditions are met. However, the train is not allowed to run separately under the following conditions:

① After taking measures, the whole train can be operated.

② No protective and anti-slip measures are taken for the left vehicles.

③ When the left vehicle is unattended.

④ When the driver cannot contact the train dispatcher and station attendant.

⑤ When the remaining vehicles stay on the line with a slope of more than 6‰.

4. Train entering signal

(1) After the train enters the annunciator, the driver shall stop immediately and report to the train dispatcher (station attendant), and shall not move the train without authorization. The station attendant shall report to the train dispatcher. After receiving the report of the driver's entering the station (receiving route)signal, the train dispatcher (station attendant)shall immediately notify the subsequent trains that have entered the section to stop and no longer release trains to the section.

(2) When the train rushes into the arrival (receiving route)annunciator, the train dispatcher (station attendant in station control)will use the train wireless dispatching communication equipment to notify the driver to enter the station after confirming that the receiving route is ready and the train operation conditions are met.

(3) When the train runs into and out of the station (departure route)annunciator, the train dispatcher (station attendant in station control)shall arrange the train to retreat after meeting the conditions. However, for departure or passing trains, the train dispatcher (station attendant in station control)can use the train wireless dispatching communication equipment to inform the driver to continue operation after confirming that the departure route is ready, the first block section is idle (automatic inter station block section is idle) and the train operation conditions are met.

5. Train operation shaking

(1) In case of train shaking during train operation, the driver shall immediately slow down and report the shaking place and train speed to the train dispatcher (station attendant), and resume normal speed operation after the train has no abnormal conditions. The station attendant shall report to the train dispatcher.

(2) When the train shakes and the running speed is below 160 km/h, the train dispatcher (station attendant)shall immediately notify the subsequent trains that have entered the section to stop, no longer release the train to the section, and notify the public works department. According to the application for on track inspection by the public works department, the train dispatcher shall timely issue the dispatching order of blocking the line and the speed limit of 160 km/h and below of the adjacent line, and then allow on track

inspection. After the public works Department inspects the equipment, the train release conditions shall be determined according to the specific situation of the site.

(3) When the train shakes and the running speed is 160 km/h or above, the train dispatcher shall issue a dispatching command with a speed limit of 120 km/h to the first train, and the speed limit position shall be determined according to 1 km before and after the shaking place reported by the driver. After the train passes through the shaking place, the driver shall immediately report the operation to the train dispatcher. If the train shaking continues, the train dispatcher shall immediately notify the subsequent trains that have entered the section to stop, no longer release the train to the section, notify the public works Department, and timely issue the dispatching order of blocking the line and the speed limit of 160 km/h or less of the adjacent line according to the application of the public works department. After the public works Department inspects the equipment, the train release conditions shall be determined according to the specific situation of the site. If the train does not shake, the speed shall be increased step by step at 160 km/h, 250 km/h and normal speed.

In the process of step-by-step train speed increase, in case of train shaking again, the train dispatcher shall immediately notify the subsequent trains that have entered the section to stop, no longer release the trains to the section, notify the public works Department, timely issue the dispatching order of blocking the line and limiting the speed of adjacent lines to 160 km/h and below according to the application of the public works department for on-the-road inspection, and then allow on-the-road inspection. After the public works Department inspects the equipment, the train release conditions shall be determined according to the specific situation of the site.

6. The train stops at the phase separation dead zone of OCS

(1) When the EMU train stops in the neutral area of OCS and cannot continue to operate, the driver shall immediately lower the pantograph and report to the train dispatcher (station attendant), and the station attendant shall report to the train dispatcher. The train dispatcher (station attendant)shall immediately notify the subsequent trains that have entered the section to stop and no longer release trains to the section.

(2) When the EMU is equipped with self-rescue through changing pantograph, retreating and breaking points, the driver shall accurately report the parking position of the EMU, and the train dispatcher, power supply dispatcher and EMU driver dispatcher shall jointly determine the self-rescue scheme and organize self-rescue according to the type of EMU, parking position and traction power supply equipment.

(3) When the EMU does not have the conditions for self rescue, but can transmit power remotely to the neutral area, after the power failure of the catenary power supply arm behind the

split phase, the train dispatcher shall go through the procedures for transmitting power remotely to the neutral area to the power supply dispatcher, notify the train stopped in the split phase to raise the pantograph, and after the train leaves the split phase area, Then inform the power supply dispatcher to restore the original power supply mode and send power to the rear catenary power supply arm to restore the normal operation of subsequent trains.

(4) When the EMU does not have the conditions for self-rescue and cannot send power to the remote control in the neutral area, the train dispatcher shall issue the dispatching command with the speed limit of 160 km/h and below the adjacent line, the driver shall organize relevant personnel to protect the train according to the regulations, confirm the length of the no power area of the catenary in front and rear of the train, and report to the train dispatcher. The train dispatcher shall determine the rescue plan and organize rescue according to the driver's report on the length of no power area of front and rear catenary.

7. Foreign matters in train collision

(1) When the collision of foreign matters during train operation affects the traffic safety, the driver shall immediately take parking measures, and report the location of the collision of foreign matters, the situation of the collision of foreign matters and the parking location to the train dispatcher (station attendant). The driver of EMU train shall also notify the onboard mechanic. The station attendant shall report to the train dispatcher. The train dispatcher (station attendant)shall immediately notify the subsequent trains of the line that have entered the section to stop and will not release trains to the section. When it is necessary to get off the train for inspection, the train dispatcher shall timely issue the dispatching command with a speed limit of 160 km/h and below on the adjacent line according to the driver's request. The driver shall get off the train for inspection after receiving the oral instruction that the train dispatcher has issued the relevant dispatching command (the EMU train shall notify the onboard mechanic to get off the train for inspection).

(2) When the EMU train can continue to operate after inspection, it shall resume operation (the EMU train shall operate according to the requirements of the onboard mechanic), and the driver shall report the inspection to the train dispatcher. If no abnormality is found in the inspection, the train dispatcher shall issue oral instructions to the subsequent first train of the line to operate at a speed limit of 160 km/h. The speed limit position shall be determined according to 2 km before and after the place where the foreign object collides. The train driver shall strengthen the lookout, confirm whether there is any abnormality in the line and catenary, and report to the train dispatcher immediately after passing the speed limit place. After receiving the report of no abnormality from the driver, Organize the subsequent trains of the line to resume normal operation; In case of abnormal conditions affecting the train operation, the train dispatcher shall, according to the driver's report, detain the follow-up train or organize the speed

limit operation of the follow-up train, and timely notify the relevant departments to check and deal with it according to the regulations. When it is confirmed that it cannot continue to operate after getting off the vehicle, it shall request rescue in time and protect it according to regulations.

(3) When EMU trains collide with foreign matters, which invade the adjacent line and affect the traffic safety of the adjacent line, the train dispatcher (station attendant)shall immediately notify the train on the adjacent line that has not passed the place to stop, no longer release the train to the section of the adjacent line, and notify relevant departments to check and deal with it according to the regulations.

(4) When the collision of EMU trains with foreign matters is unknown and it is uncertain whether it will affect the adjacent line, the train dispatcher shall immediately issue oral instructions to the first train of the adjacent line that has not passed the place, with a speed limit of 160 km/h. The speed limit position shall be determined according to 2 km before and after the collision of foreign matters.

The driver of the first train on the adjacent line shall strengthen the lookout, confirm whether the line and catenary are in abnormal state, and report to the train dispatcher immediately after passing the speed limit place. After receiving the report of no abnormality from the driver, the train dispatcher shall organize the follow-up trains on the adjacent line to operate normally. In case of abnormal conditions affecting the train operation, the train dispatcher shall, according to the driver's report, detain the follow-up train or organize the speed limit operation of the follow-up train, and timely notify the relevant departments to check and deal with it according to the regulations.

(5) The public works, electricity and power supply departments shall use the skylight time to focus on the inspection of the equipment within 2 km before and after the collision of foreign objects.

[Task detection]

1. What are the basic requirements for EMU drivers during abnormal driving?

2. What to do when the EMU stops in the phase separation and no power area of the catenary?

Task 2 Train Operation Method for EMU in Disastrous Weather

[Task Description]

(1) Get familiar with driving operation methods in disastrous weather.

(2) Master the technical equipment for driving in disastrous weather.

Ⅰ. *Operation Principle of Train Operation in Disastrous Weather*

(1) In case of equipment failure affecting train operation (except train equipment failure), in principle, the failure shall be handled first and then the train operation shall be organized. If the equipment fault cannot be repaired temporarily, and it is really necessary to organize the driving, the driving shall be organized according to the relevant driving restrictions.

(2) In case of a storm, snow or earthquake, equipment management units such as public works, electricity and power supply shall strengthen the inspection of key sections and equipment. Outside the skylight time, inspectors shall not enter the shoulder and bridge deck. If necessary, they shall block or speed limit, and conduct inspection after protection. If it is found that the traffic safety is affected, the train dispatcher shall be notified in time to operate at a speed limit or block the line.

Ⅱ. *Traffic Organization in Disaster Weather*

1. Driving in windy weather

(1) Disposal when receiving the gale alarm information from the wind speed monitoring subsystem of the natural disaster and foreign matter intrusion monitoring system.

(2) When the wind speed monitoring subsystem prompts the gale alarm information, the train dispatcher issues the dispatching command of speed limiting operation to relevant trains according to the alarm prompt. For trains that are too late to issue dispatching orders, immediately notify the driver to operate at a speed limit. The driver shall take measures immediately after receiving the dispatching order or notice.

(3) In case of windy weather, when the wind speed monitoring subsystem sends out the alarm message of prohibiting operation, the train dispatcher shall close relevant signals in time (notify the station attendant to close relevant signals during station control)and notify the driver to stop. After receiving the notice, the driver shall immediately take parking measures.

(4) In case of strong wind during train operation, the driver shall control the train operation speed according to the situation and report to the train dispatcher. The train dispatcher shall inform the driver of the first subsequent train to pay attention to operation in this section; After the train passes through this section, the driver shall report to the train dispatcher in time.

(5) In case of strong windy, the train dispatcher issues the speed limit dispatching command according to the alarm prompt of the wind speed monitoring subsystem. In case

of unstable wind speed or multiple wind speed alarms in the same section, the train dispatcher can set them together and issue the speed limit dispatching command according to the minimum speed limit value.

(6) After the speed limit alarm of the wind speed monitoring subsystem is released, the train dispatcher shall cancel the previous speed limit dispatching command in time to restore normal traffic.

(7) The speed limit of EMU trains in case of strong wind is as follows:

① It can operate at normal speed when the ambient wind speed is not greater than 15 m/s; When the ambient wind speed is not greater than 20 m/s, the operating speed is not greater than 300 km/h; When the ambient wind speed is not greater than 25 m/s, the operating speed is not greater than 200 km/h; When the ambient wind speed is not greater than 30 m/s, the operating speed is not greater than 120 km/h; When the ambient wind speed is greater than 30 m/s, EMU trains are strictly prohibited from entering the wind area.

② When EMU trains pass through the main line and arrival departure line with the center line of the line 1,750 mm away from the edge of the platform, the speed shall not exceed 80 km/h under the condition that the ambient wind speed is not greater than 15 m/s; When the ambient wind speed exceeds 15 m/s, the operating speed of EMU shall not exceed 45 km/h, and pay attention to the operation.

(8) Disposal in case of failure of wind speed monitoring subsystem of natural disaster and foreign matter intrusion monitoring system.

① When the train dispatcher finds the fault of the wind speed monitoring subsystem, he shall immediately notify the equipment management unit and register it in the inspection register of running equipment; When the equipment management unit finds the fault of the wind speed monitoring subsystem, it shall immediately report it to the train dispatcher and register it in the train operation equipment inspection register of the dispatching office.

② During the failure of the wind speed monitoring subsystem, in case of gale weather of level 7 or above in the weather forecast in the fault section, the public works department shall timely submit the weather forecast information to the train dispatcher, and the train dispatcher shall issue the speed limit dispatching order to the relevant trains according to the maximum wind level in the weather forecast. Relevant speed limit regulations are as follows: when the maximum wind speed reaches level 7, the operating speed shall not be greater than 300 km/h; At level 8 and 9, the operating speed shall not be greater than 200 km/h; At level 10, the operating speed shall not be greater than 120 km/h; When level 11 or above, the train is prohibited from entering the wind area. The speed limit mileage shall be determined by the public works department according to the fault conditions and weather forecast information, and then notified to the train dispatcher.

2. Driving in rainy days

(1) Disposal when receiving the alarm information from the rainfall monitoring subsystem of the natural disaster and foreign matter intrusion monitoring system.

When the rainfall monitoring subsystem prompts the rainfall monitoring alarm information, the train dispatcher issues the dispatching command of limited speed operation to relevant trains according to the alarm prompt. For trains that are too late to issue dispatching orders, immediately notify the driver to operate at a speed limit. The driver shall take measures immediately after receiving the dispatching order or notice.

(2) When the train passes through key flood control sections, the driver shall strengthen the lookout and take necessary safety measures at any time.

During the operation of EMU train, if the driver finds that the ponding is higher than the rail surface, he shall stop immediately, confirm the driving conditions or request rescue together with the on-board mechanic according to the site conditions, and immediately report to the train dispatcher (station attendant), and the station attendant shall report to the train dispatcher. The train dispatcher (station attendant)shall immediately notify the subsequent trains that have entered the section to stop (avoid stopping in the tunnel)and no longer release trains to the section.

When the flood reaches the shoulder, the train shall run at the specified speed limit; In case of falling stones, fallen trees and other obstacles endangering driving safety, the driver shall stop immediately, remove the obstacles and confirm that they are safe before continuing to run.

When the train encounters sudden situations endangering traffic safety such as line collapse and ballast bed empty, the driver shall immediately take emergency safety measures and immediately notify the tracking train, adjacent train and train dispatcher (adjacent station). The train equipped with train protection alarm device shall immediately use train protection alarm.

(3) In case of rainy weather, when the rainfall in key flood control sections reaches 45 mm or more within 1 h, the train speed limit is 120 km/h; When the rainfall reaches 60 mm and above in 1 h, the train speed limit is 45 km/h. When the rainfall drops to 20 mm or less within 1 h and lasts for more than 30 min, the speed limit can be gradually lifted.

The train dispatcher shall cancel the speed limit or unblock the line in time after receiving the report that there is no abnormality from the dispatching desk of public works and other relevant disciplines.

(4) Disposal in case of failure of rainfall monitoring subsystem of natural disaster and foreign matter intrusion monitoring system.

When the train dispatcher finds the failure of rainfall monitoring subsystem, he shall immediately notify the equipment management unit and register it in the inspection register of running equipment; When the equipment management unit finds the failure of rainfall monitoring subsystem, it shall immediately report to the train dispatcher and register it in the train operation equipment inspection register of the dispatching office. During the failure of rainfall monitoring subsystem, the public works department shall register the speed limit or blockade in the running equipment inspection register of the dispatching office according to the rainfall.

3. Driving in ice and snow

1) Disposal in ice and snow weather

(1)When the snow depth alarm value of the snow depth monitoring subsystem of the natural disaster and foreign matter intrusion monitoring system reaches the warning value, the train dispatcher shall timely issue the dispatching command of speed limit operation to relevant trains according to the alarm information and speed limit prompt. For trains that are too late to issue dispatching orders, the driver shall be informed to operate at a speed limit immediately.

In case of failure of the section without snow depth monitoring subsystem or snow depth monitoring subsystem, the public works and electrical affairs departments shall register the speed limit application in the traffic equipment inspection register of the dispatching office according to the snowfall conditions and needs, and can apply for speed increase or further speed limit according to the change of snow cover, and the train dispatcher shall issue the dispatching order in time.

(2) In the section where the dynamic image detection system (TEDS)for EMU operation fault is installed, the TEDS monitoring center shall strengthen the monitoring and analysis of EMU bogie icing, snow and other conditions. If it is found that the EMU bogie icing requires speed limit operation, it shall immediately report the train number and speed limit requirements to the EMU dispatcher as required. The motor train dispatcher shall notify the train dispatcher for disposal.

During the operation of the train, when the on-board mechanic finds that abnormal conditions such as abnormal noise at the bottom of the EMU and beating of the EMU require the speed limit of the train, he shall immediately notify the driver of the speed limit. The driver operates according to the speed limit requirements of the on-board mechanic, and reports the hit location mileage to the train dispatcher. The train dispatcher will no longer issue the speed limit dispatching order. The train dispatcher notifies the motor train dispatcher to remind the driver of the next first train and the on-board mechanic to pay attention to the train operation status at the beaten place; The motor car dispatcher shall immediately notify the TEDS monitoring point ahead for key monitoring. After the train passes through the hit place, the driver and on-board machinist shall report relevant operation conditions in time.

(3) In case of snow, the turnout snow melting device shall be started in time according to the snow condition of the line. When the snowfall reaches moderate snow or above, and it is difficult for the station turnout to rotate, in order to reduce the turnout pulling, the station can adopt the method of fixed receiving and departure route to handle the receiving and departure train operation, and one receiving and departure route shall be fixed up and down respectively. When it is difficult for stations with a large number of departure and arrival trains to execute, several lines with less cross interference and less change of turnout position can be selected for relatively fixed receiving and departure operation. Larger passenger stations shall try to stop at lines convenient for water supply and sewage absorption.

(4) When manual snow removal is required, the registration and signing system shall be implemented for the upper and lower roads. The train dispatcher shall stop receiving and Dispatching Trains and shunting on this line according to the application of relevant units, and the speed limit of trains on adjacent lines is 160 km/h and below.

(5) In case of snow on track bed, ice on overhead contact system and poor current collection of pantograph, the driver shall take deceleration measures first and report to the train dispatcher in time. The train dispatcher shall notify the relevant professional dispatcher, and the professional dispatcher shall notify the relevant equipment management unit in time. The equipment management unit shall find out the situation in time, apply for speed limit according to the regulations, and the train dispatcher shall issue the speed limit dispatching order in time.

(6) The power supply department shall master the icing condition of OCS conductor. When the train speed limit is required, it shall immediately register the running equipment inspection register and apply for speed limit to the train dispatcher. When the OCS de icing is required, the power supply department shall apply for de icing, and the train dispatcher shall timely arrange the OCS de icing vehicles to run on line.

In case of icing on the conductor of the overhead contact system, the power failure operation of the skylight can be canceled, and the EMU and single machine can be operated during the skylight time for hot sliding and ice melting.

(7) When the on-board machinist finds that the bogie of the EMU is frozen, the pantograph cannot be raised, the EMU is hit and other abnormal conditions need to be handled at the departure and turn back stations, he shall timely notify the driver. The driver shall report to the train dispatcher, and the train dispatcher shall notify the motor train dispatcher. The motor train dispatcher shall apply for replacing the underbody or speed limit according to the situation reported by the on-board machinist and the vehicle application, And organize the snow and ice removal of the warehousing EMU.

(8) After the snowfall, the equipment management unit proposing the speed limit shall check and confirm the relevant driving conditions and restore the normal speed operation in time. When the speed increase conditions are met or the speed limit is eliminated, an application shall be submitted to the train dispatcher, who shall issue relevant dispatching orders in time. The specific procedures and methods for resuming normal speed operation after snow shall be stipulated by the railway administration.

(9) When the train dispatcher finds the fault of snow depth monitoring subsystem, he shall immediately notify the equipment management unit and register it in the train operation equipment inspection register; When the equipment management unit finds the fault of the snow depth monitoring subsystem, it shall immediately report to the train dispatcher and register it in the train operation equipment inspection register of the dispatching office.

2) Speed limit requirements in ice and snow weather

(1) When the sleeper plate or ballast surface is covered by moderate snow or snow in the operation section, the speed limit of ballastless track section is 250 km/h and below, and that of ballasted track section is 200 km/h and below; In case of heavy snow and blizzard in the operation section, the speed limit of ballastless track section is 200 km/h and below, and that of ballasted track section is 160 km/h and below. The definition of moderate snow, heavy snow and Blizzard shall be subject to the announcement or observation of the meteorological department.

When the snow thickness of sleeper plate in ballastless track section is more than 100 mm, the speed limit is 200 km/h and below; When the snow thickness of ballast area in ballasted track section is more than 50 mm, the speed limit is 160 km/h and below.

(2) When the conductor of OCS is frozen and the current collection of pantograph is not smooth, the speed limit is 160 km/h and below.

(3) When the speed limit of the train is required for the icing of the bogie of the EMU, the speed limit of the ballastless track section is 250 km/h and below, and the speed limit of the ballasted track section is 200 km/h and below.

4. Foreign matter intrusion alarm

(1) After receiving the foreign object intrusion disaster alarm information of the foreign object intrusion subsystem, the train dispatcher shall immediately notify the train that has entered the alarm location and has not passed the alarm location in the section to stop immediately, and will not release the train to the section. At the same time, he shall report to the duty Director (deputy director on duty)of the dispatching office, and the duty Director (deputy director on duty)Immediately notify the equipment management unit to rush to the site for inspection and treatment.

(2) Before the inspectors of the equipment management unit arrive at the alarm point, the train dispatcher shall check the on-site situation through the video monitoring system. If there is any abnormality or cannot be confirmed, the train operation can be organized only after the equipment management unit has inspected and handled it and met the conditions for releasing the train. If there is no abnormality, it shall be handled according to the following provisions:

① After confirming that one block zone at the alarm location is idle, the train dispatcher shall orally notify the driver to resume operation one by one for the trains that have entered the alarm location and have not passed the alarm location in the section, and cross the block zone where the alarm point is located at the speed that can stop at any time in case of obstacles (the maximum speed of EMU trains shall not exceed 40 km/h, and the maximum speed of other trains shall not exceed 20 km/h), Before indicating that the rear train resumes operation, it must be confirmed that the front row has completely crossed the alarm point, one block partition at a time, and get a report that there is no abnormality in the front row.

② The driver stops in front of the annunciator (section signal signboard)in the block section where the alarm point is located, waits for 2 min, crosses the block section at a speed that can stop at any time when encountering obstacles (the maximum speed of EMU train is no more than 40 km/h, and the maximum speed of other trains is no more than 20 km/h), and runs through the annunciator display (train control on-board equipment display)one time. The driver shall strengthen the lookout, stop immediately in case of any abnormality, and report to the train dispatcher; If there is no abnormality, the driver shall report to the train dispatcher in time after confirming that the train has completely crossed the alarm point and one block zone at a time. While parking and waiting, the driver must contact the train dispatcher. If it is confirmed that there is a train in the block section ahead, he shall not enter.

③ After the section is idle, train operation shall be organized between stations before the red light band of the block section where the alarm point is located is canceled.

(3) After the on-site inspection and handling by the equipment management unit, the train dispatcher shall organize the train operation according to the traffic restrictions registered in the traffic equipment inspection register by the equipment management unit. When the conditions are met, the train dispatcher shall cancel the registration of the red light band in the block zone where the alarm point is located according to the permission of the equipment management unit, and use the temporary traffic button to cancel the red light band of foreign matter intrusion disaster alarm.

(4) Before the fault is not repaired, the equipment management unit must send personnel to watch on the site and report the site situation to the train dispatcher in time.

After the red light band of the block zone where the alarm point is located is canceled, the train dispatcher shall issue the dispatching command of paying attention to operation with a speed limit of 120 km/h and below. The speed limit position is the block zone where the alarm point is located, and the driver shall strengthen the lookout.

(5) After the fault is repaired, the train dispatcher unlocks the recovery button in the natural disaster and foreign matter intrusion monitoring system to restore the system to the normal state and restore normal traffic organization.

(6) Disposal in case of power grid disconnection alarm of foreign matter intrusion subsystem of natural disaster and foreign matter intrusion monitoring system.

When one power grid of the dual power grid is disconnected, the foreign matter intrusion subsystem sends the fault alarm information of the foreign matter intrusion sensor, and the natural disaster and foreign matter intrusion monitoring system does not send the disaster alarm information to the train control system, which does not affect the normal driving. After receiving the power grid disconnection alarm information of the foreign object intrusion subsystem, the train dispatcher shall organize the train operation as normal and immediately notify the equipment management unit for inspection and treatment.

(7) Disposal when the foreign matter intrusion subsystem of the natural disaster and foreign matter intrusion monitoring system fails to reflect the site conditions.

① When the train dispatcher finds that the system cannot reflect the on-site situation due to the fault of foreign matter intrusion subsystem, he shall immediately notify the equipment management unit and register it in the inspection register of running equipment; When the equipment management unit finds the fault of foreign matter intrusion subsystem, it shall immediately report to the train dispatcher and register it in the running equipment inspection register of the dispatching office.

② Before the fault of foreign matter intrusion subsystem is not repaired, the equipment management unit must send personnel to watch on the site and report the site situation to the train dispatcher in time. The train dispatcher shall issue the dispatching command of paying attention to operation with a speed limit of 120 km/h and below. The speed limit position is the block section where the monitoring point is located, and the driver shall strengthen the lookout. In case of foreign matters invading the limit, the watchman shall immediately notify the train dispatcher, who shall call the train to stop.

③ Before the watchman arrives at the monitoring point of foreign matter intrusion, the train dispatcher shall issue a dispatching command to pay attention to the operation with a speed limit of 120 km/h and below (40 km/h and below when the monitoring point of foreign matter intrusion is the tunnel entrance). The speed limit position is the block zone where the monitoring point is located, and the driver shall pay attention to the operation there.

5. Earthquake monitoring and alarm

After receiving the earthquake monitoring alarm information of the earthquake monitoring subsystem or the on-site earthquake report, the train dispatcher shall immediately close the relevant signals (in the case of station control, it is to notify the station attendant to close the relevant signals)and notify the relevant trains to stop. The train driver shall organize the train crew to take emergency measures according to the actual situation on site.

The train dispatcher shall immediately report to the on-duty director (deputy director on duty)of the dispatching office and notify the equipment management units such as public works, electrical affairs, power supply, communication and housing construction for inspection. After inspection and handling, the equipment management unit shall organize driving according to the driving restrictions registered by the equipment management unit.

6. Difficulties in recognizing the driving signal in bad weather

(1) Disposal when receiving bad weather report.

In case of bad weather and the signal display distance is less than 200 m, the driver or station attendant shall immediately report to the train dispatcher. When the train operates according to the ground signal display, the train dispatcher shall issue the dispatching order in time and change to the method of driving according to the illegible signal in bad weather.

(2) Driving method with illegible signal in bad weather:

① The train operates according to the display of locomotive signal. When approaching the ground signal, the driver shall confirm the ground signal. In case of inconsistency between the ground signal and locomotive signal, the driver shall immediately take deceleration or parking measures.

② When the display of departure (route)annunciator cannot be recognized, after the train meets the departure conditions, the driver starts the train according to the display of locomotive signal, and accelerates after confirming that the display of departure (route)annunciator is correct.

③ When the weather gets better, it shall be reported to the train dispatcher in time to issue dispatching orders and resume normal traffic.

[Task Detection]

1. What is the train operation method in disastrous weather?
2. What is the speed limit requirements for EMU in windy weather?
3. What are the regulations on speed limit in disastrous weather?
4. How to organize train operation when receiving earthquake monitoring and early warning?
5. What is the driving method in case of bad weather and illegible signal?

Task3 Emergency Handling Measures for EMU Emergencies

[Task Description]

(1) Master the handling methods of various emergencies of EMU.

(2) Get familiar with the speed limiting operation conditions of EMU.

Ⅰ. *Fault and Disposal of EMU*

(1) In case of failure during the operation of EMU, the driver shall handle immediately according to the tips of on-board information monitoring device and steps; when it needs the cooperation of on-board machinist, the driver shall notify the on-board machinist. When it is confirmed that it cannot operate normally, the driver shall choose to maintain operation or stop and use it according to the tips of on-board information monitoring device and the requirements of on-board machinist The train wireless dispatching communication equipment shall report to the train dispatcher or station attendant.

(2) When the EMU is forced to stop in the section, the onboard machinist and passenger crew shall obey the command of the EMU driver and deal with matters related to driving, train protection and accident rescue.

(3) When the EMU is rescued, the connection and decomposition of the transition coupler, special air duct and electrical connecting line shall be in the charge of the onboard mechanic with the cooperation of the EMU driver. If the conditions for pantograph raising power supply are met, the EMU is allowed to raise pantograph for power supply.

(4) In case of failure of automatic conversion between CTCS-2 section and CTCS-0/1 section, the driver shall immediately report to the station attendant and train dispatcher and handle it according to the following provisions:

① In case of operation from CTCS-2 level to CTCS-0/1 level, stop and switch manually.

② If CTCS-0 /1 operates to CTCS-2, it can continue to operate in LKJ mode.

(5) When the train control on-board equipment fails and the motor train signal display is abnormal, the driver shall turn the train control on-board equipment into isolation mode and deal with it according to the motor train signal failure.

(6) When the EMU driver or the personnel of the equipment maintenance unit find the balise fault, they shall timely report to the attendant of the adjacent station, and the station attendant shall timely report to the train dispatcher.

Ⅱ. The EMU Operates at a Speed Limit under the Following Conditions

(1) When the braking system of EMU fails, when 25% braking force is removed, the speed limit is 160 km/h; when 50% braking force is removed, the speed limit is 120 km/h.

(2) In case of an air spring failure, the speed limit of CRH2/CRH380A/AL EMU is 120 km/h, and that of other models is 160 km/h.

(3) When the car seal fails due to the damage of window glass, the speed limit is 160 km/h.

Ⅲ. Hot Standby EMU Dispatch

1. Starting time of hot standby EMU

When the fault of EMU cannot be repaired in time, the hot standby EMU shall be started in time. When starting the standby EMU, first consider using the hot standby EMU. When there is no hot standby EMU or the fixed number of hot standby EMUs is less than the actual number of faulty EMUs, the routing of online operating EMUs shall be adjusted. If possible, other EMUs shall be used as the bottom of the rescue vehicle. When the above measures cannot be realized, the nearby idle ordinary bus bottom shall be used as the rescue vehicle bottom.

2. Dispatch of hot standby EMU

The standby driver of the hot standby EMU must be equipped to undertake the task of the EMU of each line. When on duty in the locomotive dispatching room of the locomotive depot, Handle attendance according to the tasks of each line undertaken by the hot standby EMU (including transmitting dispatching orders and IC cards). After reporting to the dispatching room of the EMU, go to the train apartment or locomotive depot close to the stopping place of the EMU (EMU Operation Station)shall be on duty and have a full rest to ensure that they can be on duty at any time after calling. When the hot standby EMU is dispatched to rescue the inter Bureau EMU, it shall be under the unified command of the dispatching department of the railway corporation.

(1) The EMU dispatcher of the dispatching office of the dispatching department of the Transportation Bureau of China Railway Corporation shall immediately report to the director on duty, the dispatching director and the director of the dispatching department (deputy director)and notify the vehicle, locomotive, power supply and electrical dispatching of China Railway Corporation as needed; the vehicle, locomotive, power supply and electrical dispatching of China Railway Corporation shall notify the director of passenger train, the director of locomotive operation, the director of power supply and the director of signal respectively.

(2) After receiving the instruction from the leader of the emergency rescue command center to dispatch the hot standby EMUs, the on-duty director of the dispatching office of the dispatching department of the Transportation Bureau of the Railway Corporation shall immediately arrange the EMU dispatching console to issue the dispatching order for the dispatch and operation of the hot standby EMUs to the relevant railway bureau.

(3) After receiving the dispatch order of EMU, the dispatching office of hot standby EMU allocation bureau shall immediately (within 3 min)issue the dispatching order of the hot standby EMU to the relevant units. The relevant units must complete the shunting, servicing, driver and passenger staffing and other work of the hot standby EMU within 10 min after receiving the order, and meet the departure conditions. When the hot standby EMU rescue is dispatched, the division, on-board machinist and passenger crew of the service shall be undertaken by the allocation Bureau.

(4) When the hot standby EMU and the standby driver act as the train number in the section not in the charge of the EMU of the Bureau, the original EMU driver of the railway bureau shall act as the driver. If the vehicle model is inconsistent, the standby driver shall act as the driver. The original driver of the railway Bureau shall be responsible for leading the track and providing the train timetable carried by the EMU driver.

(5) Priority shall be given to the EMU trains responsible for transfer to ensure timely arrival and return. When organizing passenger transfer in the station, it shall be arranged on two station platforms of the same platform as far as possible. When organizing passenger transfer in the section, the train dispatcher shall organize the EMU trains responsible for transfer to enter the designated position of the adjacent line for parking. The train responsible for transfer shall arrive at the adjacent line After stopping at the designated position of the line, the driver shall report to the train dispatcher. The train dispatcher informs the conductor to organize passengers to transfer through the driver of the train applying for transfer. The conductor in charge of the transfer task shall notify the driver after confirming that the passengers have transferred. The driver shall be notified by the conductor, confirm that the door is closed, start the train when the driving conditions are met, and report to the train dispatcher.

(6) The railway administration shall refine the management measures for standby and dispatch of hot standby EMUs, and clarify the time limit standards for hot standby EMUs, personnel, spare parts, daily management and dispatch, so as to ensure that the equipment is intact and dispatched on time.

3. Operation and return of hot standby EMU

(1) When the hot standby EMU is dispatched to run and return to its place between the departure station and the connecting station, add "R" in front of the connected train number,

and the driving language is "hot standby EMU" ×× (Times)", matters related to train operation shall be handled according to EMU. The original train number shall still be used for the subsequent train number.

(2) The non-hot standby EMU shall be dispatched from the bottom of the train to operate and return to the original position between the departure station and the connecting station. The train number shall be added with "T" or "K" before the connected train number according to the vehicle type at the bottom of the train. The driving language is: "express EMU" ×× (Times)"," fast EMU " ×× (Times)".

(3) The passenger car bottom of hot standby EMU and temporary replacement of faulty EMU shall be released in priority to ensure timely arrival and return Homing.

Ⅳ. *Passenger Organization in Case of EMU Failure*

1. The EMU organizes passengers to transfer due to failure

(1) When the hot standby EMU is used to organize passengers' transfer, the station shall strengthen the station train organization, do a good job in the food supply and logistics services of transfer passengers according to the regulations, and the two trains shall be arranged at the same platform as far as possible to facilitate passengers' transfer. At this time, the station and depot emergency leading group shall rush to the site immediately, and if necessary, the members of the Railway Bureau emergency leading group shall rush to the site for organization and command.

(2) When the hot standby underbody of non EMU is used to replace EMU to operate passenger train, the train number shall be relatively fixed (in principle, the original EMU train number shall be changed to express or express passenger train number). The start-up order must be issued 1 h before the start-up. For inter Bureau passenger trains, the China Railway Corporation and the passenger dispatching department of the railway bureau shall issue the dispatching order to stop the EMU and start the passenger train. The passenger dispatching order shall specify the train number of the stopped EMU, the Bureau under the train, the running train number Marshaling sequence, vehicle type, model, personnel quota, arrival and departure time of parking station, crew responsible unit, etc.

(3) After receiving the order to start the hot standby train, the station shall reserve enough zero according to the fare difference, and designate a special person to organize and guide passengers to recover the original ticket of EMU passengers, issue new tickets and refund the fare difference at the designated place. When passengers request to change to other trains, the station shall go through the ticket change procedures in time and change the ticket to a seat ticket as far as possible. There is no service charge for ticket refund and change.

(4) During transfer, the station train shall carefully organize ticket inspection. Passengers holding tickets of other train numbers are strictly prohibited from getting on the train. Passengers holding tickets of decommissioned EMUs must change new tickets before getting on the train.

2. EMU is delayed and passengers are stranded due to fault

(1) The dispatching office of the railway bureau shall forecast and report the delay information of EMUs according to the regulations.

(2) When the EMU is more than 30 min late at the departure station, the station shall timely notify the passengers. When the passengers ask for ticket refund or ticket change before taking the train at the departure station, the station shall handle ticket refund or ticket change in time; the passenger transport office or passenger transport depot of the Railway Bureau at the departure station shall send section chief or team leader cadres to take the train, and organize the train crew to serve, explain and comfort the passengers.

(3) When the EMU is late on the way, the conductor shall timely contact the passenger transport dispatcher of the railway bureau to understand the reasons for the delay, report the situation in the train and the problems requested to be solved, and organize the steward to actively provide services. When the delay is more than 30 min, the conductor shall apologize and explain to the passengers. The passenger police shall cooperate closely with the conductor, often patrol the carriage and maintain the public order in the train Preface.

(4) After receiving the notice that the EMU will arrive 30 min or more late, the station master and police station master shall lead the relevant personnel of passenger transport and public security to meet the train at the platform, organize the passengers to get off and leave the station, and apologize and explain to the passengers. The destination is where the railway bureau is located, and the passenger transport department and Railway Public Security Bureau of the Railway Bureau (Department)leaders shall meet the train at the platform to help guide the station to do emergency disposal.

(5) When passengers ask the railway for compensation for delay or air conditioning failure by detaining the train, the station staff shall focus on persuasion and sincere apology, patiently and carefully explain and publicize relevant laws and regulations, stabilize their emotions, resolve their grievances, and strive to obtain the understanding and cooperation of passengers.

(6) The public security department shall actively cooperate with the passenger transport department, earnestly carry out the persuasion and persuasion of stranded passengers, and strive for understanding and support. At the same time, it shall publicize legal knowledge to passengers, inform passengers that they can safeguard their legitimate rights and interests through other legal channels and methods, persuade passengers to

follow the arrangement of station staff, negotiate and solve at the designated place, and assist station staff to guide passengers Passengers get off. The public security department shall not carry guns in the process of assisting in persuading them to leave.

When the passenger transport department publicizes and persuades passengers to leave the carriage, there shall be public security personnel on site to maintain order; After repeated work, the public security personnel shall announce the notice on maintaining the railway transportation order and ensuring the normal operation of the train issued by the former Ministry of Railways and the Ministry of public security, organize sufficient public police force, and take measures to take away the persons who refuse to get off the train according to law. Individual personnel who incite passengers to stay in carriages, disrupt train security, disrupt railway transportation order, and confront law enforcement by violent means shall be seriously investigated and taken evidence, and their legal responsibilities shall be investigated according to law. Dissuasion should be conducted in accordance with laws and regulations, with reason and discipline, and law enforcement in a civilized manner.

3. Emergency treatment of air conditioning failure

(1) When the air conditioner fails for more than 20 minutes and cannot be recovered, but the train can operate normally, the conductor may notify the driver to request the train dispatcher to stop at the nearest passenger station ahead, and the train dispatcher shall arrange the train to stop at the nearest passenger station ahead. After the train is installed with protective net at the parking station and some doors are opened, the train dispatcher shall report to the driver according to the driver's report (including the rescue driver during rescue)and all stations along the way issue the dispatching command to open the door with a speed limit of 60 km/h (40 km/h when passing the line adjacent to the high platform).

(2) When the train stops for some reason and cannot maintain operation and the air conditioner fails for more than 20 minutes and cannot be recovered, the conductor shall timely communicate with the driver and on-board mechanic, make a decision to open the door according to the situation, and notify the driver to report to the train dispatcher.

(3) The conductor shall organize the train attendants to install the protective net and open the door, with the cooperation of the driver and on-board machinist. The protective net shall be installed when the train is stopped, and the installation position is at the door on the left (non-passing side)of the running direction. After the protective net is installed and the door is opened, the conductor shall organize the train staff to be on duty until the door is closed. The conductor shall report to the driver after confirming that the protective net is firmly installed and the care is in place.

(4) When it is necessary to organize passengers to get off or transfer to other trains, it

shall be carried out at the station platform. When passengers must be organized to get off or transfer in the line or section not adjacent to the platform in the station, it shall be approved by the deputy director in charge of transportation (Chief dispatcher)of the Railway Bureau.

Ⅴ. *Emergency Disposal of EMU Equipment Failure*

1. Failure of EMU vehicle equipment

(1) After the EMU arrives at the station and stops stably, in case of failure of the automatic door opening and closing device, the driver shall timely notify the conductor and on-board machinist to open and close the door manually.

(2) In case of smoke from the vent, the driver shall stop immediately according to the situation or timely report to the train dispatcher and arrange to stop at the nearest front station to check whether the dust net has foreign matters.

(3) When the bearing temperature exceeds the temperature alarm, stop the train immediately, and call the stations at both ends or the train dispatcher with the train wireless dispatching communication equipment to report the parking reason and parking position. The on-board mechanic gets off the train to check the faulty axle and reports to the driver according to the actual axle temperature inspection. The driver puts forward the speed limit operation request to the train dispatcher, and the train dispatcher reports to the driver according to the actual axle temperature inspection Upon request of the engine, issue the speed limit operation command.

(4) According to the requirements of the on-board machinist, when stopping for inspection on the defect of wheel set tread, the driver shall timely report to the train dispatcher and ask the front station to stop for inspection. When the defect of wheel set tread exceeds the limit, the train dispatcher shall issue the speed limit operation command according to the driver's request.

(5) When receiving the report that the wheel set is locked due to the clamping stagnation of gearbox and connecting shaft, the driver shall stop immediately and assign the on-board mechanic to get off the vehicle for inspection and treatment. If the locking fault cannot be eliminated, request rescue in time.

(6) In case of abnormal sound, peculiar smell and abnormal conditions in the running part and windshield connecting part during operation, the on-board mechanic shall report to the driver according to the specific conditions and put forward a parking request. The driver shall stop immediately or report to the train dispatcher according to the fault conditions reported by the on-board mechanic and request the front station to stop for inspection. The operation can be continued only after the parking inspection is confirmed to be unimpeded or emergency treatment.

(7) When receiving the report of an air spring failure, the train dispatcher shall issue the dispatching with a speed limit of 160 km /h command.

(8) When the braking system fails, the train dispatcher shall issue the dispatching order according to the following requirements:

① When the foundation braking device fails to release the wheel locking, the driver shall stop immediately, call the stations at both ends, track the train and train dispatcher with the train wireless dispatching communication equipment, and report the parking reason and parking position. The on-board mechanic gets off the vehicle for inspection and treatment, and cuts off the braking operation of the vehicle.

② When 25% braking force is removed due to the failure of the braking system of EMU, the speed limit is 160 km/h; When 50% braking force is cut off, the speed limit is 120 km/h.

(9)When receiving the report that the car seal fails due to the damage of window glass, the train dispatcher shall issue the dispatching command with a speed limit of 160 km /h.

2. Catenary power failure

(1) In case of OCS power failure during EMU operation, the driver shall immediately stop and lower the pantograph, report the parking reason and parking position to the train dispatcher (station attendant), notify the on-board mechanic (vehicle steward)and the conductor, and the station attendant shall report to the train dispatcher. When the power supply dispatcher finds the OCS power failure, he shall immediately confirm the power failure range and notify the train dispatcher.

(2) After receiving the report of OCS power failure, the train dispatcher (station attendant)shall immediately stop the relevant trains that have not entered the power failure area, and notify the driver to stop the trains that have entered the power failure area. The train dispatcher shall immediately notify the power supply dispatcher to confirm the power failure scope, inform the power supply department to check and deal with it, and set the power failure sign on the CTC.

(3) After the passenger train pulled by electric locomotive stops in the section due to catenary power failure, the driver shall take pressure maintaining measures. When the wind pressure is insufficient for long-time parking, the driver shall notify the vehicle steward to organize the passenger crew to tighten the manual brake of the whole train.

(4) When the OCS trips and overlaps or the power transmission is successful, and the reason is unknown, the power supply dispatcher shall immediately notify the train dispatcher of the OCS trip, the mileage of the location indicated by the fault calibration device and the speed limit requirements. The train dispatcher shall immediately issue oral instructions to the first train of this line and adjacent lines that has not passed through the

location. Pay attention to the operation with a speed limit of 80 km/h. In principle, the speed limit position shall be in accordance with the fault mark 2 km before and after the location indicated by the positioning device. The driver shall pay attention to the status of OCS equipment, stop immediately and report to the train dispatcher in case of abnormal conditions affecting train operation. The train dispatcher shall immediately notify the subsequent trains that have not passed through the abnormal place to stop, shall not release the trains to the section, and immediately notify the power supply department for inspection and handling. The train dispatcher shall organize train operation according to the traffic restrictions registered by the power supply department; If there is no abnormality, the driver shall report to the train dispatcher immediately after passing the speed limit place. The train dispatcher shall organize the normal operation of subsequent trains on the line according to the report of the driver of the line confirming that there is no abnormality on the line, and organize the normal operation of subsequent trains on the adjacent line according to the report of the driver of the adjacent line confirming that there is no abnormality on the adjacent line.

(5) The power supply dispatcher shall immediately organize the power supply personnel to board the train of this line or adjacent lines to inspect the equipment. The power supply personnel shall timely apply to the train dispatcher for handling the fault by using the EMU train, and the train dispatcher shall arrange in time.

3. Signal, interlocking and blocking equipment affecting EMU Operation

1) Failure of blocking equipment

(1) In CTCS-2 section, when the basic block method is out of service and the telephone block method is used, the train dispatcher shall arrange the EMU to stop, issue the dispatching command to the driver, turn the train control on-board equipment mode into isolation mode and drive in LKJ mode.

(2) At the terminal station where the train operates according to the telephone blocking method, the train dispatcher shall arrange the EMU to stop, issue the dispatching command to the driver, exit the isolation mode and convert it to the train control on-board equipment mode.

(3) If the terminal station of train operation by telephone blocking method and the front routing is CTCS-0 section, the EMU does not need to stop, and the train dispatcher will no longer issue dispatching orders. After the EMU stops according to the drawing, the driver shall timely place the main machine disconnector of train control on-board equipment in the "normal" position.

2) The section passing signal fails

When the EMU is running in the section and the train control on-board equipment displays the stop signal, the train must stop immediately, and the driver shall use the train wireless dispatching communication equipment to notify the on-board mechanic. When the train stops and waits for 2 min, and the train control on-board equipment still does not receive the signal allowing operation, the driver will turn the train control on-board equipment into the visual driving mode and stop the train Continue to operate at the speed that can stop at any time in case of obstruction, and the maximum speed shall not exceed 20 km/h until the train control on-board equipment receives the allowable operation signal and operates according to the display of train control on-board equipment. While parking and waiting, one must contact the train dispatcher and station attendant. If there are trains in the front block section, anyone is not allowed to enter.

3) Departure (departure route)annunciator failure

In CTCS-2 section, in case of departure (departure route)annunciator failure, the driving certificate of EMU is a green license, and the visual driving mode of train control on-board equipment shall be manually selected for operation; when the signal allowing operation is received, it shall be operated according to the display of train control on-board equipment.

4) Inbound (receiving route)annunciator fails (mechanical guidance)

When the track circuit information received by the train control on-board equipment is HB code, it will automatically turn into guidance mode after crossing the inbound annunciator.

5) Station coding failure

In case of station coding failure or other reasons, the EMU shall stop immediately when it fails to receive the allowable driving information in front of the arrival, departure and route annunciator. After the EMU stops, the driver shall report to the station attendant and train dispatcher and turn to the visual driving mode according to the dispatching command; when the train control on-board equipment receives the allowable running signal When running, it shall run according to the display of train control on-board equipment.

4. Fault of automatic phase separation ground equipment

(1) The driver shall immediately report to the train dispatcher (station attendant)if he finds that the automatic phase crossing cannot be realized. After receiving the report, the train dispatcher (station attendant)shall notify the subsequent trains to pay attention to the operation and inform the equipment management unit to check and deal with it; when the equipment management unit finds the fault of the automatic phase crossing ground equipment, it shall immediately report to the train dispatcher (station attendant).

(2) Before the fault of on-board automatic phase separation device is repaired, the train dispatcher (station attendant)shall notify the driver to use manual phase separation

according to the registration of the equipment management unit. Before the EMU runs to the phase separation insulation area, the driver shall confirm the train number of raising the pantograph in advance. When running to the phase separation insulation area, he shall concentrate, strengthen the lookout, timely cut off the traction force and "cut off the power" , confirm that the network voltage rises and stabilizes before "power on".

(3) After receiving the fault notification of automatic phase separation "sensor device", the station attendant shall notify the adjacent multiple units (trains pulled by electric locomotives)timely and report to the train dispatcher. The train dispatcher shall immediately use the train wireless dispatching communication equipment to report to the multiple units The driver and the station (of the train pulled by the electric locomotive)shall issue the dispatching order for the shutdown of the automatic phase separation system according to the regulations, and report to the relevant equipment management unit and the public security organ. After the automatic phase separation "sensor device" is repaired, the train dispatcher shall issue the dispatching order for the restoration of the automatic phase separation system in time to restore the normal traffic organization.

5. Automatic pantograph lowering during operation

(1) When the train drops the pantograph for unknown reasons during operation, the driver shall immediately cut off the main circuit breaker and stop, check the kilometer sign of the pantograph dropping place, report to the train dispatcher (station attendant), and the station attendant shall report to the train dispatcher. Train dispatcher (station attendant)shall immediately notify the subsequent trains in the section to stop and not release the train to the section. The train dispatcher shall report the pantograph lowering to the power supply dispatcher. The on-board machinist of EMU train shall give timely feedback on the fault occurrence time and other information to the driver according to the fault information record. The driver shall report to the train dispatcher, and the train dispatcher shall report to the power supply dispatcher in time.

(2) Train dispatcher according to the driver (the EMU train is the request of the on-board machinist through the driver)to get off the train for inspection or climbing operation, and issue the dispatching order with the speed limit of 160 km/h and below the train on the adjacent line; when climbing operation is required, the train dispatcher shall also notify the train in the power supply arm to stop and lower the pantograph, go through the formalities of OCS power failure with the power supply dispatcher, and after receiving the notice of OCS power failure from the power supply dispatcher, Issue the scheduling command to allow the top job.

(3) The driver shall get off the train for inspection after receiving the oral instruction issued by the dispatching order with the speed limit of 160 km/h and below on the adjacent

line (for the EMU train, the driver shall notify the on-board mechanic to get off the train for inspection). The driver can only climb the top according to the dispatching order with the permission to climb the top and the oral instruction issued by the dispatching order with the speed limit of 160 km/h and below on the adjacent line (the driver of the EMU train informs the onboard machinist to climb the top for operation).

(4) After inspection and treatment, the driver shall immediately report to the train dispatcher after the train resumes operation. The train dispatcher shall immediately issue oral instructions to the first train on the line that has not passed the place. The speed limit shall be 80 km/h. pay attention to operation. In principle, the speed limit position shall be determined according to 2 km before and after the fault location reported by the driver. The driver shall pay attention to observing the status of OCS equipment and find abnormal conditions affecting driving The train dispatcher shall immediately stop and report to the train dispatcher. The train dispatcher shall immediately notify the subsequent trains that have not passed through the abnormal place to stop, no longer release the trains to the section, and immediately notify the power supply department for inspection and handling. The train dispatcher shall organize the train operation according to the traffic restrictions registered by the power supply department. If there is no abnormality, the driver shall report to the train dispatcher immediately after passing the speed limit place, and the train dispatcher shall organize the follow-up train to operate normally according to the report confirmed by the driver.

(5) After receiving the report, the power supply dispatcher shall immediately organize the power supply personnel to board the train of this line or adjacent lines to inspect the equipment. The power supply personnel shall timely apply to the train dispatcher for handling the fault by using the EMU train, and the train dispatcher shall arrange in time.

[Task Detection]

1. What are the conditions for speed limiting operation of EMU?
2. What are the regulations on the dispatch of hot standby EMUs?
3. How to organize passengers in case of EMU failure?
4. What to do in case of failure of EMU vehicle equipment?
5. What to do when the train control on-board equipment of EMU fails?
6. What to do when the ground equipment of EMU train control fails?

Project 4

Operation Specification for On-board Machinist of EMU

[Ideological and Political Classroom]

Dong Hongtao, a "train doctor" running with high-speed rail

When you sit on a stable train and watch the scenery along the way, when you arrive at your destination and run to your long-awaited relatives, do you know that such a group of people silently guard this sweetness and happiness, they are called "EMU mechanics". Dong Hongtao is one of them. He has sharpened his sword for 26 years and tried his edge once. Whether on duty or off for maintenance, he is struggling with the difficult and miscellaneous diseases of the motor car!

Dong Hongtao is the mechanic of the emergency unit of Xi'an motor car depot dispatching section, the person in charge of "Hongtao motor car difficulty diagnosis and treatment group" and "Dong Hongtao model worker Innovation Studio". In the past 26 years, he has successively won the honors of No. 1 Technical champion of Shaanxi Province, technical expert of the whole road, locomotive medal, model worker of the whole road, railway craftsman and so on. Looking back on his 26 years of railway career, Dong Hongtao, who won't "use one heart and two purposes", ridiculed himself with the word "stupid", but he interpreted the responsibility and responsibility of the "Guardian" of EMU safety with practical actions, and demonstrated the firm belief of a Communist Party member and the professional pursuit of a EMU mechanic with a strong sense of career and responsibility.

From 2015 to 2017, the multi-functional measuring ruler developed by Dong Hongtao's team, the special tool for disassembly and assembly of 32 core electrical connector plug for EMU rescue, and the quick installation torque wrench of pantograph gas tube round nut won 5 national patents. As a leader, Dong Hongtao has solved more than 300 problems and investigated nearly 2000 faults since his establishment. After the establishment of the emergency desk in 2015, it handled more than 200 emergencies during the operation of EMUs and provided nearly a thousand technical support for on-board mechanics. A persistent belief, the loyalty of a guardian, such as the EMU guarded by Dong Hongtao, as long as running on the road, the only obsession is to move forward bravely and be a good leader.

[Project Description]

At the end of this project, students are expected to learn the post responsibilities of EMU on-board machinist, and get familiar with the items and quantities of EMU on-board tools and spare parts; Be able to complete one round-trip operation of on-board machinist according to standards and fill in relevant records, plus handle sudden faults of EMU according to the prompt of on-board information system.

Task 1 Operation Standard for On-board Machinist of EMU

[Task Description]

(1) Get familiar with the post responsibilities and requirements of EMU on-board machinist.

(2) Be able to operate according to the one-time round-trip operation standard of the on-board mechanic of the EMU.

Ⅰ. *Post Responsibilities of EMU On–board Machinist*

As an on-board mechanic, he is mainly responsible for the on-board crew of EMU Operation (operation, test, pick-up, etc.), responsible for ensuring the safe operation state of EMU, maintaining the normal hardware environment in the vehicle, mastering and transmitting the dynamic operation information of EMU equipment, emergency handling and repairing equipment faults in operation, Conduct daily condition inspection and quality handover for the upper facilities of EMU. Specific responsibilities are as follows:

1. Monitor the technical status of EMU operation

(1) During operation, the train operation and equipment working status are monitored in the crew (monitoring)room through the on-board information system.

(2) During patrol inspection of vehicle equipment during operation, problems found shall be correctly judged and dealt with decisively.

(3) Technical inspection shall be carried out at departure and turn back stations.

(4) Timely and accurately report the fault and abnormal environment of EMU to the superior department. When endangering the driving safety, it can directly put forward the

speed limit or parking requirements to the driver.

2. Manage and operate EMU equipment

(1) Operate EMU equipment and facilities as required.

(2) Cooperate with the passenger transport department to control the air conditioning and ventilation device in the vehicle and set the operation mode of regulating the air conditioning and ventilation device; Control the lighting of passenger compartment in the train, and set and adjust the lighting conditions; Open the passenger information system and train number setting information as required.

(3) Guide the passenger service personnel to correctly use the equipment in the vehicle.

(4) During on-board operation, check the storage position of on-board tools, materials, driving spare parts and safety protection articles of EMU according to the fixed location management diagram of EMU, and do not move them without permission. In case of missing, damaged and expired spare parts (requiring calibration), report them to the affiliated workshop in time, and the workshop will organize replenishment, replacement and calibration.

3. Emergency treatment of sudden faults on the way

(1) In case of sudden failure during operation, actively carry out emergency treatment. After discovering or receiving the notice of vehicle equipment fault, the fault shall be identified in time and handled according to the manual for emergency fault treatment on the way of EMU and relevant regulations; In case of abnormal operation or shutdown, the onboard mechanic shall immediately report to the motor train dispatcher of the group company where the fault occurs.

(2) The sudden faults of EMU are divided into three categories: if they are handled independently by the driver, it is necessary to strengthen contact with the driver to understand the fault handling; If it is handled in cooperation with the driver, it shall be handled jointly under the command of the driver; If it is handled independently by the on-board mechanic, the situation and operation requirements shall be reported to the driver in time after the treatment is completed.

(3) In case of faults or other emergencies endangering driving safety, the on-board mechanic can use the emergency braking device to stop or notify the driver to take parking measures. After emergency braking and start-up of the EMU, strengthen the patrol inspection of the EMU and pay attention to monitoring the running state of the wheel set.

(4) The on-board machinist of EMU shall deal with the fault emergency on the way. When the interval exceeds 20min and the station exceeds 30min, and the fault cause is still unable to be determined or cannot be handled, the driver shall be notified to request rescue.

After requesting rescue, the on-board mechanic of the EMU shall immediately report to the EMU dispatcher of the group company where the accident occurs, obey the command of the dispatcher of the group company where the accident occurs, and make rescue preparations or fault emergency disposal as required.

(5) In case of severe ice and snow weather, when the on-board mechanic finds that the speed limit is required due to abnormal noise at the bottom of the EMU and beating of the EMU during train operation, he shall immediately notify the driver of the speed limit.

4. Information report

(1) When the EMU train operates abnormally or stops due to EMU failure, the onboard mechanic shall timely report the information to the EMU dispatching of the group company with dispatching command authority at the place of the incident, and timely report to the EMU Depot dispatching according to the specified procedures.

(2) If the EMU stops due to fault, it shall carefully check and confirm the status of all parts of the EMU. If it cannot operate normally, it shall be handled in time. If it is necessary to operate at a speed limit or request rescue, it shall be reported to the driver immediately and according to the regulations.

(3) Do a good job in communication with EMU drivers and passenger passengers.

5. Storage of EMU outside and handover of departure, return and boarding

(1) After entering the depot (storage point), the EMU shall hand over the onboard key, CRH EMU onboard mechanic crew log and EMU fault handover record to the dispatching room (duty room).

(2) Two hours before the EMU leaves the warehouse, the on-board machinist shall go to the duty room of the local workshop (the duty room of the storage point)to receive the alcohol content test, register on the on-board machinist exit and return record form, and handle the handover according to the regulations.

(3) The on-board machinist shall inspect the EMU according to the requirements of receiving operation at the storage point, focusing on the review of overnight operation contents, timely report the existing problems to the local workshop duty room (shift room at the storage point), deal with them in time, and make records.

(4) Be responsible for checking whether the thermal insulation, pollution discharge and other work of EMUs stored in other places are carried out and whether the operation quality is qualified. If there are problems, report to the local workshop duty room and the workshop duty room in time.

6. Undertake some functions of train operation organization

(1) Before the EMU leaves the warehouse, the onboard machinist shall inform the

driver to remotely cut off the pantograph not used on that day through the monitoring screen, and then raise the pantograph used on that day. After the EMU is put into storage, the onboard mechanic shall inform the driver to remotely restore the removed pantograph through the monitoring screen.

(2) To ensure the balanced service time of the pantograph of the same EMU, the pantograph can be raised according to the principle of raising the front pantograph in a single day and raising the rear pantograph in two days (the pantograph not used in the previous day shall be selected when the EMU leaves the warehouse in a different place overnight).

(3) In case of forced parking in the section due to EMU failure or other reasons during operation, strengthen contact with the driver, master the situation, timely report to the motor train dispatcher of the local group company, and do a good job in driving and safety protection under the command of the driver.

(4) When the EMU is rescued, be responsible for the disassembly and assembly of the transition coupler and special air duct, the connection and disconnection between the train locomotive and the EMU transition coupler, the connection and disconnection of the hose, the connection and disconnection of the electrical connecting line, guide the rescue coupling, confirm the coupling status, and cooperate with the driver.

7. Pantograph operation in winter

(1) When the external temperature is lower than -5 °C, the EMU will not change pantograph in the EMU station, storage yard, departure station and turn back station, and the same pantograph will be used for operation on the same day.

(2) In case of pantograph failure to rise, automatic pantograph drop, no network voltage of the train and other faults of the EMU, the operation shall be carried out according to the emergency fault handling manual on the way of the EMU, and the pantograph replacement operation shall be carried out according to the situation.

Ⅱ. *Post Management of On-board Machinist of EMU*

Because the on-board machinist of EMU has great responsibility during the operation of EMU, in order to ensure its work specification, the EMU crew management organization is set up in the EMU Depot to inspect, supervise and manage the on-board machinist's work such as boarding, handover, return and operation. Specific requirements are as follows:

(1) The on-board mechanic of EMU shall work with certificates; Wear a badge when working (as shown in Fig. 4-1), send railway telegrams, board and lodging in apartments or guest houses, and enter and leave the station with the badge and work permit.

Fig. 4-1 Style of chest plate of on-board machinist of EMU

(2) The motor car depot shall uniformly standardize the standards for filling in the crew log of on-board machinist of CRH motor car unit and the fault handover record of motor car unit, with neat handwriting, complete items and specific contents. The motor car depot shall specify the director (director)and deputy director (deputy director)who guide and manage the crew work according to the actual situation, check the cycle and frequency of the crew log of on-board machinist of CRH EMU and sign it.

(3) The abnormal information occurred during the on-board mechanic's duty shall be fed back timely and accurately by telephone. The feedback information shall include the following contents:

① Information on abnormal parking, late departure and late arrival of EMU.

② Equipment failure affecting the equipment function and operation safety of EMU.

③ Emergencies and major events inside and outside the vehicle during operation.

④ Bad weather (wind, snow, rain)status and speed limit operation information of EMU Operation section.

⑤ Relevant leaders of the head office and the group company get on the train to check the work.

(4) Quality requirements for crew work of on-board machinists

① Strictly implement the regulations and requirements of railway technical management regulations, rules for investigation and handling of railway traffic accidents, rules for emergency rescue of railway traffic accidents, rules for operation and maintenance of railway EMUs, manual for handling emergency faults on the way of CRH EMUs and other rules and regulations.

② Take a full rest before going on duty to ensure that you are energetic. Dress and carry tools according to regulations when on duty, carefully listen to and record the work requirements conveyed and deployed by the duty officer and leaders at all levels, strictly implement the operation standards, and conduct a comprehensive technical inspection on the EMU on duty to ensure that it meets the outbound quality standards.

③ Monitor the operation status of the EMU in strict accordance with the regulations, carefully inspect the carriages according to the operation standards, and timely and accurately five feedback on the safety and fault information of the EMU during operation.

④ The fault of EMU can be accurately judged and quickly handled to ensure the normal use of EMU equipment and facilities. Conduct timely and correct emergency treatment for sudden faults during EMU Operation to ensure the safe operation of EMU.

⑤ Strengthen the supervision of the upper facilities of EMU, and immediately stop the damage and incorrect use of EMU equipment and facilities.

⑥ Various statements and accounts shall be filled in timely, accurately, well and without omission.

⑦ Consciously abide by relevant regulations on labor safety to prevent injury to themselves and others.

⑧ No liability accident, no violation of rules and disciplines.

Ⅲ. *One Time Operation Standard for On-board Machinists of EMU*

1. On duty

(1) Before going on duty, the mechanic on board shall have a full rest and drinking is strictly prohibited.

(2) When on duty, the on-board machinist shall dress according to the regulations, wear chest cards, carry corresponding certificates and portable tools, go to the dispatching room (shift room at the storage point) of the EMU for alcohol test, and receive the status inspection record of fixed service facilities of EMU, joint inspection record of outgoing quality of EMU according to the regulations Crew log of on-board machinist of EMU, EMU fault handover record, on-board key, GSM-R handheld terminal, wireless intercom equipment, etc., listen to commands, tasks, requirements and precautions, and understand the maintenance, fault handling and previous operation of EMU.

2. Receiving operation

(1) Before operation, safety protection measures shall be set according to regulations.

(2) Check and confirm that the head cover of the EMU is locked in place, the coupler at the reconnection end is in good condition, the skirts and cover plates on both sides are locked in place, the air spring is free of air leakage, and the connecting pipeline at the train end is free of falling off.

(3) Remove safety protection measures after operation.

(4) After the EMU is powered on, turn on the air conditioner, lighting and passenger information system to confirm the working state.

(5) Check the onboard tools, materials and running spare parts.

(6) Patrol the operation of the EMU, confirm that the doors and windows of the cab at

the non-operating end are locked, and deal with abnormalities in time.

(7) Confirm the disposal of key faults.

3. Original departure operation

(1) After arriving at the station, check at the platform side to confirm that the side door, external display and pantograph are in good condition.

(2) Go to the crew (monitoring)room, hand over the status inspection record of fixed service facilities of EMU with the conductor, and monitor the on-board information system.

(3) During Original departure, monitor the operation of EMU in the cab.

4. Operation on the way

(1) After departure, patrol and inspect the technical status of main service facilities in the train and monitor the train operation status.

(2) During operation, patrol inspection must be carried out as required, and the train operation and equipment status must be monitored in the crew (monitoring)room. In case of fault and alarm, it shall be handled according to the specified procedures and recorded.

(3) Before the driver of the EMU continues to ride, the on-board mechanic of the EMU shall understand the operation from the driver of the EMU. After the EMU driver takes over, he shall hand over the technical status of driving and control equipment in the cab with the next driver and sign on the EMU fault handover record.

5. Turn back station operation

(1) Before the train arrives at the station, the mechanical engineer of the EMU shall go to the cab to understand the operation and make records.

(2) After the train arrives at the station, check at the platform side to confirm that the side door, external display and pantograph are in good condition.

6. Transfer operation

(1) The on-board mechanic needs to pick up the train at the transfer station 15 minutes in advance

(2) Before the train arrives at the transfer station, the on-board mechanic of the returning EMU shall fill in the crew log of the on-board mechanic of CRH EMU and the EMU fault handover record sheet, and sort out the handover items.

① During transfer at the turn back station, the following EMU on-board machinist shall stand at the starting point of turn back to pick up the train, monitor the train operation sound, check the status of pantograph and other visible parts. After the train stops stably, go to the crew (monitoring)room to handle the handover of items received during attendance and train operation status with the returning EMU on-board machinist.

② When transferring through the station, the following EMU on-board machinist shall stand on duty to pick up the train, and the following and returning EMU on-board machinist shall handle the handover of items received during attendance and train operation status in the crew (monitoring)room.

(3) After handover, take the EMU with the train, and the machinist shall stand at the platform side to deliver the train.

(4) After transfer at the turn back station and before departure, the on-board mechanic of the EMU shall go to the crew (monitoring)room to monitor the on-board information system and wait for departure.

(5) In case of EMU failure requiring emergency treatment during transfer operation at turn back station, the on-board machinists of returning and succeeding EMUs shall cooperate and deal with it together.

7. Final operation

(1) Before the train arrives at the station, learn about the operation from the EMU driver and make records.

(2) After the train arrives at the station, patrol the carriage together with the conductor, handle the status handover of fixed service facilities in the train, fill in the status inspection record of fixed service facilities of EMU, fill in the crew log of onboard machinist of CRH EMU, and sort out the handover items.

(3) Key faults shall be reported to the motor car depot in advance, and wait in the crew (monitoring)room for the train to enter the motor car depot.

(4) On the way to the motor car depot, the operation status of the motor car unit is monitored through the on-board information system.

(5)After entering the EMU, accept the alcohol test as required, and hand over the onboard keys and corresponding record sheets. In case of not joining the exchange, it shall be implemented in accordance with the relevant management measures of the local group company.

8. Off duty

(1) Hand over the technical status with the driver of the EMU after entering the depot and stopping the EMU stably.

(2) After entering the depot, the on-board machinist shall report the operation condition to the dispatching room of the EMU depot, sign the handover log, hand over the key faults, and return the on-board mobile phone, relevant keys of the EMU, crew log, etc.

Ⅳ. *Working Terms for On-board Machinist of EMU*

1. Working contact terms

(1) During the normal operation of EMU, when the onboard mechanic needs to enter the cab at the main control end, the contact terms are as follows:

Machinist: the driver of ××× times, and the machinist makes an inspection tour of the cab.

(2) After the EMU stops temporarily in the section or station due to the failure of power supply, public works, communication, signal and other equipment, the driver shall immediately report the parking reason to the train dispatcher. Use the hand-held radio to inform the conductor and the on-board mechanic of the reasons for parking. The contact terms are as follows:

Driver: conductor and mechanic of ××× train, who stops in the train section or station due to ××× fault or reason.

Conductor: the conductor of ××× understand.

Mechanic: the mechanic of ××× understand.

(3) In case of EMU equipment failure, after temporary parking in the section or station, the driver shall immediately report the parking reason to the train dispatcher. According to the fault information reported by the vehicle status display screen, the hand-held radio is used to inform the conductor and the on-board mechanic of the parking reason and fault information. The contact terms are as follows:

Driver: the conductor and mechanic of train ×××. If the train stops in the section (or station)due to ××× fault, please ask the mechanic to find and deal with it.

Conductor: the conductor of ××× understand.

Machinist: the machinist of ××× understand and dispose immediately.

(4)When the equipment fault is handled or abnormal driving is adopted, the driver shall report to the train dispatcher that the train dispatcher is qualified for driving, and the driver shall use the handheld radio to inform the conductor and on-board mechanic that they are qualified for driving. The contact terms are as follows:

Driver: conductor and mechanic of ××× train, qualified for start-up.

Conductor: the conductor of ××× understand.

Mechanic: the mechanic of ××× understand.

(5)After the fault treatment of EMU is completed, the mechanic will use the handheld radio to notify the driver that the fault treatment is completed (or the driver cannot handle the request for rescue), and the driver will report the situation to the train dispatcher. The contact terms are as follows:

Mechanic: driver of ×××. ××× fault is handled, it is ready for start-up (or the fault cannot be repaired and rescue is requested).

Driver: the driver of × × × understand.

(6)When the EMU business station temporarily opens the door during detention, the conductor uses the handheld radio to inform the mechanic and driver. The driver shall immediately report to the train dispatcher or station attendant. The contact terms are as follows:

Conductor: machinist and driver of × × ×, need to open the door of × train × position.

Mechanic: mechanic of × × × understand.

Driver: driver of × × × understand.

(7) After the completion of relevant operations during the detention period of EMU business station, the conductor shall use the handheld radio to inform the mechanic and driver. The driver shall immediately report to the train dispatcher or station attendant. The contact terms are as follows:

Conductor: mechanic and driver of × × ×, the door of × train × position has been closed.

Mechanic: mechanic of × × × understand.

Driver: driver of × × × understand.

(8) The contact terms in other cases shall be contacted by the on-board mechanic and the driver according to the actual situation, and shall strive to be standardized, accurate and concise.

2. Reporting language after occurrence of driving information

When the EMU train operates abnormally or stops due to EMU failure, the on-board mechanic shall timely report the information to the EMU dispatching of the group company with dispatching command authority at the place of the incident, and timely report to the EMU Depot dispatching according to the specified procedures. The language of the report is:

Mechanic: "I am × × × on-board mechanic × × ×, × × × past × × ×, × × × section, × × × EMU appears × × situation, report over ".

Ⅴ. *Tools and Spare Parts for EMU*

The on-board tools and driving, emergency and passenger transport spare parts of EMU shall be equipped, fixed and stored quantitatively according to the structural characteristics of vehicle model (see table 4-1). All departments shall strengthen the maintenance and management of spare parts of EMU, conduct regular inspection and maintenance, and keep the technical state in good condition.

Tab. 4-1 On-board tools and spare parts

category	Number	Name	Quantity	Remarks
On-board tools	1	Tong-type ammeter	1	
	2	Infrared thermometer	1	
	3	Rim tread checker	1	
	4	38 piece tool set	1	
	5	9-piece box wrench	1	
Onboard tools	6	Adjustable wrench	1	
	7	Wire-nippers	1	
	8	Tape measure	1	
	9	Pipe wrench (12 inch)	1	
	10	Pipe wrench (18 inch)	1	
	11	Round file	1	
	12	Semicircular file	1	
	13	Set screwdriver	1	
	14	Hand hammer	1	
	15	Crowbar	1	
	16	Flat shovel	1	
	17	Notebook computer	1	According to the needs of vcHicle mode1
Running Spare Parts	1	Torpedo	6	
	2	Torch	2	
	3	Short circuit copper wire	2	
	4	Hand signal lamp	2	
	5	Signal flag	2	
	6	Protective signal lamp	2	
Emer-gency spare parts	1	Transition coupler	2	Vehicle adaptation module and locomotive adaptation module
	2	Rescue air duct	2	
	3	Wire	20	
	4	Grounding rod	2	
		Electric pole	1	
	6	Insulating boots	1	
	7	Insulating gloves	1	
	8	Safety helmet	1	
	9	Safety belt	1	
	10	Climbing ladder	1	
	11	Iron shoes		Configure according to the vehicle type
	12	Wheel skid		Configure according to the vehicle type
	13	Pantograph binding supplies		According to the needs of vehicle model

Continue

Passenger transport spare parts	1	Emergency gangway foot plate	2	
	2	Emergency ladder	2	
	3	Door protective net		Configure according to vehicle model
	4	Emergency lamp(hand torch)	6	
	5	Megaphone	1	
	6	Emergency Hammer		Configure according to vehicle model

[Task Detection]

1. Briefly describe the post responsibilities of the on-board mechanic of EMU.

2. What EMU equipment does the EMU onboard mechanic need to manage and operate?

3. What work does the on-board mechanic of EMU need to do in case of sudden failure during emergency treatment?

4. What are some functions of train operation organization undertaken by the on-board machinist of EMU?

5. What is the content of pick-up operation in the one-time round-trip operation standard for on-board machinists of CRH380A EMU? And draw the line diagram of receiving operation.

6. What are the running spare parts and emergency spare parts of EMU?

7. What is the standard language for the EMU accompanying machinist to report to the EMU depot dispatching when the EMU train operates abnormally or stops due to EMU fault?

Task 2 Emergency Fault Handling of On-board Machinist of EMU

[Task Description]

(1) Get familiar with the responsibilities and division of labor of on-board staff during emergency fault disposal of EMU.

(2) Be able to handle the sudden failure of EMU according to the prompt of on-board information system.

Ⅰ. *Principles for Emergency Disposal of EMU Failure*

Basic principles for emergency disposal of EMU faults: ensuring safety, ensuring transportation, unified command and scientific disposal. Firmly change the train without hesitation, and put an end to taking the train blindly; Strengthen the purpose of process management of emergency disposal, and eliminate blind command and disorderly command.

(1) In case of vehicle equipment failure during the operation of EMU train, the driver shall handle it in time according to the prompts of on-board information monitoring device; When it needs to be handled by the on-board mechanic, the driver shall notify the on-board mechanic. The on-board machinist shall deal with the fault in the way of EMU according to the emergency treatment manual and relevant regulations. The dispatching emergency command center of EMU Depot shall be responsible for remote technical support and enable the emergency command system as required. When it is confirmed that it cannot operate normally after treatment, the driver shall choose to maintain operation or stop according to the prompt of on-board information monitoring device and the requirements of on-board machinist.

(2) In case of failure of EMU, the emergency commander shall make full use of ground traffic safety monitoring system, EMU on-board information wireless transmission system, pantograph video monitoring device and other safety monitoring equipment to cooperate in emergency disposal. In case of pantograph catenary fault of EMU, the onboard machinist shall immediately confirm the pantograph status through the pantograph video monitoring device.

(3) After the fault shutdown of EMU, the on-board machinist shall inform the driver to request rescue when the fault reason cannot be determined or cannot be handled and cannot continue to operate after 20 min of interval parking and 30 minutes of station parking. When the failure causes the failure of the air conditioner of the whole train, the onboard mechanic shall immediately notify the driver for rescue. The dispatching emergency command center of the motor car depot shall timely remind the onboard machinist to apply for rescue within the specified time.

After requesting rescue, the on-board mechanic must immediately report to the motor train dispatching of the group company where the fault occurs, and strictly obey the rescue command of the group company where the fault occurs.

(4) During rescue, EMU shall be used first, followed by locomotive. Under special circumstances, the multiple unit can be handled by changing the end of the multiple unit and decomposing the multiple unit into a single unit; When the control end fault of EMU train needs to return to the rear station, it must be handled by changing the end of the whole train; If there is no hot standby EMU nearby, the standby EMU can be started or the routing of online operating EMU can be adjusted for rescue. When using EMU rescue, it shall be handled according to the requirements of EMU mutual rescue method, and when using locomotive rescue, it shall be handled according to the requirements of unpowered return operation procedure in EMU return method.

When the EMU is rescued, the driver shall understand and master the direction of the rescue train, and inform the on-board mechanic to make rescue preparations in the direction of the rescue train.

(5) When the hot standby EMU is used for cross-group routing, the application for train replacement can be submitted only with the consent of the dispatcher of China Railway Group.

(6) When the EMU stops without power, for the EMU with parking braking device, the driver shall be responsible for putting the EMU in parking braking state; When there is no parking brake device for the EMU or there is no power to stay in the section with a slope of more than 20‰, the driver shall notify the on-board mechanic to prevent sliding, and iron shoes shall be used to keep close to it.

(7) Boarding and alighting process and requirements.

① The on-board mechanic must apply for operation according to relevant regulations before getting off the train for operation. The speed limit requirements and inspection conditions shall be put forward to the train dispatcher through the driver according to the actual needs. The blocking requirements shall be put forward when the operation may invade the gauge of the adjacent line. After receiving the oral instruction of the train dispatcher that the dispatching order of the speed limit or blocking of the adjacent line has been issued, the driver shall notify the on-board mechanic. After both parties sign each other, the on-board mechanic shall get off from the non-meeting side to check and deal with the fault, The passenger train crew shall take good care of the door, and keep close contact with the driver and on-board machinist.

② After the on-board machinist completes the operation, take all the tools, spare parts, materials and accessories on the train. When speed limit operation is required, the driver shall be informed of the speed limit requirements, and the driver shall operate according to the speed limit requirements after reporting to the train dispatcher (station attendant). If it cannot continue to run, ask for rescue in time.

(8) Release conditions.

① When the station staff find or receive the following situations or information during the operation of EMU trains, they must immediately take parking measures:

a. There are dragging, pulling, hitting, up and down vibration and continuous friction sound at the lower part of the vehicle; The vehicle jumps up and down suddenly, and the vehicle body swings violently; When the joint sags obviously.

b. Temperature alarm of axle box bearing, gearbox bearing, traction motor bearing and stator.

c. The on-board information monitoring device indicates that the shaft does not rotate or lock.

d. Abnormal conditions such as insufficient braking force are found.

e. Pantograph automatically drops or hangs foreign matters for unknown reasons.

f. Outer door failure occurs during operation.

g. Accidental de marshaling of multiple unit, poor transmission between marshaling rooms and coupler failure at multiple coupling end.

h. When the EMU collides with foreign matters and affects the driving safety.

i. The skirt and external lifting cover plate of EMU are opened.

j. TEDS predicts faults requiring immediate shutdown inspection.

k. The electrical equipment of EMU is on fire and smoke, and other equipment of EMU is on open fire.

l. Other situations that affect the driving safety of EMU.

② When the following faults occur during the operation of EMU, the emergency disposal is invalid, and the rescue must be requested.

a. The braking of the whole train fails.

b. There is no traction on the whole train.

c. Mechanical failure of running gear, unable to continue operation.

(9) In case of EMU failure, the EMU Depot shall actively send personnel to pick up the train on the way or rush to the site, and continue to track until the EMU is put into storage.

(10) In case of abnormal operation or stop of EMU due to fault, the driver shall immediately report to the train dispatcher or station attendant of the group company where the fault occurs, and notify the on-board mechanic.

(11) The on-board machinist shall immediately report to the motor train dispatching of the group company of the failure Bureau, and then report to the dispatching emergency command center of the section. After receiving the report, the dispatching emergency command center of the motor car depot shall immediately start the fault emergency disposal procedure, assist the on-board mechanic in fault disposal, and report the fault information and disposal to the motor car dispatching of the group company.

(12) After the fault handling of EMU is completed, the on-board machinist shall timely notify the driver that he can start the vehicle, and report the inspection and handling results to the EMU dispatching and emergency command center of the group company of the fault occurrence Bureau, and the EMU dispatching emergency command center shall timely report to the EMU dispatching of the group company after receiving the report.

Ⅱ. Emergency Fault Handling Process for On–board Machinist of EMU

1. When the train stops during operation, the on-board mechanic gets off the train to check the process

When the on-board machinist needs to get off the high-speed railway (railway of 200 km/h and above and railway of 200 km/h and below only running EMU trains)to check and deal with faults, he must handle the operation application according to relevant regulations before getting off the train, put forward the speed limit requirements and inspection conditions to the train dispatcher through the driver according to the actual needs, and put forward the blocking requirements when the operation may invade the gauge of adjacent lines, The request includes: parking place, reason for getting off, speed limit value of adjacent line, etc. After receiving the notice that the driver has issued the dispatching order with the train speed limit of 160 km/h and below on the adjacent line, the on-board machinist shall sign and confirm with each other. After wearing protective equipment, the on-board mechanic shall get off the train from the non-meeting side to check and deal with the fault, notify the conductor to take good care of the door, pay attention to the status of facilities under his feet when getting off the train, keep close contact with the driver, and pay attention to personal safety during operation; When it is necessary to get off the train for inspection and troubleshooting on ordinary speed railways (Railways below 200 km/h, except those running EMU trains only), the on-board machinist can get off the train from the non-passing side for inspection after obtaining the consent of the driver, notify the conductor to take good care of the door, pay attention to the status of facilities under his feet when getting off the train, keep close contact with the driver, and pay attention to personal safety during operation. After the on-board machinist completes the inspection and treatment, take all tools, spare parts, materials and accessories on the train and notify the driver of the inspection and treatment results. When speed limit operation is required, the driver shall be informed of the speed limit requirements. If the operation cannot be continued, the driver shall request rescue in time. (pay attention to carrying lighting tools when getting off in long and long tunnels for inspection). When the on-board mechanic gets off the train for inspection, he shall use a video flashlight to record the whole process.

2. The on-board machinist needs to go to the top to check and deal with the fault process

(1)The on-board machinist shall first contact the driver to confirm whether the overhead contact system above the parking position of the EMU crosses the split phase, and make a request to the train dispatcher through the EMU driver. After receiving the dispatching command of the train speed limit of 160 km/h and below on the adjacent line, the overhead contact system has been powered off and the dispatching command of permission to climb the top (if the parking position crosses the split phase area, the two split phase areas shall be powered off at the same time), Inform the driver to remove the damaged pantograph and raise another good pantograph. Confirm with the driver that there is no network voltage. After discharging (CRH2A/B/C/E/G and CRH380A/AL multiple units, the on-board machinist shall notify the driver to close the main circuit for discharge), and the on-board machinist shall wear protective articles and get off the train for operation (the on-board mechanic manually opens the door and strengthens the lookout after getting off to ensure personal safety).

(2) The on-board machinist shall first check the power of the catenary with an electroscope at the non-passing side of the line to confirm that the catenary has been powered off. Within the operation range of the fault part at the non-passing side, a grounding rod shall be hung at both ends adjacent to the cantilever of the catenary before climbing on the roof to check and deal with the fault (in case of multiple fault parts, a grounding rod shall be hung adjacent to the catenary cantilever outside the two fault parts at the farthest distance. If the section or non-passing side of the station does not have the conditions for hanging the grounding rod of the catenary cantilever, the grounding rod shall be hung on the catenary at the head of both ends of the EMU). The roof climbing operation shall not exceed the range of the catenary between the grounding rods hung at both ends (as shown in Fig. 4-2). to firmly connect the grounding wire with the steel rail, the rust on the contact part of the steel rail must be removed before connecting the grounding wire with the steel rail to ensure good grounding effect. The grounding wire hanging in front of the control end shall be watched by the driver, and the other grounding wires shall be watched by the train staff designated by the conductor. (the nursing content is: when the grounding wire falls off or is removed by someone, timely notify the onboard mechanic to stop operation and get off the train).

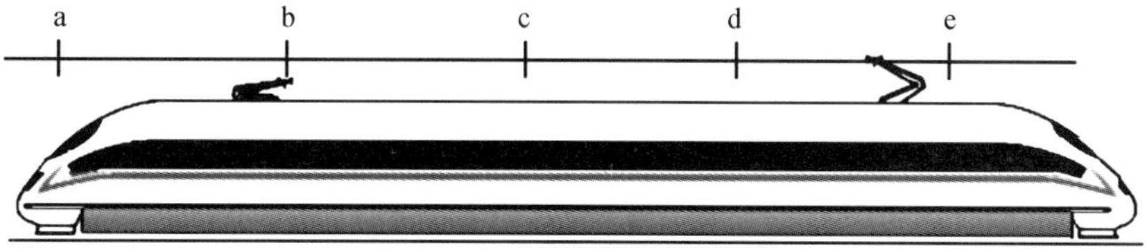

Fig. 4-2 Schematic diagram of catenary hanger position

Note: a, b, c, d and e respectively represent the cantilever position of OCS.

① As shown in the Fig. 4-2, the raised pantograph is damaged, and the grounding rod is hung at the cantilever arms d and e.

② As shown in the Fig. 4-2, the pantograph is lowered and damaged, and the grounding rod is hung at the cantilevers a and c.

③ As shown in the Fig. 4-2, both pantographs are damaged, and the grounding rod is hung at the cantilevers a and e.

(3) The on-board machinist shall check and handle the roof (the climbing ladder shall be installed firmly, in the correct direction and on the non-passing side), bind the damaged pantograph, and ensure that the distance from the damaged pantograph to the catenary is greater than 300 mm, there is no risk of parts falling off, and the distance from the high-voltage device on the roof is greater than 300 mm; After the damaged pantograph is inspected, the on-board mechanic shall also inspect all other pantographs of the EMU to ensure that there is no risk of parts falling off and that the distance from the high-voltage device on the roof is greater than 300 mm. After the climbing operation, the on-board machinist is responsible for removing the grounding wire at the cantilever end of the overhead contact system, and then removing the grounding wire connected with one end of the steel rail. After collecting and counting the tools, get on the train, sign on the driver's account, and inform the driver to use the pantograph in good condition and operate normally. While waiting for power supply, the on-board machinist shall count the tools and collect the protective articles and tools.

(4) When the on-board machinist needs assistance in hanging and removing the grounding wire, transferring, installing and removing the climbing ladder and night operation auxiliary lighting, the on-board machinist shall be responsible for assistance in reconnection and marshaling; In case of single marshaling, the driver of EMU shall be responsible for assistance. In case of single driver in a single shift, the conductor shall assign train staff to assist.

3. Brake cut-off inspection process is required for EMU fault

(1) When brake cut-off operation is required due to EMU failure: CRH380A (L)EMU needs to be operated under shutdown, and CRH380B (L)and CR400BF EMUs need to be operated at a speed below 200 km/h.

(2) When the air brake and parking brake are cut off at the same time or separately due to the fault of EMU: the cutting operation involving parking brake needs to be carried out in the parking state. The driver and on-board machinist shall take anti-slip measures for the train according to the regulations. After the cutting operation of parking brake and air brake, it is necessary to shake the brake clamp with parking brake cylinder, confirming that all parking brake clamps have been released. The on-board machinist shall inform the driver to conduct rolling test at a speed not higher than 5 km/h. During the test, the on-board machinist shall confirm whether there is real locking and abnormal sound at the running part. After the test (for EMUs that only need to cut off the parking brake, the air brake air supply shall be restored), the on-board machinist shall report the test results (recovery)to the depot safety production dispatching command center. After getting on the train, confirm

that the parking brake has been cut off through the display screen, check the relevant axle temperature monitoring data of the cut off braking vehicle, and confirm that the results are normal, Inform the driver of the completion of the test and handle the mutual signature confirmation procedures with the driver. When the on-board mechanic fails to carry out the rolling test or fails to pass the rolling test, he shall not start the vehicle.

(3) After handling, the on-board mechanic shall inform the driver of the removal of braking force and speed limit requirements, and sign with the driver to confirm the speed limit operation requirements.

(4) When the EMU resumes operation after the brake is cut off, the on-board machinist shall take the vehicle with the brake cut off as the focus of inspection and patrol. In addition to necessary inspection and patrol, the rest of the time shall focus on the control in the compartment with the brake cut off to monitor whether there is abnormal sound and vibration during operation. In case of abnormal vibration or noise, the driver shall be notified to stop and get off the vehicle for inspection immediately.

(5) After the braking of the EMU is cut off and restored to operation, the on-board machinist shall apply to the train dispatcher for parking inspection at the front station through the driver. After parking at the front station, the on-board machinist shall get off the train according to the regulations, point the temperature of the brake disc, traction motor, gearbox and shaft end of the cut-off braking vehicle, compare the point temperature with the adjacent vehicle, and focus on the inspection of the tread state of the cut-off braking vehicle, Confirm whether there is holding brake. After the inspection is completed and the operation conditions are met, the on-board machinist shall report to the train dispatcher (station attendant)through the driver, and the driver shall resume operation according to the requirements of the on-board machinist.

4. Treatment measures for pantograph fault during EMU operation

In case of pantograph catenary fault during the operation of EMU train, the onboard machinist shall strengthen fault judgment and disposal. In principle, the climbing operation shall not be carried out in the section, and the operation requirements shall be strictly observed when climbing operation is necessary.

(1) For EMUs equipped with pantograph video monitoring device, the on-board machinist shall immediately confirm the appearance status of pantograph through the pantograph video monitoring device, and timely check the playback video. If it can be confirmed that the visible part of pantograph status has no obvious abnormality or does not exceed the limit and there is no risk of falling off, inform the driver to operate normally after pantograph replacement.

(2) If the pantograph status cannot be confirmed through the pantograph video

monitoring device, or it is necessary to get off the train for inspection, or if the EMU is not equipped with pantograph video monitoring device, get off the train for inspection according to the off the train inspection process.

(3) Get off and check. When the conditions are met, the on-board machinist can use binoculars, self photographing rods and other auxiliary means under the vehicle for further inspection and confirmation.

① After preliminary inspection, if it is confirmed that the visible part of the pantograph appearance has no obvious abnormality or does not exceed the limit, and there is no risk of falling off, but the cause of pantograph lowering cannot be determined, the on-board mechanic shall immediately report the inspection and the requirements for parking at the front station to the driver, and the driver shall report to the train dispatcher. The driver shall cut off the lowered pantograph according to the requirements of the on-board mechanic, change the pantograph and run at the speed limit of 160 km/h to the front station for further inspection and disposal.

If the front station is the terminal station, the on-board machinist shall apply to the driver and the motor train dispatcher of the group company for starting the replacement of hot standby motor train units. The replaced faulty motor train units shall apply for speed limit conditions not higher than 160 km/h according to the roof fault condition and return to the motor train station for treatment.

If the front station is not the terminal station, the on-board machinist shall conduct further inspection and confirmation with a telescope or pantograph video monitoring device after stopping the station. If it is confirmed that the appearance of pantograph is normal or does not affect the operation safety, the EMU shall maintain operation at normal speed; If it cannot be confirmed, it must be inspected and handled on the top.

② If it is found that the pantograph is slightly damaged and there is no risk of parts falling off during the inspection, the on-board machinist shall notify the driver to remove the damaged pantograph and report the requirements for parking inspection at the front station to the train dispatcher. After changing the pantograph, run at a speed not higher than 120 km/h and stop at the front station. After parking, the on-board machinist shall get off the train for further confirmation, Check and confirm that normal speed operation can be restored when operation is not affected; If the damaged part of the pantograph is found to be expanding, it must be inspected and handled on the top. If the pantograph is seriously damaged, but does not invade the limit, has no risk of falling off, and meets the minimum spacing requirement with the catenary (300 mm), the faulty pantograph can be removed, and the pantograph can be replaced and run to the front station at a speed of no more than 40 km/h for further treatment.

③ If it is found that the pantograph is scratched or damaged seriously during the inspection, and there is a risk of parts falling off, the onboard machinist shall carry out the top climbing operation according to the top climbing inspection and fault handling process.

(4) When the on-board mechanic finds that the pantograph is broken, displaced, attached foreign matters and other high-voltage accessories are seriously damaged and cannot be handled alone, the driver shall apply to the train dispatcher to dispatch the power supply operation vehicle, catenary detection operation vehicle, etc., and the power supply personnel shall assist in climbing the top for treatment. If it is confirmed that all pantographs (including those in use and those not in use)are seriously damaged after climbing on site, inform the driver to request rescue, bind the damaged pantograph, and confirm that the distance between the damaged pantograph and other parts of the roof from the catenary is greater than 300 mm. While waiting for rescue, the driver and the on-board machinist shall prevent the train from sliding according to the regulations. At the same time, the driver shall place the brake handle at the maximum braking position and keep the emergency light in the passenger compartment on, and the headlights and rear marker lights on. The on-board mechanic starts the emergency ventilation device, and the driver monitors that the battery voltage meets the regulations. If it is lower than the specified value, turn off the battery; When there is no emergency ventilation device or the battery voltage is lower than the specified value, inform the conductor to organize the installation of protective net, open the designated door for ventilation and protection, and inform the driver to report to the train dispatcher.

5. Disposal measures for foreign matters hanging on pantograph

After receiving the notice of foreign matters hanging on the pantograph, the on-board mechanic shall immediately check the appearance state of the pantograph through the pantograph video monitoring device to confirm whether it affects the normal operation of the EMU. If it does not affect the operation, it can maintain (or speed limit)operation to the front station for inspection and treatment. The on-board machinist shall put forward the disposal scheme and speed limit requirements according to the specific situation. In case of large dust net winding pantograph, it is difficult to dispose quickly at the moment, priority shall be given to starting the hot standby vehicle.

(1) For EMUs equipped with pantograph video monitoring device, the on-board machinist shall immediately confirm the foreign matter and pantograph appearance status through the pantograph video monitoring device, and timely check the playback video. If it can be confirmed that the visible part of the pantograph status has no obvious abnormality or does not exceed the limit, there is no risk of falling off, and does not affect the operation, inform the driver of normal operation after pantograph replacement. When the EMU can stop at the front (passenger handling)station for disposal, the onboard machinist shall notify

the driver, the driver shall report to the train dispatcher, and the train dispatcher shall organize the power supply department to assist the on-board machinist to climb the top and remove foreign matters at the front (passenger handling)station.

In case of abnormal pantograph, affecting operation or EMU without pantograph video monitoring device, get off the train for inspection according to the getting off inspection process. The on-board mechanic shall control the off-board inspection time, speed up the inspection progress and minimize the impact on the transportation order.

(2) When the on-board mechanic checks off the train and confirms that the overall appearance of the pantograph is normal or does not affect the operation safety, inform the driver to maintain the operation at normal speed after changing the pantograph;

(3) The on-board machinist shall check under the train and confirm that the pantograph sliding plate and bracket are damaged or the catenary is abnormal. The inspection results shall be reported to the driver and the train dispatcher in time.

(4) When climbing operation is required, the on-board machinist shall carry out the climbing operation according to the climbing inspection and troubleshooting process.

(5) After handling the foreign matters, report the handling results to the driver and resume normal driving. When speed limit operation is required, the on-board mechanic shall inform the driver of the speed limit operation requirements.

6. Fire handling measures in case of vehicle equipment failure

(1) During the operation of EMU, when the on-board machinist obtains or finds smoke, fire, scorch or peculiar smell caused by rubber and plastic melting of air conditioning vents, distribution cabinets and other equipment and facilities in the passenger compartment, he shall immediately notify the driver and conductor, require the driver to disconnect the main circuit breaker and lower the pantograph, and select a safe place to stop.

(2) The on-board mechanic shall arrive at the corresponding carriage in time, turn off the power supply of air conditioning, ventilation system or equipment and facilities, and notify the conductor and driver of the equipment status.

(3) After parking, the on-board mechanic shall check the vehicle equipment, make accurate judgment and deal with it decisively. When it is confirmed that it will not affect the driving safety, inform the driver and sign for confirmation.

(4) In case of fire, the on-board mechanic shall timely call the local "119" for rescue.

7. Handling measures for bearing temperature alarm detected by on-board axle temperature detection system

(1) When the temperature of axle box bearing, gearbox bearing and traction motor bearing of running part is too high during the operation of EMU, the EMU driver shall stop immediately, report the parking reason and parking position to the train dispatcher, and

notify the onboard mechanic for treatment.

(2) The on-board mechanic switches the mon screen to the "axle temperature real-time detection" screen, confirms the temperature of the faulty equipment and records it.

(3) The on-board mechanic shall get off the train for inspection and temperature confirmation according to the specified procedures, and conduct comprehensive inspection in the order of primary and secondary. Focus on the inspection of gearbox, coupling, traction motor, axle box, brake disc, wheel set tread and other parts. Requirements: the gearbox is free of damage and oil dripping, and the oil level of the gearbox is normal (for straight roads, if there are superelevation and ramps on the line, the oil level will change or even cannot be observed. It is necessary to check the oil level of adjacent gearbox of the same bogie for auxiliary judgment. The oil level of gearbox on one side decreases or even cannot be observed, and the oil level of gearbox on the other side increases to normal; if the oil level of adjacent gearbox of the same bogie cannot be checked, the phase of two adjacent bogies shall be checked The oil level of the gearbox at the same position. If there is a ramp or ultra-high, the oil level of the gearbox will drop or even cannot be observed; the coupling will be free of damage, deflection, oil dripping and discoloration; the traction motor will be free of damage; the axle box will be free of damage and discoloration; the speed sensor of the motor (shaft end)will be free of disconnection and damage, and the connector will be free of looseness and deformation. It shall be measured with an infrared thermometer "Point temperature of key parts of the running gear" is compared with that of the same parts adjacent to the vehicle. If the point temperature of the alarm part is normal, it is necessary to confirm the point temperature of other parts of the faulty shaft. Report to the driver according to the measured temperature and inspection conditions.

Parts that must be checked: gearbox oil level, temperature patches of all parts, rubber parts.

For the parts with narrow space and difficult to be visually inspected, the on-board machinist shall use the self photographing rod to take photos and give information feedback. The section emergency commander shall compare the photos for item-by-item confirmation.

(4) If the alarm is judged to be true, if it is confirmed to be abnormal or the temperature rise is too high, sign on the driver's manual account according to the regulations and operate at a limited speed.

① Apply for rescue in case of serious mechanical failure and serious mechanical failure that cannot maintain operation;

② When the gearbox, coupling and traction motor are abnormal, if the gearbox is damaged, dripping oil, the coupling is damaged, skewed, dripping oil and discolored, the traction motor is damaged, the axle box is damaged and discolored, and the point temperature of the axle box exceeds the standard, but there are no other abnormalities within the visible range, after the manual rolling test, the speed limit is 40 km/h to maintain the operation, and apply for rescue at the front station.

③ When the point temperature of gearbox and traction motor exceeds the standard, if the point temperature of gearbox and traction motor exceeds the standard but there are no other abnormalities within the visible range, after the manual rolling test, the speed limit is 140 km/h to maintain the operation, and apply for rescue at the front station.

(5) Check that there is no abnormality and confirm that the axle temperature is normal. In case of false alarm, inform the driver to resume normal speed operation and sign on the driver's manual account.

In case of response to excessive bearing temperature of the running gear of the allocated EMU, the on-board machinist shall get off the train for inspection and confirmation, take disposal measures according to the provisions of the emergency manual according to the specific situation, and operate according to the following speed limit table(Tab. 4-2) if there is no abnormality within the visual range and no other faults.

Tab. 4-2 Speed limit table

Level	Axle box bearing	Gearbox bearing	Bearing
Warning Leve(Level 1)	200 km/h	200 km/h	200 km/h
Warning Leve(Level 2)	40 km/h	40 km/h	40 km/h

(6)The on-board machinist shall focus on monitoring the faulty vehicle during maintaining operation or restoring normal speed operation. Pay close attention to the [real-time detection of axle temperature] information on the way. In case of abnormal vibration or abnormal sound, immediately inform the driver to stop and get off for confirmation. At the end of this operation or at stations with train replacement conditions, the underbody shall be replaced, and the faulty train set shall be stopped and returned to the depot for treatment.

8. Disposal measures in case of emergency braking and shutdown during the operation of EMU train

(1) In case of emergency braking and shutdown of EMU due to equipment failure of the vehicle, the on-board machinist shall deal with it according to the provisions of emergency fault handling manual on the way of EMU. Before driving, the on-board mechanic shall monitor and control the driver to conduct a brief braking test. After confirming that the braking performance is good, inform the driver to run at a speed limit of 60 km/h. After driving, patrol the whole train, focusing on monitoring whether there is abnormal sound and abnormal vibration in the running part. If there is no abnormality,

inform the driver to resume normal operation.

(2) In case of emergency braking and shutdown of EMU train due to other abnormal conditions, the on-board machinist shall deal with it according to relevant plans after mastering the specific conditions. Before driving, the driver shall be monitored for a brief braking test. After confirming that the braking performance is good, the driver shall be notified to run at a speed limit of 60 km/h. After driving, the whole train shall be inspected, focusing on monitoring whether there is abnormal sound in the running part If there is no abnormal vibration, inform the driver to resume normal operation.

(3) In case of emergency braking and parking of EMU train due to other abnormal conditions, the on-board machinist shall handle it according to the relevant plans after mastering the specific conditions. Before driving, the driver shall be monitored to conduct a brief braking test. After confirming that the braking performance is good, the driver shall be notified to operate at a speed limit of 60 km/h. After driving, the whole train shall be inspected to focus on monitoring whether there is abnormal sound in the running part If there is no abnormal vibration, inform the driver to resume normal operation.

(4) During the inspection of the whole train, if any abnormal sound or abnormal vibration is found in the traveling part, the on-board machinist shall timely notify the driver to stop, get off the train as required, check the traveling part of the whole train, put forward the operation speed limit conditions or apply for rescue to the driver according to the inspection, and timely report to the motor train dispatching of the group company with dispatching command in the place of the accident.

9. Emergency response measures for separated operation in case of abnormality of Multiple Unit EMU

When one unit of multiple unit cannot continue to operate for some reason and needs to be separated for operation according to the dispatching order, the driver of the multiple unit and the on-board mechanic shall do a good job in the anti-slip work of the faulty multiple unit according to the regulations (when the EMU stops without power, the driver shall be responsible for the EMU with parking brake device in the parking brake state; when the EMU does not have parking brake device or stops without power in the section with a ramp of more than 20 ‰, the on-board machinist shall carry out anti-slip according to the notice of the driver), the on-board machinist shall cooperate with the driver to disassemble the multiple unit according to the operation procedure of EMU disassembly. The on-board machinist on duty for the faulty EMU shall do a good job in the protection of the EMU, stay in place with the faulty EMU and wait for rescue, and the normal EMU shall continue to operate according to the command.

[Task Detection]

1. Independently read *The emergency fault handling manual of CRH380 series EMU.*

2. Briefly describe the basic principles of emergency disposal of EMU faults.

3. Briefly describe the inspection process of stopping during train operation and getting off the train with the mechanic.

4. Briefly describe the disposal measures in case of emergency braking and shutdown during the operation of EMU.

Project 5

EMU Operation and Maintenance

[Ideological and Political Classroom]

The unshakable safety concept has created a 28 year defect free flaw detection-Lei Li

"Every time is the first time, and the first time should be defect free" is the safety concept Lei Li adheres to in his post. Since joining the work in October 1990, Lei Li has devoted himself to research and continuous innovation to fill the gap of flaw detection technology for ordinary speed trains. Founded the five character operation method of "calibration, cleaning, integrity, comparison and inspection" for ultrasonic flaw detection of hollow shaft of EMU, explored and developed the information flaw detection mode, successively found and eliminated more than 30 typical or major train wheel set faults, and realized flaw free flaw detection for 28 years. She devoted her youth to her beloved flaw detection career and bloomed the beautiful flower of women craftsmen.

During his work, Lei Li, who loves his job and is dedicated, has found major cracks and defects for many times. In the long-term flaw detection practice, she has the courage to innovate, seriously explores and summarizes the flaw detection processes and methods of ordinary speed trains, and puts forward the "sixteen character" flaw detection method of "crack length, hole is one point, clutter chaos and rust penetration". The short front k-value probe developed by her fully met the production needs and filled a gap in the flaw detection process of the whole disc brake wheel set at that time. On July 28, 2010, during flaw detection of a crh1a EMU, she found that there were three internal defects on one of the hollow shafts, which were hidden. She repeatedly detected by reducing sensitivity, changing shaft end face flaw detection, manual detection and other methods. It took more than 3 hours to finally determine that one of the defects had exceeded 3mm, and the wheel was changed to eliminate the hidden danger.

Facing the rapid development trend of high-speed rail EMU technology in recent years, Lei Liyong took the initiative to serve as the Deputy foreman of workshop technology office. She not only led the preparation of flaw detection operation instructions and the judgment and disposal methods of flaw detection defects of hollow axles, but also innovated and developed a new model of information flaw detection, actively organized the production backbone of flaw detection team to enter the resumes of 130 EMU hollow axles and 34 hollow axles in stock of 5 models and 3 technical platforms, and established a database, It realizes the big data analysis and tracking of the health status of the hollow shaft, effectively improves the application efficiency of the hollow shaft, makes the flaw detection of the motor car more standardized, scientific and information-based, and scientifically and effectively ensures the flaw detection quality.

Character casts high-quality products. It is Lei Li's craftsman spirit of love and dedication, perseverance, excellence and continuous innovation that has created the miracle of defect free and zero failure of her flaw detection products for 28 years. This ultimate pursuit of work and the persistence in improving product quality are the best interpretation of the craftsman spirit.

[Project Description]

At the end of this project, students are expected to master the main maintenance methods and standards of emU, and master the composition and function of EMU maintenance organization. Be familiar with the function and layout of maintenance base, and understand the use of commonly used maintenance equipment; Master the operation process of EMU operation level maintenance, and be able to complete related content according to the operation standard of grade Ⅰ and Ⅱ maintenance.

Task 1 EMU Maintenance Features

[Task Description]

(1) Get familiar with maintenance characteristics, maintenance system, maintenance methods and maintenance scope of high speed EMU.

(2) Be able to judge the maintenance mode according to the operation of EMU.

Ⅰ. *EMU Maintenance Features*

1. Adopt a large number of high-tech equipment

The Hamburg bullet train section in Germany, for example, can complete the maintenance and reconditioning work of the 412-meter-long ICE bullet train within 60 minutes because of its advanced maintenance technology and equipment.

(1) The on-board microcomputer diagnosis system transmits the fault signals detected

in the application to the bullet train section through the remote wireless communication technology, so as to make maintenance preparations in advance.

(2) Three levels of maintenance work are established to operate simultaneously under, inside and on top.

(3) The overhead track with rail bridge facilitates the inspection and replacement of walking parts.

(4) Wheelset and bogie replacement equipment with air cushion running device.

(5) Vacuum sewage treatment system and automatic cleaning device.

(6) Automatic detection of wheel tread cracks, wear and roundness diagnostic equipment.

(7) Control and management of the entire maintenance process of the microcomputer information system.

2. Maintenance from a systems engineering perspective

First, the life cycle cost (LCC) of high-speed trains is studied. Secondly, the technology, finance, management and other aspects of the comprehensive management of factors; In addition, the system engineering theory is used to study the reliability, maintainability and availability of high-speed trains, and the comprehensive analysis of each link of high-speed trains (drafting, design, manufacturing, installation, application, maintenance and renewal, etc.)is carried out. In addition, information feedback is also carried out to improve the design of manufacturing departments.

3. Extensive implementation of replacement repair and centralized repair

Replacement repair is widely implemented in the maintenance process of EMU, that is, the parts, modules or parts found to be faulty or defective are replaced with corresponding parts with intact functions (new or repaired)instead of on-site maintenance, which can greatly save the repair time and improve the utilization rate of the train. At the same time, this change and repair method is also applied to the maintenance of the corresponding units in the plant repair, called the large parts change and repair. For the main parts that can be repaired, they are sent to professional chemical plants, workshops or sections for centralized and unified repair, which can improve the quality of maintenance and save maintenance costs.

4. More reasonable maintenance system

The main framework of high-speed train maintenance system still adopts planned preventive repair system, but there is a flexible maintenance system in specific maintenance, and state repair occupies an increasing proportion. The basis and reliable guarantee of state repair are complete computer maintenance management information system, advanced communication means and precise and reliable maintenance and diagnosis equipment.

5. The maintenance outage is greatly shortened and the utilization rate is greatly improved.

At present, high-speed trains in all countries in the world adopt the new maintenance mode that is fully included in the database during overhaul. For example, the annual average mileage of The German ICE train is up to 500,000 km, and its maintenance stay time is less than 3 days, and it also has good equipment for fault repair. Another example is the French TGV train. Replacing an axle takes only about one hour, and replacing a non-powered bogie takes less than 1.5 hours.

Ⅱ. *Basic Maintenance Mode and Maintenance Mode*

1. Basic maintenance mode

Maintenance mode refers to the control of equipment maintenance timing. That is, the grasp of maintenance timing is realized by adopting different maintenance methods. At present, there are three maintenance methods: regular maintenance (also known as planned maintenance), condition-based maintenance (also known as condition based maintenance)and post maintenance (also known as fault repair).

1) Regular maintenance

Periodic maintenance, also known as planned maintenance, takes service time or running mileage as the maintenance period. Therefore, as long as the equipment is used for a predetermined time or operating mileage, the specified maintenance work shall be carried out regardless of its technical status, which is a mandatory preventive maintenance method.

The implementation of regular maintenance is guaranteed by the planned repair cycle, repair level, repair scope and relevant maintenance regulations. The repair process and period of inspection and repair of EMU shall be determined according to its structural characteristics, operation conditions, actual technical status and production level in a certain period, so as to ensure the safe and reliable operation of EMU.

2) Repair as appropriate

Condition-based maintenance, also known as condition-based maintenance, requires the EMU to determine the maintenance time according to the actual operation conditions, without fixed restrictions. By continuously monitoring the status of EMU and each subsystem, judge its performance curve, locate the system fault or failed components, and record and track the failure time and process. Since the fault does not occur instantaneously, there will always be time and opportunity to detect and take maintenance measures.

It can be seen that this method has strong pertinence, high efficiency, high cost, high requirements for maintenance equipment, conditions and personnel, and is not universal.

3) Failure maintenance

The failure maintenance method is also called fault maintenance. It does not control the maintenance time and repairs only after the machine fails. Practice has proved that even if some parts fail, they will not endanger safety and cause serious consequences. It is more economical to adopt post maintenance. For some parts with redundant technology, such as traction transmission system, it is suitable for post maintenance.

2. Main maintenance methods of EMU

High-efficiency maintenance mode is adopted for EMU maintenance. Its purpose is to greatly improve the safety and reliability of EMUs, greatly improve the service efficiency of EMUs, greatly reduce the rest time, greatly improve the operation efficiency of maintenance units, and realize the manufacturing of vehicle repair mode. The maintenance mode of EMU is based on the component life management system and supported by advanced maintenance equipment and facilities and supporting maintenance services of parts manufacturing plants. Its main forms are replacement repair, centralized repair, status repair and balanced repair. Its main characteristics are high specialization, high intensification, high socialization and high programming.

1) Replacement repair

If a component failure is found in various repair procedures, or the components need to be repaired or replaced in medium and advanced repair procedures, the method of replacement repair shall be adopted. The removed components shall be sent for repair in three cases. First, the components with relatively simple technical structure shall be overhauled by the maintenance base; Second, for components with complex technical structure and large repair range, after economic analysis, the maintenance base shall provide corresponding maintenance sites and supporting facilities, and entrust the maintenance unit set up by the manufacturing factory in the maintenance base for maintenance; Third, large parts, such as traction converter and traction transformer, shall be returned to the manufacturing factory for maintenance during the advanced repair.

2) Centralized repair

The maintenance of EMU components is mainly concentrated in the maintenance base, and the operation centre only undertakes daily routine inspection and some temporary maintenance operations. The component maintenance is concentrated in the corresponding manufacturing factory or its dispatched office.

3) State repair

Service facilities generally adopt State repair, that is, they are inspected and repaired at any time, and they are always in good technical condition; Meanwhile, according to the definition of service life, some equipment or components can not meet the use requirements and will be replaced before failure, and the monitoring state repair is adopted.

4) Balanced repair

To reduce the rest time of overhaul, some parts are arranged to be overhauled during operation or other low-level repair by means of parts replacement, so as to reduce the workload during overhaul and reduce the repair time of EMU as much as possible.

[Task Detection]

1. Combined with the maintenance of EMU, expound the definition and elements of maintenance.

2. What are the advantages and disadvantages of replacement repair and specialized centralized repair? What is the relationship between the two maintenance methods?

3. Distinguish the different maintenance modes of high-speed trains.

Task 2 EMU Maintenance Organization

[Task Description]

(1) Get familiar with the composition and function of EMU maintenance mechanism;

(2) Get familiar with the function and layout of EMU maintenance base;

(3) Understand the maintenance equipment commonly used in EMU operation.

Ⅰ. *EMU Maintenance Organization*

Following the basic principles of "centralized maintenance, decentralized storage" and "relative concentration of advantageous equipment", the EMU is equipped with maintenance base and maintenance organization with two different functions to avoid cross operation and repeated investment. The maintenance base is set at the main transportation hub. According to the needs of transportation organization, several operation stations are set with the maintenance base as the center, forming a hierarchical structure of maintenance capacity; The maintenance tasks shall be differentiated and organized scientifically. The maintenance base shall undertake all maintenance procedures from level Ⅰ to level Ⅴ (D1 ~ D5). In principle, the maintenance of EMUs shall be concentrated in the maintenance base, and the operation station shall only undertake level Ⅰ to level 2 (D1 ~ D2).

1. Setting principle of maintenance organization

The location of maintenance organization shall be determined by fully considering the passenger flow characteristics of high-speed railway, the distribution of high-speed stations, the environmental conditions around the railway and the relevant existing railways. The main considerations are as follows:

(1) Volume of passenger traffic from departure to destination.

(2) There are few empty train returns and the utilization rate of EMU is high.

(3) Near the station.

(4) Where the personnel required by the maintenance base can be easily guaranteed.

These factors considered are mainly to improve the operation efficiency of EMUs. In addition, the factors of construction land should be fully considered.

2. Composition and function of maintenance mechanism

1) Maintenance base

The maintenance base is equipped with a certain number of EMUs, which are mainly used for regular maintenance, fault handling, vehicle parking and servicing cleaning of EMUs. The maintenance base undertakes the maintenance of all maintenance levels, and is responsible for the night stay of EMUs in the base and outside the base, the long-term parking of standby EMUs, as well as passenger catering, vehicle cleaning and other servicing operations. The maintenance base shall consider not only the maintenance of the whole train formation, but also the arrival and departure of trains and night operation. The overhaul base needs to have the equipment conditions for overhaul.

2) Operation station

The operation station is matched with the maintenance base, and several are set in the main passenger stations. The reasons for setting the application are as follows:

① It is conducive to centralized maintenance and decentralized storage.

② It can greatly reduce the no-load transportation caused by the daily maintenance of EMU, and improve the operation capacity and use efficiency of EMU.

③ It can improve the departure capacity of main passenger stations and facilitate the arrangement of operation scheme.

④ The maintenance layout setting mode of foreign EMUs is fully used for reference.

The use of a small number of EMUs is mainly responsible for D1 ~ D2 level repair, servicing and temporary repair of high-speed EMUs, and a parking lot is set to meet the needs of EMUs at night.

3. Layout of a maintenance organization

(1) Layout of EMU maintenance base and operation station in China.

Referring to the operation and maintenance experience of foreign EMUs, in order to meet the maintenance needs of EMUs in China, China also has many maintenance institutions, which are EMU Depot (EMU maintenance base), EMU Operation Station and EMU storage yard from high to low.

(2) Management of maintenance base.

The EMU maintenance base shall be uniformly managed by China National Railway, and the introduction and cooperation of EMU maintenance base shall be uniformly implemented by China Railway Corporation.

Ⅱ. *EMU Maintenance Base*

1. Functions of maintenance base

1)EMU management function

The EMU maintenance base has the overall management function of managing the base, connecting the surrounding areas and radiating the whole road, and comprehensively manages the use, technical preparation, maintenance test and operation safety of EMUs. Through the connection of the information center, it can effectively manage the dispatching, servicing, operation, maintenance, accessories and equipment of EMU.

2) Check the servicing function

The inspection and servicing functions of EMU include servicing operation, level Ⅰ and level Ⅱ maintenance operation and temporary repair operation.

Servicing operation: mainly for technical servicing and passenger servicing. The operation contents include water supply and drainage, lubricating grease supplement, interior cleaning, ground receiving and treatment facilities of closed toilet system, car body skin cleaning, garbage collection and transfer in the car, etc.

Temporary repair: it mainly deals with the temporary faults of EMU, detaining and repairing the main parts of EMU, and replacing the main equipment and parts other than wheel lathing of EMU and repair at all levels, including bogie, wheel set, pantograph, air conditioning facilities, main converter, main transformer, etc.

3) Maintenance function

The maintenance of EMUs in the base focuses on prevention, inspection, replacement repair and assembly and commissioning; Manage the EMU in the way of life management; Minimize the repair time and improve the efficiency, reliability and utilization of EMUs. The replaced parts of EMU shall be overhauled by professional manufacturers in a professional centralized maintenance mode.

4) Spare parts storage and distribution function

The base shall set up storage facilities for large EMU parts, accessories and spare parts, including material warehouse, material shed, spare parts warehouse, etc. The three-dimensional storage mode is adopted for spare parts and materials, and its information management is incorporated into the EMU information system, and can automatically carry out distribution management according to the maintenance information.

5) Information management function

Information management includes production dispatching command, EMU Operation Management, on-site operation monitoring, vehicle parts life management, vehicle parts distribution support, depot detection and on-board information ground receiving and processing.

6) Sewage treatment function

The maintenance base is equipped with a closed toilet system and ground receiving and treatment facilities.

The ground receiving and processing facilities of vacuum closed toilet system shall be fixed; The toilet collection receiving operation line shall be combined with the daily inspection operation line and set in the warehouse. The main facilities for sewage discharge are placed under the working platform of the inspection shed, which can be connected with the sewage outlet on the vehicle through pipelines and quick connectors, and a mobile sewage truck is set.

2. Layout of maintenance base

The maintenance base reasonably arranges the line group, buildings, channels, various pipelines, environmental protection and other facilities in the section in combination with the station type, landform, transportation development, urban planning and other factors. The facilities in the high-speed EMU maintenance base are mainly composed of three parts: ① the EMU stays in the depot (warehouse or shed)at night; ② Main maintenance shed and repair workshop (collectively referred to as comprehensive maintenance shed); ③ EMU skin cleaning, wheel tread diagnosis, non-falling wheel lathing, train sewage discharge and other equipment.

The layout of facilities in the base shall be compact, tidy, smooth operation and advanced technical and economic indicators, so as to reflect the characteristics of daily inspection, maintenance and regular maintenance of the whole train of high-speed EMU without decoupling. Different forms of facilities in the base constitute different ways of overall layout.

(1) In-line layout. The in-line layout is shown in Fig. 5-1, and the parking lot and maintenance garage in the base are arranged vertically. This scheme is often adopted when the terrain is narrow and long and there are access operations at both ends. Its features:

① The layout is compact, the operation of EMU into the section is smooth, the number of corner running in the section is less, the number of moving and reprinting can be reduced, the running distance is short, and the maintenance efficiency can be improved.

② It is beneficial to improve the maintenance capacity and expand the maintenance site.

③ The scale and occupied area of the base are large.

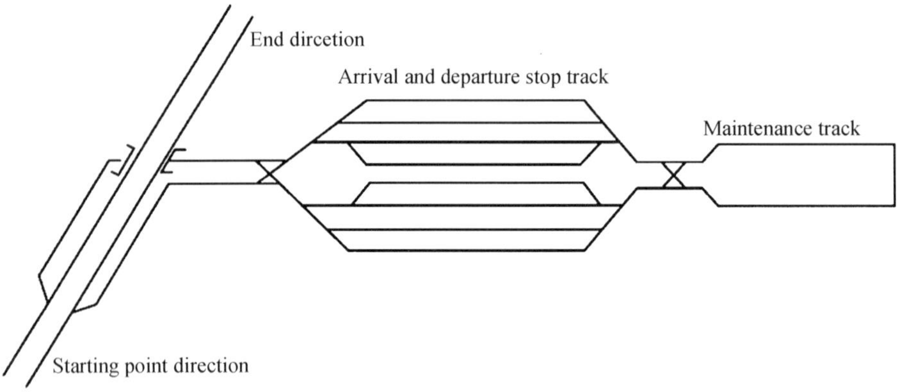

Fig. 5-1 In-line layout

(2) Parallel layout. The parallel layout is shown in Fig. 5-2. The train storage yard in the base is arranged horizontally in parallel with the service shop. This scheme has strong adaptability to topographic conditions and small floor area. Its features:

① The operation of EMU entering the depot can only be carried out after multiple corner turns. The running distance in the EMU Depot is long, and special traction lines need to be set in the depot. The operation efficiency is low, which is generally adopted when it is unavoidable due to site constraints.

② The base is restricted by the land area, and the train arrival and departure stop line is set parallel to the maintenance line, which is suitable for small-scale vehicle maintenance base with less than 10 trains.

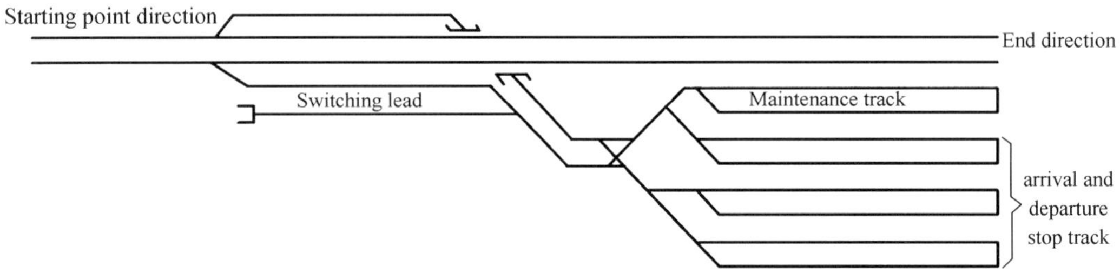

Fig. 5-2 Parallel layout

(3) Staggered layout. The staggered layout is shown in Fig. 5-3. Part of the storage yard and maintenance garage are arranged in horizontal rows, part in vertical rows or other general layout schemes controlled by the site.

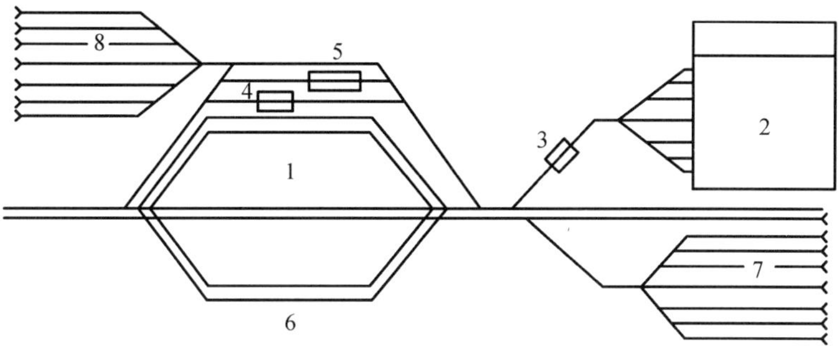

1, 7, 8—parking lot; 2—maintenance shed; 3—wheel set diagnosis library;
4—no wheel shed; 5—skin cleaning warehouse; 6—blowdown line.

Fig. 5-3 Staggered layout

In the above three layouts, due to the smooth operation of EMU entering the section in the in-line layout scheme, fewer times of corner turning and short running distance in the section, this layout is recommended if conditions permit.

After the basic type scheme of general layout is determined, the location of other lines and equipment shall be determined according to different operation requirements and site conditions. Generally, the arrival departure stop line group, the main maintenance line group, as well as the special lines for EMU sewage discharge, skin washing, non-falling wheel lathing, wheel tread diagnosis, etc. shall be arranged in a longitudinal manner. It is best to set two parking lots at both ends of the maintenance shed.

3. Maintenance shed

Along the length direction of the maintenance shed, access roads outside the shed shall be set every 100m. Catenary can be erected in all or part of station tracks in the maintenance shed, and the height of catenary can be the same as that outside the shed. At the operation place on the roof, the catenary must be equipped with section insulator and disconnector with grounding, as well as the sign lamp interlocked with the disconnector and the safety lock of the operation platform, so as to ensure the safety of operators. Low voltage power supply, independent air source and water source are set in the warehouse.

1) Warehouse line

According to different maintenance tasks (servicing, daily maintenance, bogie replacement, etc.), maintenance garages of different access levels are set in the maintenance base, and different maintenance work is carried out on different warehouse lines.

Fig. 5-4 shows the level Ⅰ~Ⅲ maintenance garage in the German EMU Depot.

Fig. 5-5 shows the overhaul depot line. On these tracks, large parts can be replaced or a carriage can be disassembled.

Fig. 5-4　M1–M3 maintenance shed of German Railway

Fig. 5-5　Overhaul depot line of German Railway

2) Design requirements

(1)Warehouse line design requirements.

The distance between two warehouse lines should be 10 m. The distance between the outer track in the depot and the axis of the side wall of the inspection depot shall not be less than 5 m. EMU water supply, drainage and sewage equipment shall be set in the depot. The clear height of the inspection shed shall consider the height requirements of the operators on the roof. For the longitudinal transportation from the bottom working surface to the floor in the warehouse, a gentle slope with a gradient of no more than 10% shall be set. The clear height of the repair garage shall be determined according to the repair process, EMU vehicle gauge, roof operation requirements, crane structure size and other factors. The top height of the traveling rail of the crane in the warehouse shall not be less than + 8.8 m, as shown in Fig. 5-6.

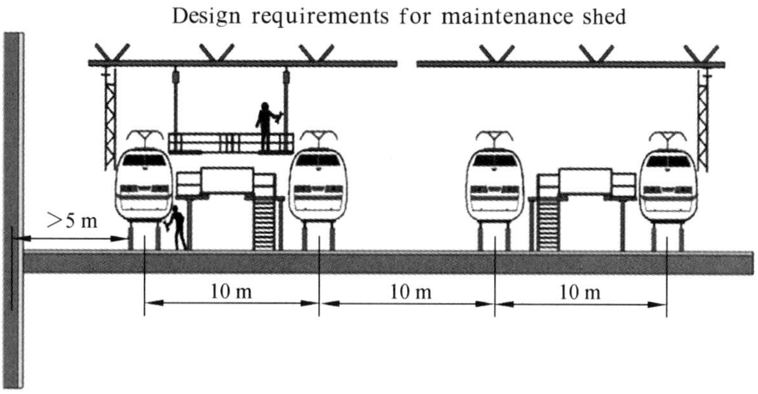

(a) Maintenance line design requirements

(b) Slope design requirements

Fig. 5-6 Warehouse line design requirements

The service shop shall be equipped with equipment for replacing the main components of bogie, wheel set, roof and under the vehicle. Bogie and wheel set replacement is preferably carried out by using movable track bridge and air cushion technology.

(2) Design requirements for overhaul depot.

Movable rigid catenary lateral displacement and control equipment can be set for the catenary above the station track in the depot. Safety protection measures shall be set to ensure the safety of operators. The three-dimensional overhaul line of the working face is set in the major repair garage, the distance between the lines is 12 m, and the distance between the outer track in the garage and the side wall axis of the repair garage shall not be less than 6.5 m. The overhaul operation adopts the whole train unwheeling mode, and the component replacement repair is implemented. Through type crown block lifting equipment is set, as shown in Fig. 5-7.

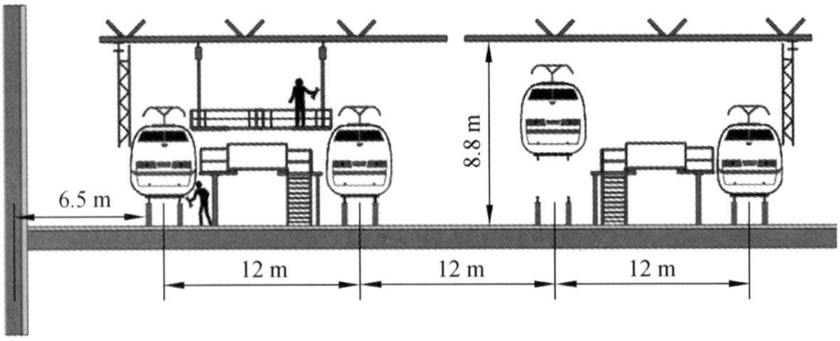

Fig. 5-7 Design requirements for overhaul depot.

4. Working face

To carry out parallel operation and improve the efficiency of maintenance, the maintenance base is generally equipped with three or four working surfaces for the maintenance of high-speed trains.

(1) Three layer operation surface, as shown in Fig. 5-8.

The first floor is set at the elevation of 0.95 m below the rail surface, which is the basic operation platform for the inspection, maintenance and material transportation of the running part and lower facilities.

The second floor is set at the elevation of 1.25 m above the rail surface, which is the operation platform of vehicle interior and side wall.

The third floor is set at the elevation of 3.8 m above the rail surface, which is the roof operation platform. Protective facilities to prevent roof operators from falling shall be set on the side without roof operation platform.

(2) Four layer operation surface is shown in Fig. 5-9.

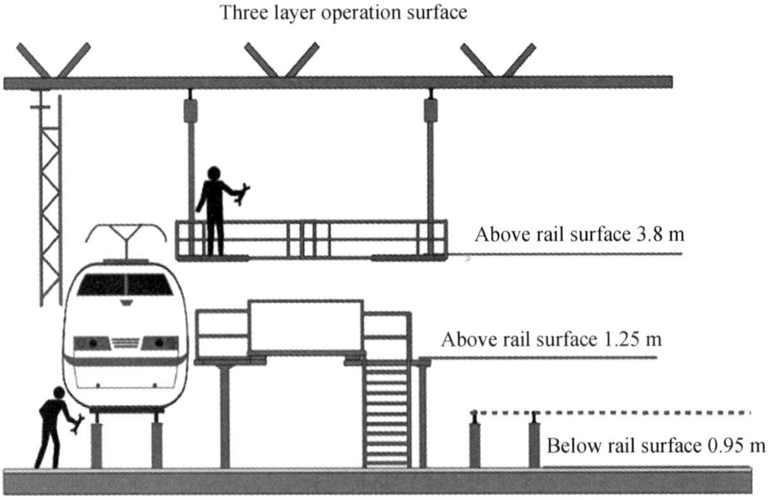

Fig. 5-8 Three layer operation surface

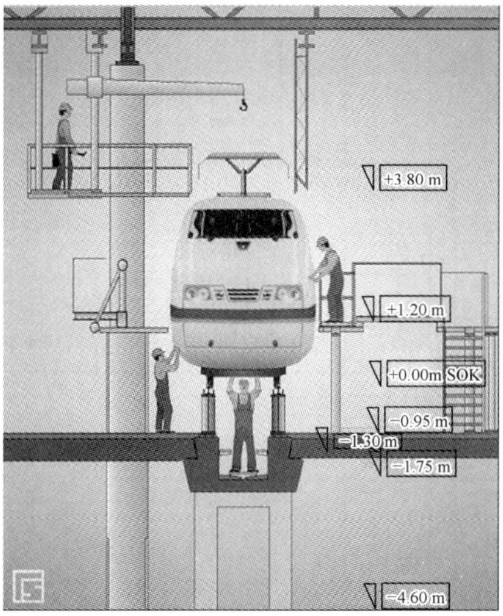

Fig. 5-9 Four layer operation surface

The first floor working face (– 0.95 m) is responsible for the inspection and repair of the train bottom.

The second floor working surface (+ 1.2 m)is used for operation in the vehicle.

The third floor working face (+ 3.8 m)adopts mobile aerial platform.

All pipelines shall be installed on the fourth floor working face (– 4.6 m)except transportation.

5. Auxiliary maintenance facilities for main parts and accessories

Appropriate places shall be set in the base for necessary maintenance of main parts, mainly including bogie room, traction motor room, transformer room, converter room, electrical and control equipment room, pantograph room, braking equipment room, air conditioning equipment room and equipment room in the vehicle. The facility capacity meets the production needs, and the layout meets the requirements of smooth process.

Repair facilities inside the base and complete the maintenance of other accessories. The repair workshop of accessories shall be set with the maintenance shed as the main body. Auxiliary workshops mainly include: battery room, measuring instrument room, material warehouse, etc.

6. Organization

Each maintenance base is equipped with several administrative agencies to coordinate work and complete maintenance tasks. An example of its organization is shown in figure 5-10.

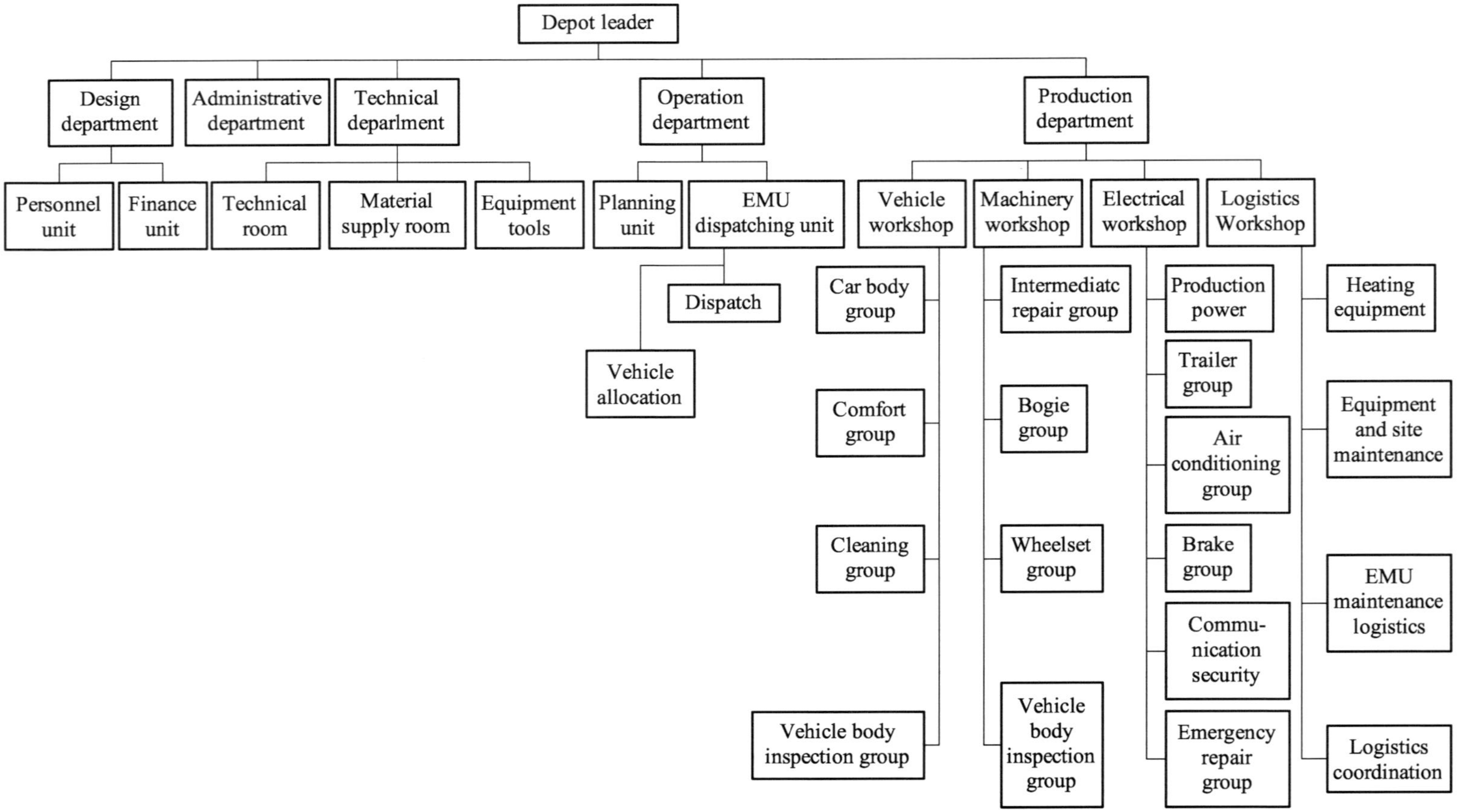

Fig. 5-10 Example of maintenance base organization

Ⅲ. *Main Maintenance Equipment of EMU*

The high-tech requirements of EMU have led to the renewal of EMU maintenance equipment. From mobile unwheeling machine to pit unwheeling machine, EMU maintenance equipment has developed at a high speed. The servicing and maintenance of EMUs is the precondition to ensure the effective use and operation quality of EMUs, and it is an important part of the comprehensive support project of high-speed railway system. In the condition monitoring and fault diagnosis of high-speed EMUs, the wide application of advanced technology and intelligent and integrated diagnosis equipment is the basic element to improve the maintenance quality and operation efficiency.

The maintenance process flow of EMU is shown in Fig. 5-11, which generally includes entering the section, external cleaning, tread diagnosis, internal repair (in warehouse operation, period of inspection and repair operation, repair operation, internal cleaning, disinfection, material supply and other items), and finally waiting and leaving the section. These processes require us to maintain more strictly and carefully.

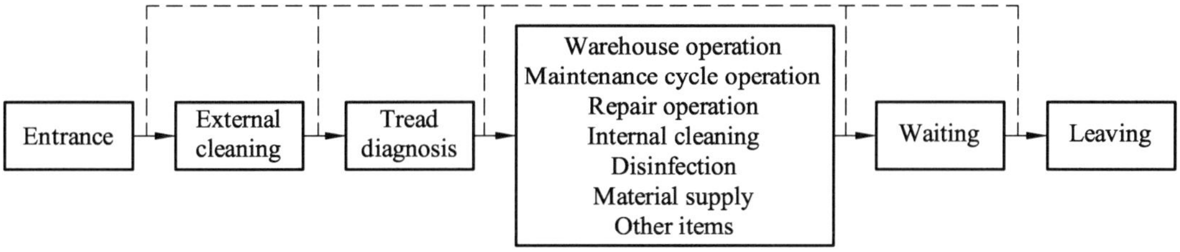

Fig. 5-11 Maintenance process flow of EMU

1. Basic configuration requirements of EMU Operation Station

(1) Automatic car body cleaning equipment.

(2) Ground sewage suction facilities shall be equipped with mobile equipment if necessary.

(3) Non falling wheel lathe device.

(4) Wheel tread detection equipment.

(5) Ground receiving and information processing equipment of train monitoring system.

(6) Sufficient storage lines.

(7) Repair shop and temporary repair shop.

(8) Necessary system testing equipment and mechanical power equipment.

(9) Production and safety information management system.

2. Basic configuration requirements for EMU maintenance base.

(1) Automatic car body cleaning equipment.

(2) Ground sewage suction equipment.

(3) Non falling wheel lathe device.

(4) Wheel tread detection equipment.

(5) Ground receiving and information processing equipment of train monitoring system.

(6) Sufficient storage lines.

(7) Car repair shop and paint shop.

(8) Bogie maintenance shed (room)and test facilities.

(9) Wheel set, bearing maintenance shed (room)and inspection and test equipment.

(10) Brake system maintenance shed (room)and testing equipment.

(11) Traction system maintenance shed (room)and testing equipment.

(12) Auxiliary power supply system maintenance shed (room)and detection and test equipment.

(13) Coupler and buffer device maintenance shed (room)and maintenance and detection equipment.

(14) Vehicle body air tightness test equipment.

(15) Other parts maintenance sites and maintenance, detection and test equipment.

(16) Single vehicle test facility.

(17) ATC test facilities.

(18) If necessary, trial operation lines shall be set in the site.

(19) Production and safety information management system.

3. Introduction of main tools and equipment

(1) Special equipment in comprehensive maintenance shed:

① Overhead track system with track bridge (or synchronous locomotive).

② Power bogie and intermediate wheel pair quick replacement equipment.

③ Wheelset rotating equipment.

④ Vacuum blowdown equipment for train urinals in the depot.

⑤ Operation lift truck.

⑥ Battery charging equipment.

⑦ Automatic sanding equipment for power car.

(2) Main special equipment for maintenance and test:

① ATC sensor.

② Sensor performance test bench.

③ Vacuum circuit breaker test bench.

④ Electrical circuit comprehensive test bench.

⑤ Electrical instrument test bench.

⑥ Automatic detection device for pantograph wear plate.

⑦ Cleaning equipment for bogie, frame, wheel set, bearing, traction electromechanical and other main parts.

⑧ Disassembly and assembly equipment of power bogie.

⑨ Performance test bench for disc brake device.

⑩ Hydraulic shock absorber performance test bench.

⑪ Performance test bench for various valves.

⑫ Three dimensional shelf and hydraulic lifting device.

⑬ Production management computer control system.

⑭ Infrared axle temperature detection repeater.

⑮ Automatic driving simulator.

(3) Wheel set and bogie replacement device.

When the wheel set and bogie of motor car and trailer of high-speed train fail, it shall be replaced. Bogie replacement equipment is essential and important equipment for maintenance base and operation, and a powerful guarantee to improve maintenance efficiency and EMU turnover efficiency. In terms of replacement mode, it can be divided into two types: movable track bridge bogie lowering mode and synchronous unwheeling mode.

Fig. 5-12 shows the bogie replacement equipment with movable track bridge, which has small equipment scale and high operator efficiency.

Fig. 5-12 Bogie equipment replacement with movable track bridge

Fig. 5-13 shows the bogie replacement equipment of synchronous bogie. When in use, four unwheeling machines are generally used for each unit to disconnect the connection between the bogie and the vehicle body, and the unwheeling machine is lifted at the same time to erect the vehicle body and push out the bogie. Because the whole train is connected through tight coupling, the coupling fit clearance is very small, so it puts forward higher requirements for the synchronization of unwheeling machine. In this way, the equipment scale is large. Generally, 4–8 vehicles are lifted together. Multiple operators are required to work at the same time, which is easy to cause operation loss.

Fig. 5-13　Bogie replacement equipment of synchronous bogie

(4) Ultrasonic flaw detection equipment.

Fig. 5-14 shows several ultrasonic flaw detection equipment. Where (a)shows an example of detecting an axle on the ultrasonic flaw detection bench; (b)shows the hollow shaft detected by the ultrasonic flaw detector, which is used to detect the internal defects of the axle; (c)shows the wheel tread ultrasonic testing equipment.

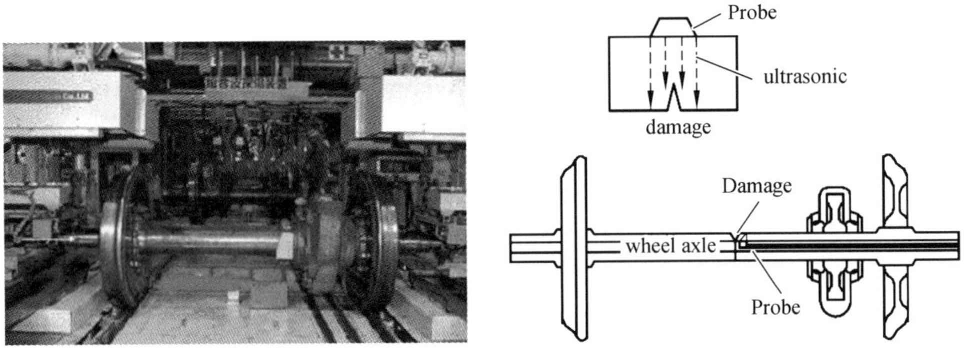

(a)

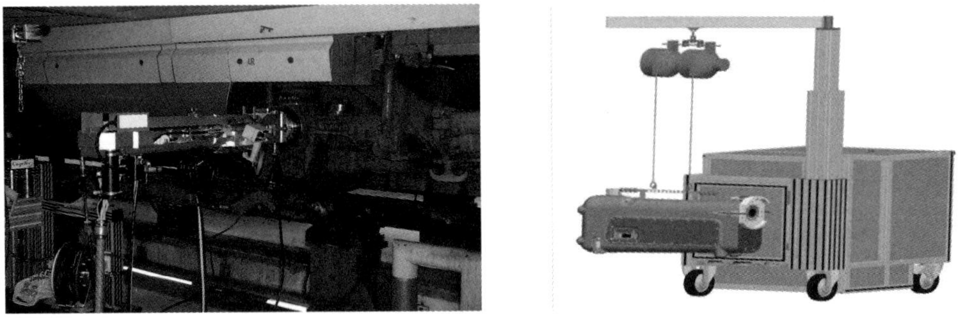

(b)

(c)

Fig. 5-14 Ultrasonic flaw detection equipment

(5) Non-falling wheel lathe device.

When the tread diagnosis device diagnoses that the wheel set is defective (scratch, etc.)or the wheel tread and rim are worn to the limit, grinding and maintenance shall be carried out in time to restore the comfort of EMU Operation and ensure driving safety. The feature of the device is that the bogie does not need to fall and separate from the EMU body. The EMU directly drives into the equipment moving track (the equipment is installed in the pit). Through the direct lathing of the equipment, the equipment lathing time and the working intensity of maintenance personnel are reduced, as shown in Fig. 5-15.

Fig. 5-15 Non-falling wheel lathe device

(6) Wheel tread detection equipment.

The shape of wheel tread directly affects the comfort and driving safety of trains, especially for high-speed trains. The wheel tread diagnosis device is the most important maintenance and diagnosis equipment in the maintenance base and application. It has the functions of detecting tread slid flat, measuring tread shape and geometric dimensions, measuring tread slid flat and concentricity, etc. The device also has the functions of data acquisition and processing, and is networked with the communication computer in the section to complete the functions of data storage, display, printing and transmission. The accuracy of the detection device directly affects the maintenance efficiency of the whole train. Fig. 5-16 shows the wheel tread detection equipment on the line.

Fig. 5-16 The wheel tread detection equipment

(7) Automatic car body cleaning equipment.

EMU skin cleaning equipment is an essential servicing equipment, which is used for automatic skin cleaning when the train returns to the depot and enters the depot. Special cleaning agent is required. To meet the requirements of environmental protection and energy conservation, water circulation treatment facilities must be established at the same time (as shown in Fig. 5-17 and Fig. 5-18).

Fig. 5-17 Schematic diagram of equipment composition of car washing machine

Fig. 5-18 Automatic car body cleaning equipment

(8) Vacuum blowdown equipment for toilet box of EMU.

The sewage collection and treatment of high-speed EMU shall be solved, and a set of sewage system shall be set in the section. The blowdown operation shall be carried out at the same place as the maintenance and servicing operation as far as possible, so as to shorten the dwell time of EMU in the section. Vacuum suction sewage system is mainly used for sewage surface facilities, as shown in Fig. 5-19.

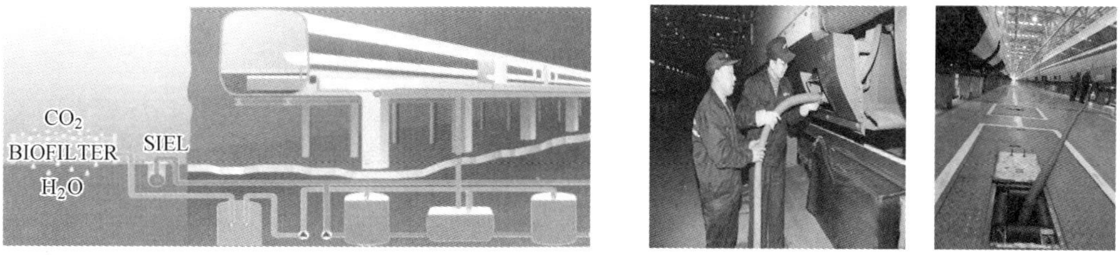

(a) Schematic diagram of sewage suction equipment (b) Suction scene

Fig. 5-19 Vacuum blowdown equipment

[Task Detection]

1. What kinds of maintenance organizations are there for EMUs in China? What are their functions?

2. Briefly describe the layout of maintenance bases and operation stations in China.

3. Briefly describe the maintenance process after the EMU is put into operation.

4. Briefly describe the concept of three and four working surfaces in the maintenance base.

5. What are the main maintenance equipment in the maintenance base?

6. Draw the in-line layout of the maintenance base.

Task 3 Operation Flow of EMU Operation and Maintenance

[Task Description]

(1) Get familiar with the operation and maintenance process of EMU.

(2) Be able to complete the operation according to the level I maintenance operation standard of EMU.

The operation division, operation procedures, operation steps and operation flow of operation level maintenance (level Ⅰ and level Ⅱ maintenance)of CRH series EMUs are basically the same, and the maintenance scope, maintenance limit, special operation contents and methods vary from model to model. The following is a detailed description of the first and second level maintenance of EMU.

Ⅰ. *Level I Maintenance of EMU*

1. Period of inspection and repair

(1) The level Ⅰ period of inspection and repair of multiple units shall comply with the cycle standard specified in the notice of China Railway Corporation on printing and distributing the rules for operation and maintenance of Railway Multiple Units (TZY [2017] No. 238). The planned preventive maintenance of EMUs is mainly based on the running kilometer cycle and supplemented by the time cycle (whichever comes first). (see table 6-1 for a specific period of inspection and repair)

(2) After the completion of temporary maintenance, secondary maintenance and advanced maintenance EMU, the primary maintenance must be carried out before the operation.

(3) The EMU must carry out a level-1 maintenance operation before taking on the hot standby; If the cumulative standby (including hot standby)time of EMU exceeds 48h, level I maintenance must be carried out before online operation; After on-line operation, it shall be implemented according to the provisions of level Ⅰ period of inspection and repair of EMU on the operation line.

2. Maintenance scope

Level I maintenance refers to the maintenance operation of rapid routine inspection, test and fault treatment for the roof, under the vehicle, both sides of the vehicle body, in the vehicle and cab of the EMU, which must be implemented in the inspection warehouse of the EMU.

3. Staffing and division of labor

(1) Short EMU (8-car formation)

One maintenance operation team (4 operators in total for ①, ②, ③ and ④), 2 other auxiliary personnel (⑤ and ⑥), and 2 catenary workers. Group ① is the leader of the maintenance group and is responsible for the overall work arrangement.

①② is responsible for the inspection of roof equipment, cab equipment, in vehicle equipment, on-board information system and other equipment; ③④ is responsible for the inspection of both sides of the car body and the trench under the car, such as car body, skirt, bottom plate, bogie, brake, coupler and buffer connection, and the setting and removal of wheel stopper; Two catenary workers are responsible for clearing the road in the warehouse and disconnecting the switch for power-off operation; Two other auxiliary personnel (⑤ and ⑥)assist in the inspection. ⑤ is specifically responsible for cooperating with the technician to download the on-board data of the EMU, cooperate with the operation of relevant integration departments, cooperate with the relevant tests of the EMU, and cooperate with the operation of lifting and lowering the pantograph during the roof operation of ① and ②. ⑥ assists the operation team in dealing with the temporary repair fault of the EMU, connecting and plugging the external power supply, receiving and sending of accessories, etc.

Roof and cab faults shall be inspected and repaired by ①② and confirmed by quality inspection; The faults found in the inspection of ③④ shall be handled by ⑥. And then confirmed and assisted in the inspection by ③ and④; In principle, the personnel ③ and ④ shall be responsible for the operation of the pick-up and transfer vehicle. When the operators are nervous, the foreman can arrange the personnel⑤ and ⑥ to be responsible, and the personnel ⑤ and ⑥ shall give timely feedback on the operation of the pick-up and transfer vehicle to the personnel ③ and ④.

Note: (1) When ③④ checking the gearbox of the driving device on each side, the traction motor connected to the gearbox shall be checked by the operator on the gearbox inspection side; (2) When working under the trench, ③④ must keep an interval of about 3M before and after; (3)the motor car depot shall arrange and implement the stand-by pick-up and delivery of motor car units.

(2) Long (multiple)EMU (16 sets)

There are 2 maintenance teams (8 operators), 2 catenary workers and 2 other auxiliary personnel.

1) Long EMU.

Each operation team shall overhaul 8 vehicles in the long EMU. The main control key, power supply and outage application, etc. shall be in the charge of No. ① of the operation team in the warehousing direction of the EMU, and the inspection of the equipment in workshops 08 ~ 09 shall be in the charge of the operation team in the warehousing direction of the EMU. The division of labor of other operators shall be defined by the motor car depot in comparison with the short EMU (8-car formation).

2) Multiple EMU.

Each operation team shall overhaul one EMU. The main control key, power supply and outage application, etc. shall be in the charge of No. ① of the operation team in the warehousing direction of the EMU. The inspection of coupler and draft gear at the reconnection end, air duct connection and other equipment shall be in the charge of the operation team in the warehousing direction of the EMU. The division of labor of other operators shall be defined by the motor car depot in comparison with the short EMU (8-car formation).

(3) Professional division of labor

① The locomotive driver shall be responsible for the sanitation in the cab, remove the sundries in the cab and sort out the equipment in the area.

② The passenger transport department is responsible for cleaning the toilets, catering equipment, passenger service facilities and other facilities in the passenger compartment of the EMU, removing the sundries in the vehicle, sorting and returning the seats in the passenger compartment, closing all refrigerators, cabinet doors and drawers, and turning off or disconnecting the power supply of electrical equipment.

③ The EMU Depot shall be responsible for the data analysis of wheel fault online detection system, pantograph and roof state dynamic detection system, EMU operation fault image detection system, car body skin cleaning, sewage unloading, disconnector operation related to EMU maintenance and major fault treatment and repair after EMU warehousing.

④ The professional maintenance of on-board LKJ, ATP, CIR, EOAS and other electrical equipment and auxiliary facilities shall be undertaken by the electrical department.

⑤ The power supply department shall be responsible for the professional maintenance of power supply equipment and auxiliary facilities such as on-board catenary detection device (3C)of EMU.

⑥ The sorting of materials and accessories, the management of tool placement and the cleaning of waste materials of each discipline after the maintenance of the motor car depot shall be carried out in accordance with the on-site management regulations of the motor car depot.

(4) Staff assign ment

With regard to the allocation and division of OCS workers and auxiliary personnel in the maintenance of short series and long series (multiple unit)EMUs, EMU Depot shall continuously adjust and optimize in combination with the actual situation.

4. Maintenance mode

(1)The level Ⅰ maintenance of EMU can adopt the operation mode of No Power (external power supply can be connected)-Power On or Power On-No Power-Power On. Main technical operation time of EMU level Ⅰ maintenance: 4 h is reserved in the inspection shed (6h when ice melting and snow removal is required).

① The level Ⅰ maintenance operation adopts the No Power-Power On maintenance mode.

a. No power maintenance items: roof, gutter, passenger compartment facilities and vehicle -181 fault treatment, etc.

b. Power on maintenance items: vehicle side inspection, power supply function test of all equipment, troubleshooting and recheck of passenger compartment facilities. Electrical and communication inspection, inspection of equipment and facilities in cab and vehicle, braking and pressure maintaining test, inspection of power supply status of vehicle equipment, vehicle dynamic-181 fault treatment, etc.

② The level Ⅰ maintenance operation adopts the power on - no power - power on leve 1maintenance mode.

a. Power on pre-inspection items: Electrical and communication inspection, equipment and facilities inspection in cab and vehicle, power supply status inspection of vehicle equipment, vehicle side inspection, vehicle operation -181 fault treatment, etc.

b. No power Maintenance items: roof and trench inspection, passenger compartment facilities and vehicle -181 fault handling, etc.

c. Power on maintenance items: power supply function test of all equipment, vehicle side inspection, troubleshooting and recheck of passenger compartment facilities, etc.

(2) The internal cleaning, skin cleaning, sewage suction and water supply of EMUs shall be organized and implemented by the EMU Depot and relevant units in accordance with the integrated management measures for operation and maintenance of EMUs and the first-class maintenance operation mode.

(3) Level Ⅰ maintenance shall fully implement the operation requirements of "must see, must point, must call and must draw" for EMU maintenance, and the specific contents shall be specified in the class 1 maintenance operation instruction.

(4) The quality inspector's inspection on the quality of maintenance operation of in vehicle service facilities can be carried out in combination with ex warehouse joint inspection.

(5) After the level Ⅰ maintenance is completed, the quality inspector shall organize each professional maintenance operation group to carry out ex warehouse joint inspection.

5. Maintenance operation flow and route

1) Primary maintenance process.

① No power - power on level Ⅰ maintenance mode, as shown in Fig. 5-20.

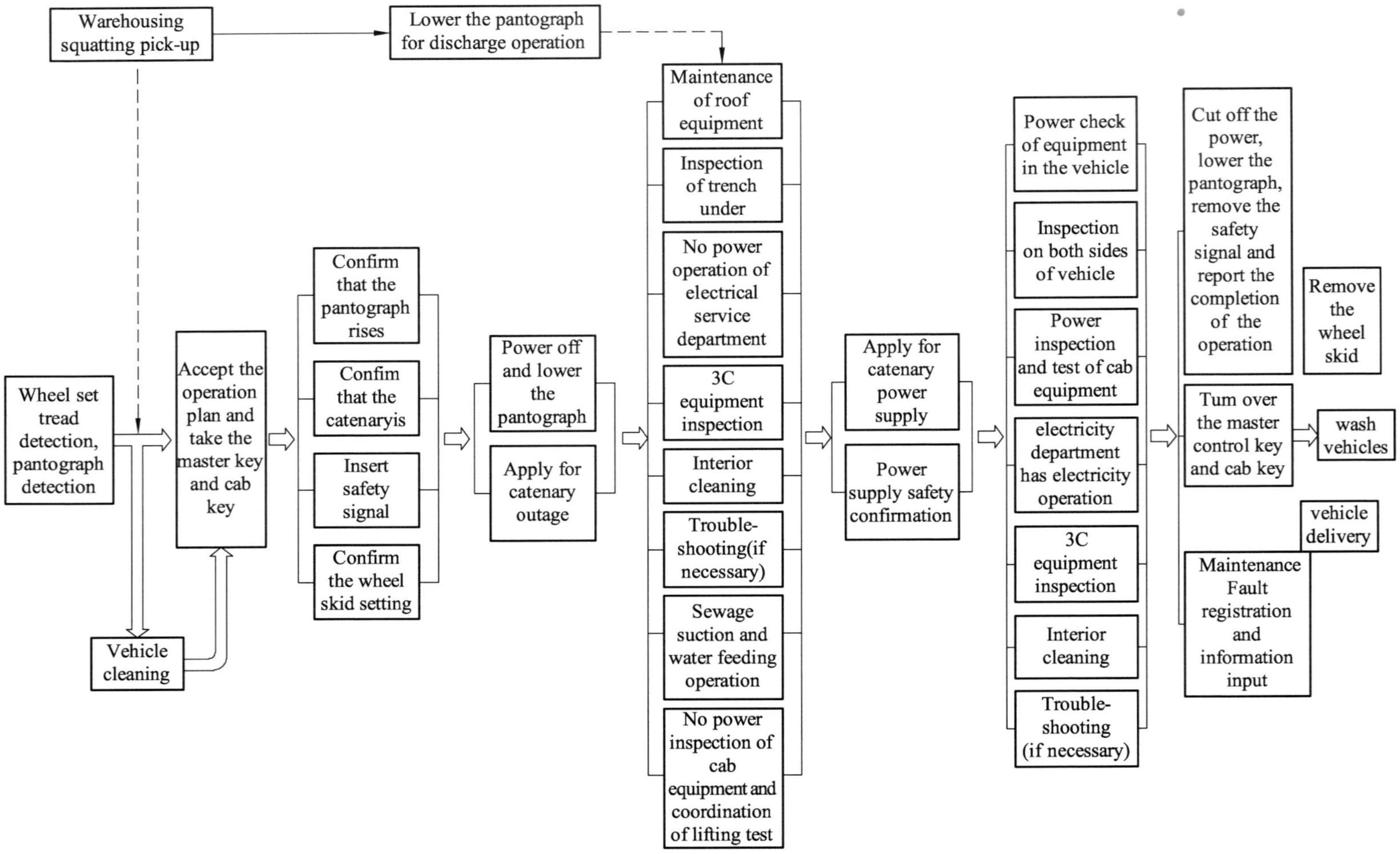

Fig. 5-20 Operation flow of level I maintenance of EMU

② Time node of level I maintenance process (no power + power on), as shown in Fig. 5-21.

Operation Department \ Time	10	20	30	40	50	60	80	90	100	110	120	150	140
Power supply and outage group							Power supply operation						
Technical group	Data download and analysis; Operation fault inspection and troubleshooting							Fault determination					
Main engine factory after sale	No power check, operation fault check, fault handling							Power on inspection and fault determination					
First level repair group (①②⑤)	Roof equipment inspection							Inspection of in vehicle facilities, function test of cab equipment and fault determination test					
First level repair group (③④)	Inspection of underbody equipment							Inspection and fault determination test on both sides of the vehicle					
Electricity Department	ATP/CIR no power check							ATP/CIR power check					
Power supply department	3C equipment power check							3C equipment no power check					
Outsourcing Department	Dirt suction, water filling, skin cleaning, filter screen cleaning and high-pressure equipment wiping												
Passenger transport department	Interior cleaning												
Note: each operation department shall operate in strict accordance with the time node, and the duty room of the bullet train station shall pay attention to the card control of the time node to ensure smooth operation.													

Fig. 5-21 Time node diagram of level I maintenance process of EMU (No Power + Power On)

2) Level Ⅰ maintenance operation line of CRH380A EMU

① No power operation route on the roof (No. ① and ② no power operation route), as shown in Fig. 5-22.

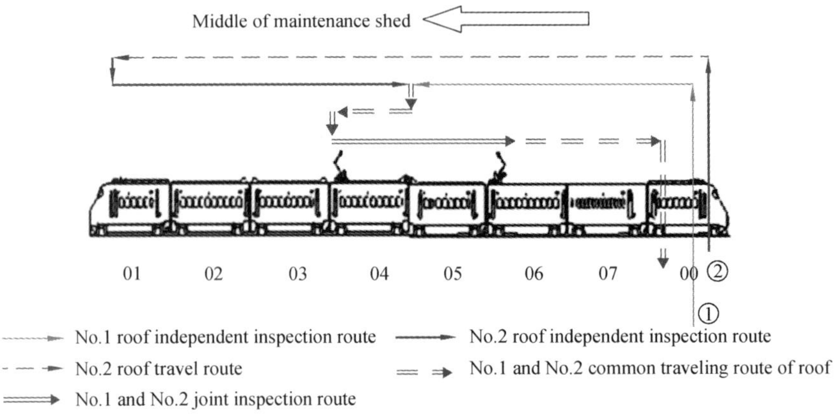

Fig. 5-22 Route of no power operation on the roof

② No power operation route under the vehicle (No. ③ and ④ no power operation route), as shown in Fig. 5-23.

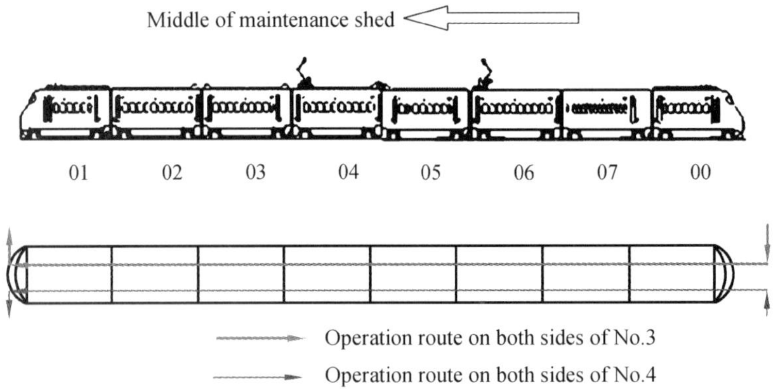

Fig. 5-23 Route of no power operation under the vehicle

③ Route of power on operation in the vehicle (No. 1and 2 power on operation routes), as shown in Fig. 5-24.

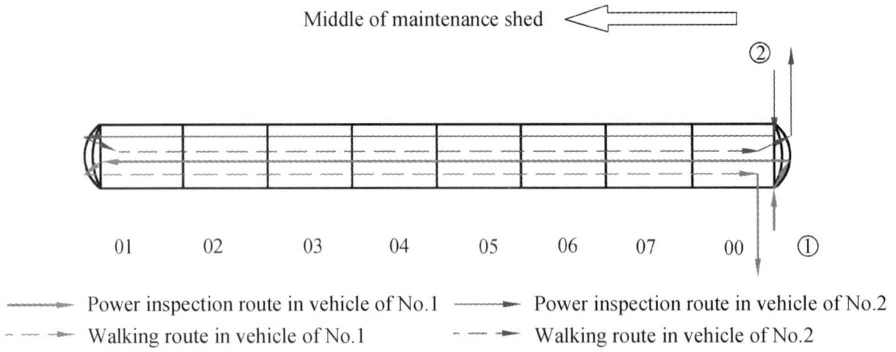

Fig. 5-24 Route of power on operation in the vehicle

④ Route of power on operation on both sides of the vehicle (No. ③ and ④ power on operation routes), as shown in Fig. 5-25.

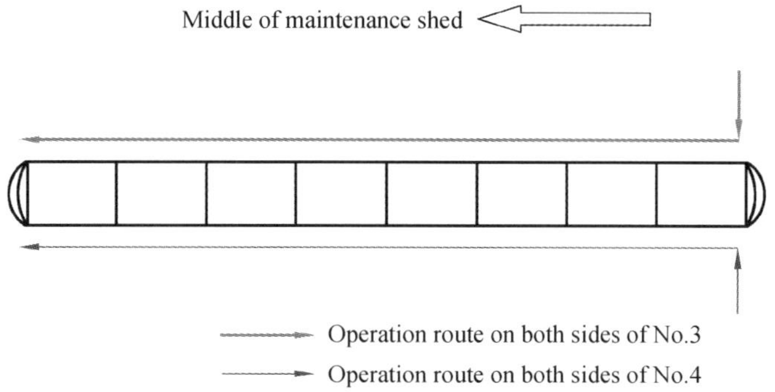

Fig. 5-25 Route of power on operation on both sides of the vehicle

3) Maintenance route of CRH380A (L)EMU

① No power operation route on the roof (No. ① and ② no power operation route), as shown in Fig. 5-26.

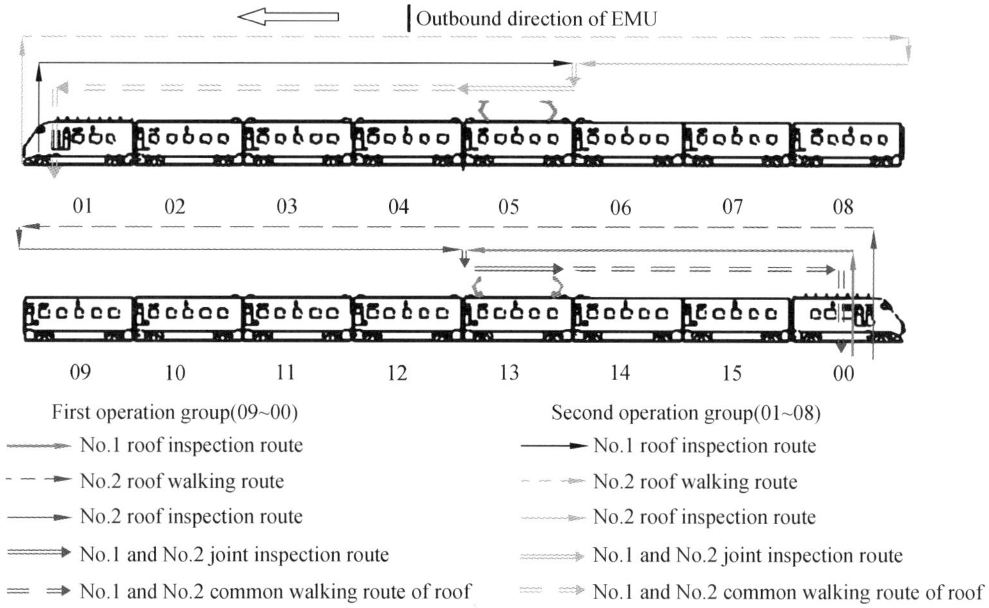

Fig. 5-26 No power operation route on the roof

② No power operation route under the vehicle (No. ③ and ④ no power operation route), as shown in Fig. 5-27.

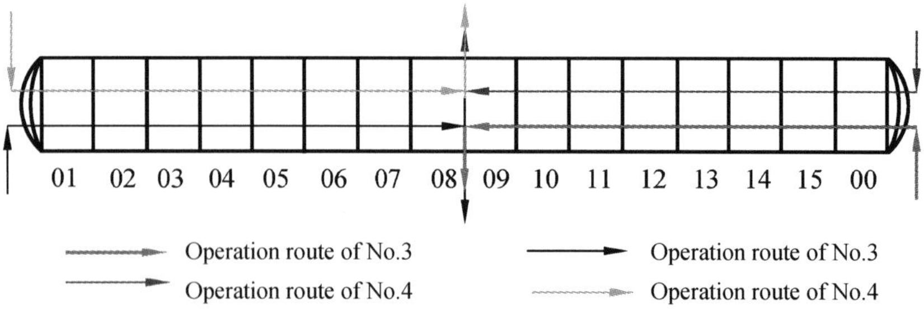

Fig. 5-27 No power operation route under the vehicle

③ Power on operation routes in the vehicle (No. ① and ② power on operation routes), as shown in Fig. 5-28.

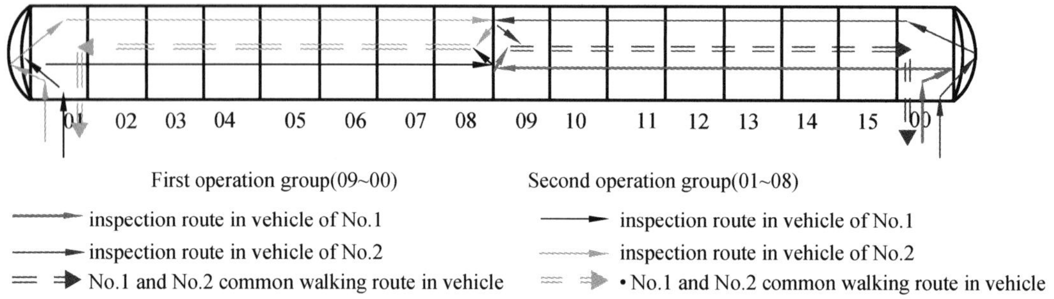

Fig. 5-28 Power on operation routes in the vehicle

(4)Power on operation routes on both sides under the vehicle (No. ③ and ④ power on operation routes), as shown in Fig. 5-29.

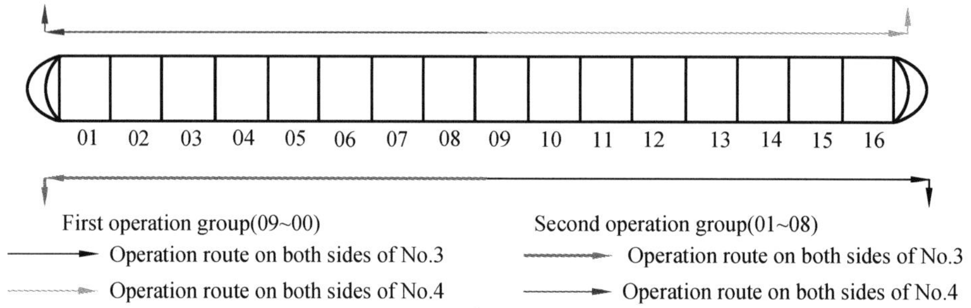

Fig. 5-29 Power on operation routes on both sides under the vehicle

6. Maintenance requirements

(1) Before the level Ⅰ maintenance of EMU is put into storage, it shall be detected by using the wheel fault online detection system, pantograph and roof state dynamic detection system and other detection equipment, and the detection data shall be subject to special analysis by a specially assigned person in time.

(2) The water level of each water tank of the EMU is more than 25%, and the dirt tank

must be evacuated to meet the maintenance and test conditions of the water supply and drainage sanitation system of the EMU.

(3) The maintenance operation team shall accept the operation plan in advance. Export the faults of the EMU to be inspected through the EMU management information system. No. ① understands the key faults of EMU operation, obtains the master control key and cab key, and makes preparations for the operation.

(4) When the EMU enters the depot, the receiving personnel must receive the vehicle at the designated position of the EMU Depot, listen to whether there is abnormal sound in the operation of the bogie and equipment under the vehicle, and check the status of equipment such as vehicle number and destination display, side door closing and indicator light display. After the EMU stops in the depot, report the receiving situation to the maintenance operation team. After the EMU stops in the depot and sets the wheel stopper, start the operation according to the level Ⅰ maintenance process, and swipe the card for confirmation according to the time node.

Ⅱ. *Level Ⅱ Maintenance of EMU*

1. Period of inspection and repair

(1) The level Ⅱ maintenance of EMU refers to the periodic maintenance, inspection and test of all systems and parts of EMU, without omission or overdue.

(2) Level Ⅱ maintenance can be carried out by detaining maintenance or combined with level I maintenance.

(3) The maintenance cycle of EMU is mainly based on running kilometers and supplemented by the time cycle, whichever comes first.

(4) The specific maintenance cycle of each project shall be subject to the cycle specified by the group company. It is allowed to delay the implementation of level Ⅱ maintenance projects implemented in the cycle of running kilometers by 10% (unless the scope of maintenance cycle is adjusted); The level Ⅱ maintenance items implemented in time cycle must be completed within the specified time.

2. Maintenance scope

The level Ⅱ maintenance project consists of preventive maintenance and corrective maintenance. Preventive maintenance defines the maintenance items, maintenance cycle and corresponding maintenance standards; Corrective maintenance refers to the maintenance implemented after failure. The motor car depot shall improve the contents and requirements of corrective maintenance items according to the application failure, solidify the maintenance items implemented in combination with the spring and autumn of motor car units, and report to the vehicle department in time.

3. Maintenance operation management

(1) The motor car depot can implement the balanced repair or centralized repair mode for level II maintenance according to the operation of motor car units.

(2) Level Ⅱ maintenance is based on parallel operation and three-dimensional operation, highlighting "special post, special person and special repair" maintenance, and eliminating cross operation. The motor car depot shall strengthen the management of maintenance tools and materials, comprehensively implement the vehicle share distribution of various projects, and standardize on-site operation.

(3) The EMU Depot shall continuously improve the EMU condition detection and personnel operation monitoring, establish and improve the management system, equip equipment maintenance and data analysis personnel, actively carry out comprehensive analysis and application of data, constantly standardize the business process, improve the maintenance process, optimize the maintenance system, and ensure smooth and orderly operation and controllable quality.

[Task Detection]

1. Briefly describe CRH380A (L)level Ⅰ maintenance process.
2. Briefly describe the division of maintenance work of CRH380A EMU.
3. Briefly describe the division of maintenance work of CRH380A (L)EMU.
4. Draw the no-power operation line for level Ⅰ maintenance of CRH380A (L)EMU.
5. Draw the electrified operation line for level Ⅰ maintenance of CRH380A (L)EMU.

项目一　动车组运用管理概述

【思政课堂】复兴号奔驰在祖国广袤的大地上

“复兴号奔驰在祖国广袤的大地上。”习近平主席在二〇一八年新年贺词中的亲切话语，是对铁路工作者的激励，是鞭策，更是对过去几年特别是党的十八大以来铁路工作成果的高度肯定。

过去几年，旅客的出行体验和幸福指数也越来越高。铁路部门不断创新服务形式，从过去基本的要求走得了，到现在高铁 WiFi、动车外卖、微信支付、刷脸进站等一系列的服务新举措，越来越满足人们走得快、走得好的需求。看似运输需求上的转变，实际是对铁路运输供给和企业发展质量的更高要求。只有时刻把以人民为中心的发展思想放在心上，才有如此的作为。

展望未来，中国铁路的发展令人期待。随着高铁，继续扩大高铁覆盖范围，形成“八纵八横”的高速铁路网，将进一步缩小人们的“生活圈”，让越来越多的人享受到了高铁的快速便捷，“出门”不再是难题，舟车劳顿也已是过去式。中国铁路将开启新征程，不断强大的自主创新复兴号将引领“中国制造”；不断完善的高铁铁路网将让大中城市的连接更加紧密；不断开放的中国铁路将在共享中贡献中国力量；不断强化的“交通强国、铁路先行”的责任使命将见证中国铁路的历史担当……

我已经看到，承载中华民族伟大复兴中国梦，承载中国人民美好生活新向往的“复兴号”，正满怀信心、全速驶向新时代的又一个春天。

【项目描述】

通过本项目学习，使学生了解国内外动车组运用基本情况及特点，正确理解动车组运用管理的工作基本任务；通过对动车组运用管理组织机构的分析，认识各级运用组织的职责及管理内容，以及相互之间的从属关系。

任务一　动车组运用概述及工作基本任务

【任务描述】

（1）了解动车组运用基本情况及特点。

（2）理解动车组运用管理工作的基本任务。

一、动车组运用基本情况及特点

1. 国外动车组运用基本情况及特点

动车组的运用方式因各国国情不同而有着较大的区别。国外高速铁路建设管理模式大致有 4 种类型：一是新建高速铁路专线，专门用于旅客快速运输，如日本新干线和法国高速铁路，均为客运专线形式，白天行车，夜间维修；二是新建高速铁路双线，实行客货共线运行，如罗马—佛罗伦萨高速铁路，客运速度 225 km/h，货运速度 120 km/h；三是部分新建高速与部分既有线混合运行，如柏林—汉诺威线，承担着客、货运任务；四是在既有线上使用摆式列车运行，这常见于欧洲国家，在美国“东北走廊”摆式列车速度也达到了 240 km/h。建设管理模式的不同，使得动车组的运用管理模式也不尽相同。

（1）日本新干线动车组运用。

日本新干线铁路从 1964 年开始营业运行，经过多年的实践，逐步总结、研究出一套具有日本特色的列车运用组织方法。其基本过程是：首先制订合理、准确地反映运输需求的列车运行计划，然后利用各种手段保证列车运行计划的实施，当发生列车运行波动时，采用必要的办法尽量快速恢复列车的稳定运行。新干线的动车组运用、检修及备用都与运行图进行了合理的配合，巧妙地运用了待避和越行等技巧，日本新干线路如图 1-1 所示。

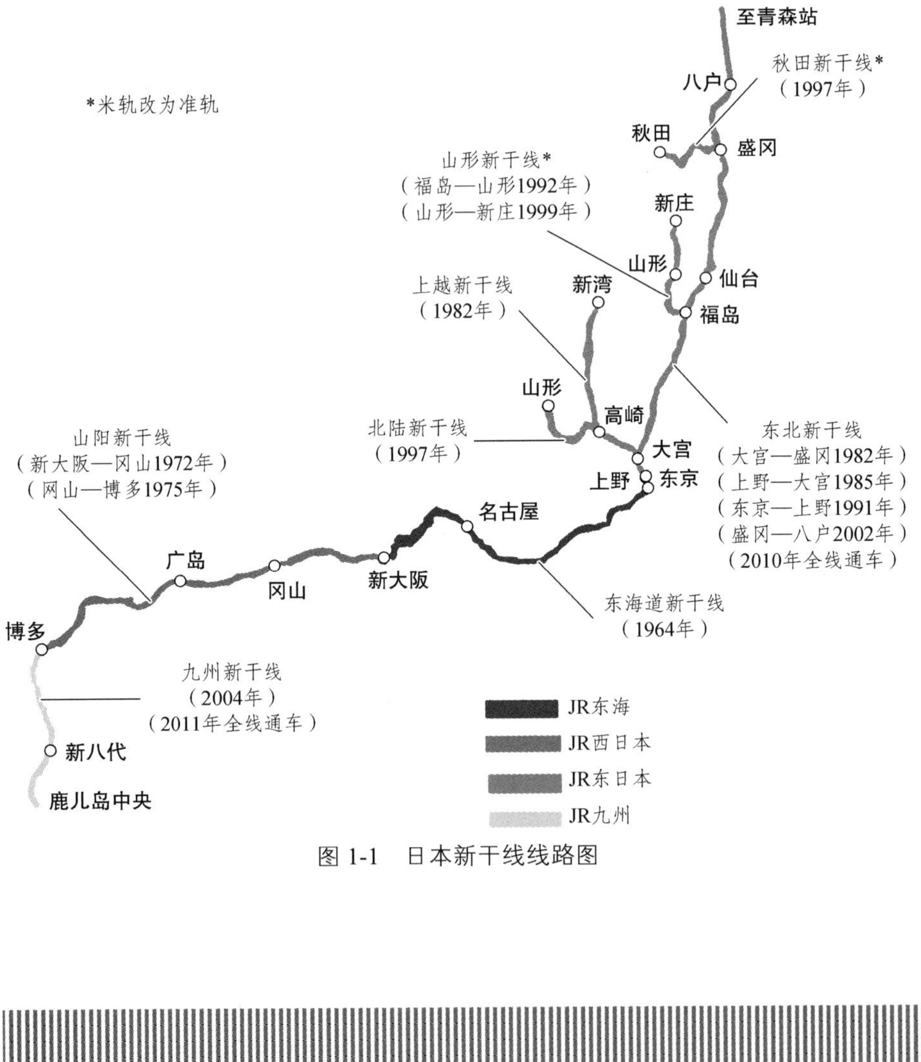

图 1-1　日本新干线线路图

（2）德国 ICE 动车组运用。

德国从 20 世纪 70 年代开始逐渐形成了四通八达的城际特快列车系统（IC 系统），连接着 30 多个重要城市和交通中心（见图 1-2）。德国高速铁路部分区段由既有线改造而来，全部高速线路均按客货列车混合运行。德国高速铁路的基本组织方式为白天不同速度的客运列车混合运行（高速列车、IC 列车），夜间客运列车、货运列车混合运行。德国之所以采用这种方式，主要是由于德国的区间通过能力比较富裕，而且既有线铁路列车技术水平与高速列车的差别不是很大。

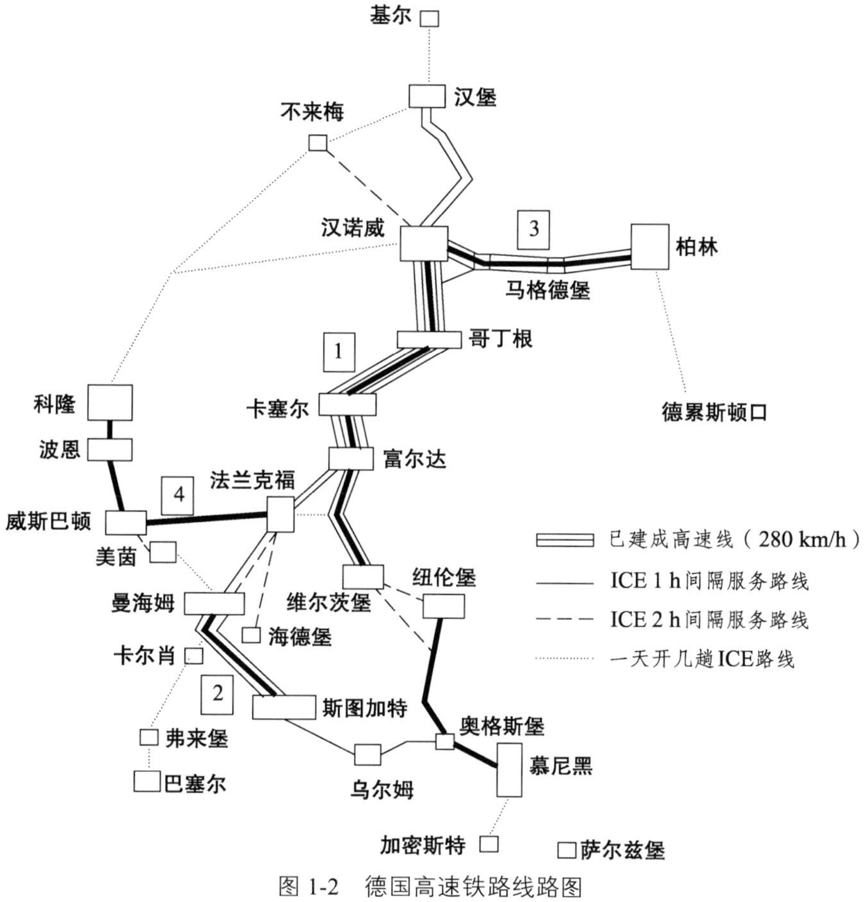

图 1-2　德国高速铁路线路图

（3）法国 TGV 动车组运用。

法国高速铁路在建设模式上采用部分修建新线、部分改造旧线的方式，以巴黎为中心向各个方向辐射，为客车专用铁路（见图 1-3）。每条高速线上只运行同一种类的高速列车，列车运行组织相对简单。列车运行线平行，列车只有停站地点和次数不同，整个列车运行图为平行运行图。为适应客流需要在高速线上运行的高速列车可以下到既有线上运行。

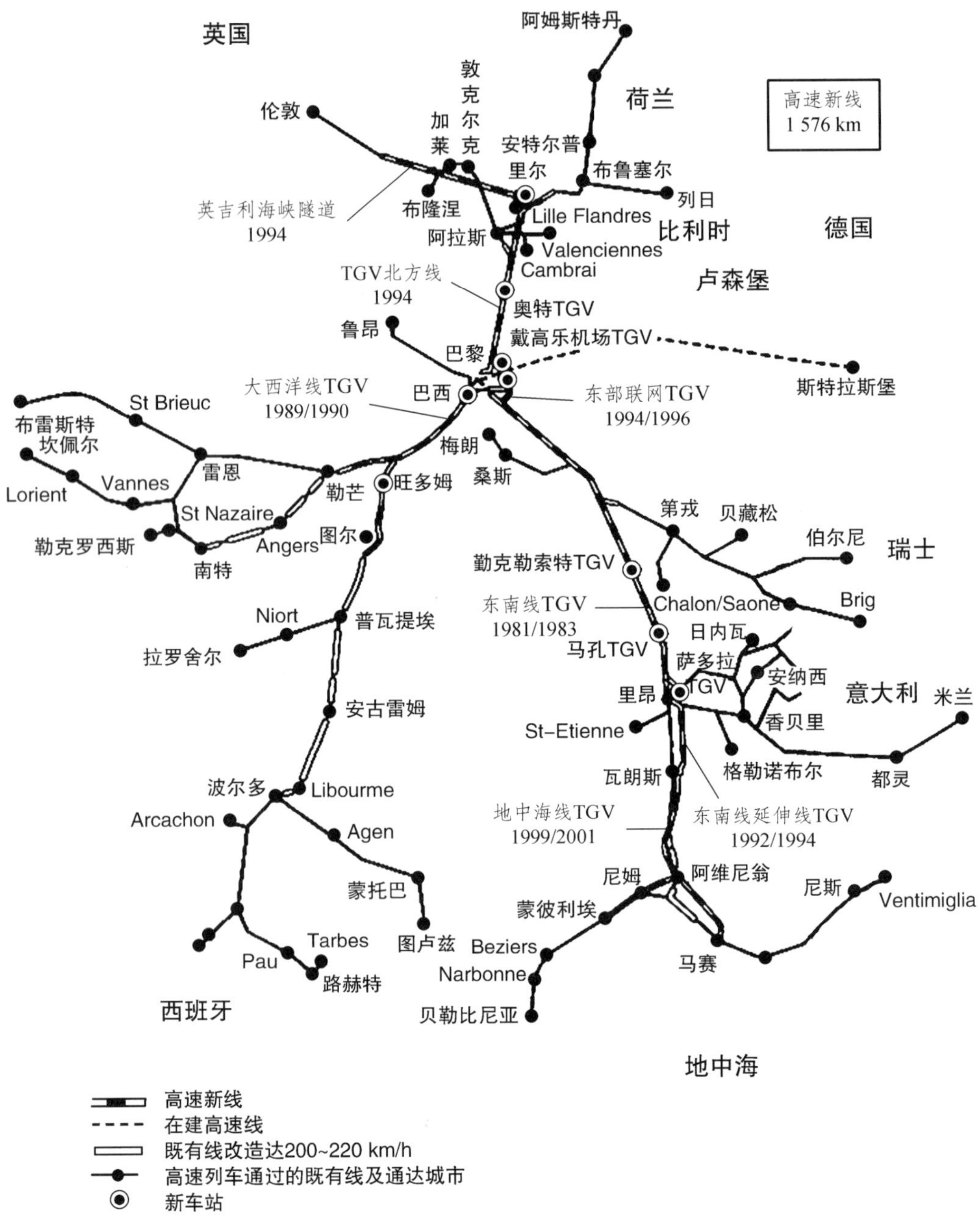

图 1-3　法国高速铁路线路图

2. 我国动车组运用基本情况及特点

1）我国高速铁路运行线路基本情况

自 2008 年 8 月 1 日中国第一条 350 km/h 的高速铁路——京津城际开通运营以来，我国高速铁路进入快速发展阶段。2009 年 12 月 26 日，世界上一次建成里程最长、工程类型最复杂的京港高铁武广段开通运营。截至 2020 年底，我国高速铁路及客运专线里程已经达到 3.9 万 km，占全球高铁里程的 70%以上。2020 年，已经提前完成了我国 2016 年 7 月 13 日发布的《中长期铁路网规划》（发改基础〔2016〕1536 号）文件中要求的“路网规模达到 15 万 km，其中高速铁路 3 万 km，覆盖 80%以上的大城市；到 2025 年，路网规模达到 17.5 万 km，其中高速铁路 3.8 万 km 左右”的目标。根据规划，2030 年基本实现内外互联互通、区际多路畅通、省会高铁连通、地市快速通达、县城基本覆盖。

（2）我国动车组运用基本特点。

到目前为止，我国已经建设完工多条客运专线，总计投入数百列动车组，组成了铁路运输中一道亮丽的风景线。我国动车组在运用中有着很多的特点：

① 运营速度高。我国高速铁路动车组在京沪线上试运行时跑出了世界高速铁路的最高运营时速 486.1 km，在武广高铁上的最高运营时速达到 394 km，而动车组在京津城际及京沪铁路上的持续运营速度也可达到 350 km/h 以上。

② 运量巨大。受到我国国情的影响，我国高速铁路动车组在现有的铁路条件下，尽可能地缩小列车的追踪间隔时间并最大限度地增加了列车载客量，实现了最短 3 min 的列车追踪间隔时间。

③ 运营可靠性高。我国 CRH 系列动车组的临界失稳时速超过 550 km，具有优异的动力学性能和出色的稳定性。此外，CRH 系列动车组还装备了新型的运行监控装置，可以实现自身参数和性能变化的实时检测、控制。而且动车组还具有故障导向安全这一功能，列车运行安全拥有可靠的保障。

④ 智能化控制。我国高速铁路动车组通过完备的网络连接成一个系统，高度智能化的计算机控制技术实现对运行系统和辅助系统的实时控制，使地面监控系统能够收集到各方面的信息从而判断车辆运行情况和状态。

⑤ 全天候运行不间断。我国高速铁路在风速 8 级以下时能够按照既定 350 km/h 的速度不间断运行，同样适用于各类风沙、雨雪等恶劣天气，达到真正意义上的全天候运行。

二、动车组运用管理工作的基本任务

动车组是完成旅客运输生产任务的重要设备，动车组运用工作是铁路运输的重要组成部分，动车组运用管理采用现代化管理手段，建立健全准确无误、反应迅速的通信网络、信息采集、数据处理系统，实行网络管理，实现有序可控。因此中国国家铁路集团有限公司编制了《铁路动车组运用维修规则》（简称《运规》，是动车组运用管理的基本大法）对动车组运用管理提出了总体要求，要求各级动车组运用人员应具备高度的责任心和求实精神，热爱本职工作；对工作做到高标准、严要求，对技术做到精益求精；顾全大局，联劳协作，服从命令听指挥；深入实际，调查研究，扎扎实实地做好各项工作。

动车组运用管理工作的基本要求是：管好用好动车组，优质高效地全面完成运输生产任务；加强安全管理，确保行车和人身安全；加强职工队伍建设，不断提高职工的政治素质、技术素质和文化知识水平；坚持改革开放，推广先进经验，遵循经济规律，促进资产回报，不断提高动车组运用效率。坚持质量第一和为运输服务的原则，贯彻修、养并重，预防为主的方针，不断加强基础工作，完善运用维修管理制度，提供质量良好的动车组，是动车组运用维修工作的基本任务。

【任务检测】

1. 概述动车组运用的特点。
2. 根据国外动车组运用管理情况，分析比较日本、德国及法国的动车运行管理模式。
3. 动车组运用管理工作的基本任务是什么？

任务二　动车组运用管理组织及内容

【任务描述】

（1）熟悉动车组运用组织机构及管理内容。
（2）认知动车组的配属使用及管理分类。

一、动车组运用管理部门的体制及职责

我国铁路运用管理工作：① 贯彻“统一指挥，分级管理”的原则，以利于充分发挥各级运用管理组织的职能作用；② 实行安全生产责任制。贯彻“党政同责、一岗双责、齐抓共管、失职追责”和“领导负责、专业负责、分工负责、岗位负责”的要求。运用管理组织机构如图1-4所示。

动车组实行总公司、铁路局、动车（客车）段三级专业管理。

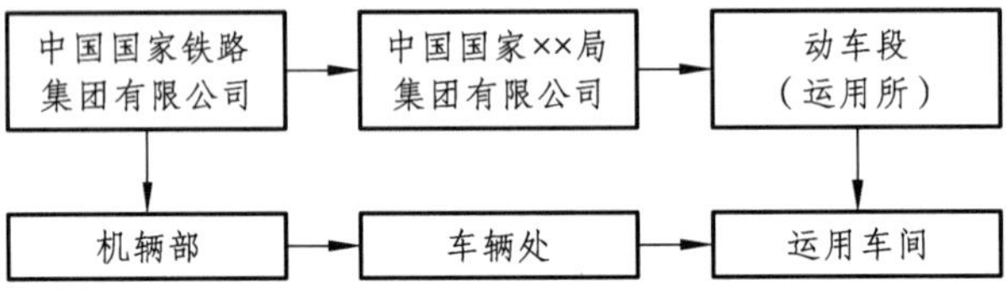

图1-4　运用管理组织机构

1. 中国国家铁路集团有限公司

中国国家铁路集团有限公司（简称“国铁集团”）负责明晰动车组相关专业管理界面；根据运输需要，规划全路动车组运用维修能力布局，统筹运力资源配置；制定动车组运用维修顶层管理规定并监督实施， 指导总公司所属运输企业开展运用维修工作。

2. 中国铁路××局集团有限公司

局集团有限公司是动车组专业管理的责任主体，负责制定动车组专业管理办法，明确运输相关专业部门的管理职能，承担所属动车组运用维修的安全、质量责任。依据总公司运用维修规则等相关管理规定及动车组技术手册等，制定相关管理办法及技术标准并组织实施。

3. 动车段

动车（客车）段（本书中以下对管理有动车组的客车车辆段及动车段全部简称为动车段，不再进行区分）是动车组车辆运用维修工作的责任主体，贯彻执行上级相关规章制度、管理办法及技术标准。规范段内各部门的人员配备及管理，优化生产组织和流程，协调联劳单位共同做好动车组运用维修工作。

二、动车组的管理

1. 动车组技术管理

采用总公司、铁路局、动车段三级动车组运用维修技术管理体系和组织机构，明确职责分工。总公司负责组织制定动车组运用维修规则等相关管理规定；铁路局负责组织制定动车组运用维修作业办法，明确检修项目、检修周期、检修内容、技术要求及检修工艺等；动车段负责组织编制动车组运用维修作业指导书，明确作业内容、作业步骤、作业标准、工装设备、安全事项等。

铁路局要根据动车组运用维修工作实际，配齐、配强专业技术管理人员。车辆处须设置动车组分管处长和运用、检修、安全、规章、设备、培训等专职管理人员；动车（客车）段实行总工程师技术负责制，配备动车组运用、检修、机械、轮轴、电气、网络、牵引、制动、空调、安全、规章、设备、培训、信息化等专（兼）职管理人员。各级管理人员要努力提高技术素养，遵守技术纪律。

动车组运用维修技术规章实行分级管理。总公司负责组织制定动车组运用检修标准，在动车组管理信息系统中发布；铁路局负责组织制定动车组运用检修作业办法，以局文形式发布；动车（客车）段负责组织编制动车组运用检修作业指导书，以段文形式发布。

运用检修作业办法须结合实际优化检修项目、内容和周期，项目、内容删减、及周期延长时，按规定报批。

作业指导书应明确作业内容、作业步骤、作业标准、工装设备、检测器具、安全事项等内容，要求文字简练、可操作性强，并根据实际及时修、建、补、废，定期发布。检修部件、设备设施发生变化时，动车（客车）段应组织对作业指导书进行验证。

铁路局要规范委外检修管理，制定运用维修委外检修管理办法，明确办理流程、资质审核、质量卡控等要求。

2. 动车组修程修制

动车组实行以走行公里周期为主（走行公里以动车组管理信息系统为准）、时间周期为辅的计划性预防修的检修体制。分为五级修程。一、二级检修为运用检修，在动车所内进行；三、四、五级检修为高级检修，在具备相应车型检修资质的检修单位进行。

3. 动车组配属管理

动车组由国铁集团统一管理，统一调配，实行配属制度。所谓配属制度，就是中国铁路总公司根据运输任务的需要和运输设备条件等因素将动车组配属给各铁路局、动车段使用和保管的制度，以完成运输生产任务。

4. 路用动车组

路用动车组包括检测、维修、试验、公务等特定用途的动车组，由总公司负责配属。

配属给非铁路局单位使用的路用动车组，须委托铁路局代管，并签订代管协议。

路用动车组车辆及电务车载设备的维修由配属（代管）铁路局负责，检测、维修、试验等专业设备设施的维修由产权单位负责。

路用动车组执行路网性检测、维修、试验任务前，使用单位须与配属（代管）铁路局沟通，制定一级、二级检修计划，保证检修不超期。其一级检修及整备作业，由检测计划指定的铁路局负责；二级检修由配属（代管）铁路局负责。

公务动车组由总公司专运处负责运用维护和保养。运营动车组改为路用动车组时，须报总公司批准。

5. 动车组报废

动车组经鉴定具备下列条件之一时，可以办理整列或部分车辆报废手续：

（1）动车组整列运用超过设计寿命，且经技术鉴定无法继续使用的。（见表 1-1）。

表 1-1　动车组设计寿命一览表

序号	车型	设计寿命（年)
1	CRH1A/1B/1E	25
2	CRH1A-A CRH1E （1229~1233)	20
3	CRH2A/2B/2E/2G/2C	20
4	CRH3C	20
5	CRH5A	30
6	CRH5G	20
7	CRH380A (L)	20
8	CRH380B(L)	20
9	CRH380CL	20
10	CRH380D	20
11	CRH6A/F	20
12	CRH3A	20
13	CR400AF/BF	30

(2)动车组整列或部分车辆发生事故或遭遇意外灾害，修理费用超过其重置价70%的；或车体结构变形、破损严重无法修复的。

报废程序：

① 动车组的报废鉴定由配属局组织。在事故发生地报废的，可由配属局委托所在地铁路局，在造修企业的由配属局委托造修企业组织鉴定，配属局应派人员参加。

② 经鉴定委员会鉴定符合报废条件的，产权单位应按规定程序办理，并报总公司批准。

③ 经总公司批准报废的动车组不允许整列或部分车辆出租、销售、转让。

三、动车组检修

1. 动车组检修计划

动车组运用检修计划按月、周、日编制，高级检修计划按年、月编制。高级检修动车组送修前应填写《动车组扣修单》。动车组二级检修月计划由动车段负责编制，报铁路局备案；二级检修周计划、运用检修日计划由动车所编制并组织实施。动车组在检查库内一级检修时间不得少于 4 h。动车（客车）段应加强动车组运用检修计划管理，努力提高动车组检修计划兑现率。对未按计划兑现的组项，应及时调整，不得超期失修。

2. 动车组一级检修

一级检修是对运用动车组的车顶、车下、车体两侧、车内和司机室等部位实施快速例行检查、试验和故障处理的检修作业，须在动车所库内检查实施。动车（客车）段（所）应结合动车组密集入（出）所、每班工作量等，合理确定作业小组数量。停留超过 48 h 的动车组上线运营前须进行一级检修。动车组一级检修原则上应在本所进行，下列情况除外：

（1）动车组图定入外所检修。配属段须与承修段签订委托检修协议，明确质量、安全责任、检修费用等相关内容。

（2）遇恶劣天气等特殊情况可能造成动车组一级检修过期，需入外局动车所检修。担当局应及时向所在地铁路局提出检修申请，所在地铁路局须积极组织安排，担当局做好配合。

动车组入外所检修时，配属段须与承修段签订委托检修协议，明确质量、安全责任、检修费用等相关内容。一级检修修竣后须填写《动车组一级检修竣工单》。

3. 动车组二级检修

二级检修是对动车组各系统、零部件实施的周期性维护保养、检测、试验，不得漏项、超期。扣车集中检修时须填写《动车组扣修单》，修竣后须填写《动车组扣修竣工单》。动车（客车）段应对“周期相同、部位接近、性质类似”的检修项目合理组合，均衡安排检修计划，优化生产组织。二级检修可采用扣车检修或结合一级检修的方式进行。

4. 动车组临修作业

动车组发生故障需扣车临修时，须填写《动车组扣修单》，修竣后须填写《动车组扣修竣工单》。

5. 动车组加装改造

动车组结构改变、参数调整、软件升级等加装改造须按有关规定审批，加装改造可在动车组造修企业或具备改造条件的动车（客车）段、动车所内进行。

6. 动车组信息化管理

动车组管理信息系统（以下简称信息系统）应与动车（客车）段、动车所同步设计、同步建设、同步使用，形成全面覆盖、高度集成的信息化平台，实现管理现代化、决策科学化。

信息系统应遵循国家和铁路信息安全相关规定。信息系统应满足总公司、铁路局、动车（客车）段（造修企业）、动车所四级管理和生产需求。动车（客车）段、动车所自动化设备及其他相关系统应与信息系统实现信息交互。铁路局应制定信息系统使用维护管理办法，积极推进信息系统的建设、使用、维护相关工作；依托信息系统，通过运用、检修数据的积累和分析，不断规范业务流程，改进检修工艺，优化修程修制。

7. 动车组技术变更

动车组结构改变、性能参数调整、软件优化升级等技术变更须按有关规定审批。技术变更可在动车组造修企业或具备实施条件的动车段、动车所内进行。

四、动车组运用

1. 动车组运行图

动车组列车运行图是动车组运用工作的主要依据。为确保运行图正常实施，编图时须充分考虑动车组的车型、数量、主要技术参数、检修作业标准，以及动车所的检修、存放、整备能力等因素。热备动车组数量及热备地点应相对固定，具体由铁路局确定。铁路局车辆部门应积极参与动车组列车开行方案论证、车底交路勾画；严格落实动车组技术作业标准，确保安全；优化动车组运用，提高效率。动车（客车）段应依据动车组运行图，动车所检修、存放、整备能力，检修标准等，科学编制动车组运用计划，提高上线率，合理使用动车组，最大限度地疏解高级检修密集到期；科学编排动车组随车机械师乘务计划，合理安排值乘交路，严禁超劳。各铁路局应根据实际情况铺画动车组试运行交路，根据试验项目在条件允许时可利用综合检测、周末、高峰等运行线进行试运行。

2. 动车组编组

单列动车组为固定编组，运用状态不得解编。两列同型短编（8 辆编组）动车组可重联编组。重联、解编作业执行《动车组重联及解编作业办法》。动车组禁止加挂各型机车车辆（无动力调车时的调车机或公铁两用车、救援或无动力回送时的机车及回送过渡车除外）。动车组禁止编入其他列车。

3. 动车组摘挂

采用机车调车作业时，随车机械师或动车（客车）段（所）胜任人员负责过渡车钩、专用风管和电气连接线的连接和分解并打开车门，调车人员负责车钩连结与摘解、软管摘结。

4. 动车组运行

严禁检修过期动车组上线运营。

动车组在始发、终到、通过站不安排客列检进行技术作业。铁路局应积极推广使用动车组运行故障动态图像检测系统，有效提高动车组运用安全防范能力。

红外线轴温探测系统必须对运行动车组轴温进行探测。探测动车组热轴报警时，红外线值班员按规定程序向列调报警，但不进行列车拦停。列调须立即通知动车组司机，动车组司机立即通知动车组随车机械师，由动车组随车机械师根据车载轴温检测系统探测情况，确定动车组是否继续安全运行，由动车组司机将处理情况反馈列调，列调反馈红外线值班员。

动车组列车运行中出现故障时，动车组司机应按车载信息监控装置的提示，按规定及时处理；需要由动车组随车机械师处理时，应通知动车组随车机械师。经处置确认无法正常运行时，动车组司机应按车载信息监控装置的提示和动车组随车机械师的要求，选择维持运行或停车等方式，并报告列车调度员。

动车组随车机械师发现或接到车辆设备故障通知后，应及时判明故障，按《动车组应急故障处理手册》正确处置，并按规定报告故障信息。担当所须在故障发生后 1 h 内将故障信息录入动车组管理信息系统。

动车组随车机械师下车检查、处理故障前需按照相关规定申请邻线限速。

救援动车组可采用动车组、机车两种救援方式，优先采用动车组救援。具体按《动车组相互救援办法》执行。

CRH2C 型和 CRH380A 型动车组不允许超员，其余动车组超员率不得超过 15%。运行中人员过于集中时应进行疏散。

5. 动车组调车

动车组调车原则上采用有动力方式。机务部门须在动车（客车）段、动车所内设动车组地勤司机，负责调车作业。

采用机车调车作业时，动车组随车机械师或动车段（所）胜任人员负责过渡车钩、专用风管和电气连接线的连接和分解并打开车门，调车人员负责车钩连结与摘解、软管摘结。

动车组通过检修、检测设备的限速按具体设备技术条件执行，主要设备限速规定如下：

踏面诊断设备：通过限速 30 km/h；检测限速 8 ~ 12 km/h。

不落轮车床、转向架更换及落轮设备：通过限速 5 km/h。

洗车机：自走行时限速 3 ~ 5 km/h；牵车机牵引时限速 1.5 ~ 3 km/h。

轨道桥：限速 10 km/h。

6. 动车组的回送

动车组因新配属、调拨、出租、检修等需要时要进行回送。动车组的回送一般采用专列方式进行。按动车组动力可使用状态划分，可分为有动力回送和无动力回送两种，亦称为有火回送和无火回送。动车组的回送规范和既有线机车、车辆的回送有着较大的区别，详见项目三相关内容。

动车组回送按旅客列车办理，原则上采用 ATP 控车的有动力回送。高铁线路与既有线并行时，尽可能安排高铁线路回送。两列同型短编（8 辆编组）动车组，可重联回送。无动力回送时，最高限速 120 km/h。回送途中，应尽可能避免实施紧急制动；发生紧急制动后，动车组司机须通知动车组随车机械师下车确认过渡车钩状态良好后，方可开车。需加挂回送过渡车时，过渡车由使用单位与主机企业协商确定，要求派员押送，确保回送安全。

7. 动车组交接

动车组新造出厂、高级检修、转属、租用时，须办理技术状态、随车工具备品、技术履历、技术资料（仅限新造出厂）、检修记录（最近一次二级检修记录）等交接。动车组的接、送车工作由车辆部门牵头组织。新造出厂、局间转属和租用时，接入局应成立机务、电务、车辆专业组成的接车组；高级检修时，配属局应成立机务、电务、车辆专业组成的接（送）车组。

8. 动车组试运行

遇下述情况时，须安排动车组试运行：

模拟、专项试运行由总公司组织安排。新造、高级检修、临修试运行由铁路局组织。由动车（客车）段请令，调度所负责安排。涉及跨局试运行时，由铁路局调度所根据车辆部门的申请向总公司调度请令。试运行前，动车（客车）段应组织相关部门进行动车组检修整备作业，确保其技术状态良好。遇下述情况时，须安排动车组试运行：

（1）模拟试运行（新型动车组正式上线运行前或新线开通时）。

（2）动车组新造出厂、高级检修修竣后。

（3）临修更换转向架、轮对、万向轴、主变压器、牵引电机后。

（4）专项试运行。

【任务检测】

1. 简述动车组运用管理部门的体制及职责。
2. 动车组的配属原则是什么？
3. 动车组管理的分类有哪些？

项目二　动车组运行组织管理

【思政课程】走自主创新之路，中国高铁走向世界

20 世纪 90 年代初，就已经提出高速铁路兴建计划。但是，在修建方法上却引发了长达十多年的争议和论证。“磁浮派”和“轮轨派”之争是中国高铁技术理论奠基史上的显著标志，当时磁悬浮派认为磁悬浮列车代表着未来高铁技术发展趋势，而轮轨派认为无论从技术上还是从工程造价上来看，修建轮轨高铁才是当务之急。这场历时 18 年的争论堪称一场关于高速铁路的思想启蒙。期间对为如何建设高铁、以什么样的标准建设高铁等问题的反复研讨与摸索，这恰恰奠定了扎实的技术理论基础。最终，考虑到与我国现有的轮轨技术兼容问题和造价问题，选择了轮轨技术。

2004 年初，中国准备全国普及高铁，但是自己无法设计和制造。于是中国铁道部门举行了一次国际竞标。很多国际竞标者比如日本川崎、德国西门子、加拿大庞巴迪和法国阿尔斯通都参加了。中国铁路部门并没有选择某个竞标者，而是要求每个企业设计和生产各自类型的高铁列车，条件是必须接受中国的信号标准。就这样，中国高铁网络运行着不同国家品牌企业的各种列车。在这一阶段，中国通过引进消化吸收，基本掌握了时速 200 ~ 250 km 的高速列车制造技术。

接下来，中国对列车提出了新要求，那就是时速达 380 km。为了克服技术障碍，自 2008 年底开始，中国建立了一个特殊团队，这个团队的作用是解决关键技术问题。这个团队由青岛四方、中国中车、中车唐山公司以及中国的 25 所大学，56 个关键实验室和 500 家原始设备制造商组成。其中包括了约 500 多名研究员和约 10 000 名工程师。在所有人的努力下，2010 年，中国成功设计了自己的车辆，集成空气动力学、拓扑学、承重体系、动态传输、刹车系统、列车控制操作系统、牵引动力供应以及关键材料部件等等，提首个自主设计的中国高铁列车 CRH380A 正式推出。

截至目前，中国已经掌握了设计、制造适应各种运行需求的不同速度等级的高速动车组列车成套技术，具备极强的系统集成、适应修改、综合解决并完成本土化的自主创新能力，最终形成自主技术标准与设计，完成从“中国制造”向“中国创造”的转身。

目前，中国高铁技术已经处于世界先进前列，并开始角逐全球高铁市场承建了世界高铁网络中的 60%，主要涉及如下几个国家：印度尼西亚、巴基斯坦、老挝、泰国、俄罗斯、埃塞俄比亚等。中国高铁正在大步走向世界。

我国动车组的发展之路就是自主创新之路，也只有自主创新才能够走在世界高速铁路前列。

【项目描述】

通过本项目学习，使学生了解动车组各专业主要岗位职责，熟悉动车组专业接口管理规定；熟悉动车组安全管理规定以及发生火灾爆炸事故应急处置预案；掌握动车组行车组织规则，熟悉动车组接发及运行方面的要求，熟知各种应急预案的规定；了解动车组停放防冻管理办法。

任务一　动车组专业管理规定

【任务描述】

（1）了解动车组各专业主要岗位职责。
（2）熟悉动车组专业接口管理规定。

一、动车组各专业人员配备与隶属

（1）动车组本务司机、地勤司机隶属机务段管理。
（2）随车机械师、存放点车辆调度人员、地勤机械师隶属动车段管理。
（3）客运乘务人员（列车长、列车员）隶属客运段管理。
（4）动车组人员配备与隶属关系见图 2-1 所示。

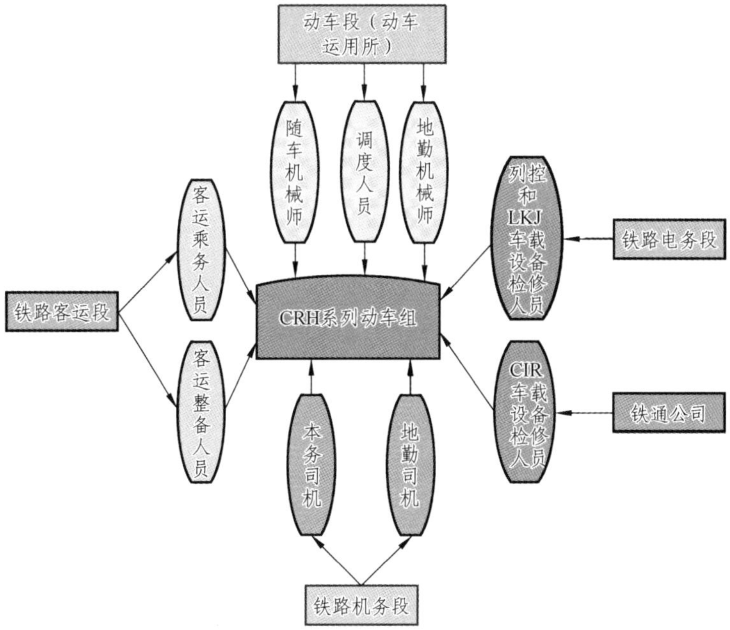

图 2-1　动车组人员配备与隶属关系

二、主要岗位职责

1. 本务司机

（1）认真执行规章制度，服从命令听从指挥，切实履行规定职责。

（2）动车组在区间被迫停车时，负责指挥随车机械师、客运乘务组处理有关事故救援等事宜。

（3）出所后，负责动车组的车门集控开关。在车站，负责将列车停稳在规定位置，开启车门；开车前，根据客运乘务组通知，关闭车门。

（4）动车组运行中出现故障时，按车载信息监控装置的提示，按步骤及时处理；需要由随车机械师配合处理时，通知随车机械师。

（5）负责在运用所内（或存放点）在动车组操纵端司机室与地勤司机办理动车组驾驶、列控车载设备、LKJ、CIR 设备及制动系统技术状态、主控钥匙、司机室门钥匙及列控车载设备柜钥匙交接。

2. 地勤司机

（1）认真执行规章制度，服从命令听从指挥，切实履行规定职责。

（2）动车组出入运用所（存放点）时，负责与本务司机办理动车组驾驶、列控车载设备、LKJ、CIR 设备及制动系统技术状态、主控钥匙、司机室门钥匙及列控车载设备柜钥匙交接。

（3）动车组出所时，负责确认行车安全设备技术状态，与相关行车安全设备检修单位办理行车安全设备合格证交接；负责与动车所质检员办理驾驶设备技术状态交接。

（4）负责动车组调车作业。

（5）负责检修库以外停放的动车组防溜设置及撤除。

3. 随车机械师

（1）认真执行规章制度，服从命令听从指挥，切实履行规定职责。

（2）负责在运行途中监控动车组的技术状态，发现故障及时将有关信息通知司机，并采取措施，妥善处理。

（3）动车组出入所时，负责与运用所（质检员）办理技术交接；与调度员或地勤机械师办理车门集控开关钥匙交接。

（4）在司机指挥下，处理有关事故救援等事宜。

（5）发生危及行车安全故障或其他紧急情况时，使用紧急制动阀停车或通知司机采取停车措施。

4. 客运乘务员

（1）认真执行规章制度，服从命令听从指挥，切实履行规定职责。

（2）发生危及行车和旅客生命安全的紧急情况时，使用紧急制动阀停车或通知司机采取措施；需要组织旅客撤离列车时，通知司机，由司机向列车调度员报告或通知就近车站值班员；在司机指挥下，处理有关事故救援等事宜。

5. 动车组存放点车辆调度人员

（1）负责按照作业计划组织、协调各专业作业，传达命令和作业前后的登记。

（2）负责随车机械师出退乘报到及动车组主控钥匙、司机室门钥匙、车门集控开关钥匙及列控车载设备柜钥匙等管理。

（3）负责组织协调处理动车组相关事宜并及时报告。

6. 动车组存放点地勤机械师

（1）负责动车组设备使用及管理。

（2）负责配合存放点的调车、客运整备、保洁、吸污作业，检查吸污作业质量。

（3）负责动车组防冻。

（4）负责与存放点的动车组随车机械师办理交接。

三、动车组专业接口管理

（1）动车组运用管理。

车辆（动车）段运用所按规定的修程、修制，完成动车组的运用检修，确保动车组出所时技术状态达到标准要求。机务段在动车运用所设派班室和待乘室，安排本务司机按计划出乘。

（2）动车组车载设备管理。

电务段负责列控车载设备和 LKJ 设备，铁通公司负责 CIR 设备，车辆段负责车载广播设备的检修。在运用所内设上述设备的检修点，负责相关出入所检测、检查及维护工作。

（3）车内设备使用和管理。

动车组配电盘、车内空调、照明及旅客信息系统设备由随车机械师操作。自动广播装置的广播内容由客运段负责按规定要求录制，车辆段负责输入自动广播装置。客运乘务员发现设备故障时，通知随车机械师及时处理。运行中发生设备损坏时，随车机械师与列车长共同确认，并填写上部设施破损记录，双方签字。

（4）动车组的整备和保洁管理。

动车组的客运整备和车内保洁由客运部门负责，动车组外皮清洗和吸污作业由车辆部门负责。

（5）动车组看管，由铁路局指定部门负责。

（6）动车组作业管理。

车载行车安全设备（列控车载设备设备、CIR 设备、LKJ 设备）的检修、客运整备及保洁作业，须统一纳入动车组运用检修计划，由运用所统一管理。作业前，地勤司机、地勤机械师、客运整备人员、吸污作业人员、看管人员等有关作业人员，应向运用所调度人员报到，接受命令；各专业作业结束后，应到调度人员处进行登记，填写检修竣工单。

（7）动车组调车管理。

动车组出入所（存放点）的操纵由各铁路局根据具体情况自定；动车组转线及所内（或存放点）调车等作业，根据动车所的安排，地勤司机负责操纵。各铁路局根据具体情况制订详细的调车作业办法。

（8）动车组存放点管理。

① 铁路局设置的动车组存放点须具备动车组存放条件，并报部核准。

各局在动车组存放点应设调度人员、地勤机械师及地勤司机，并建立作业登记制度、钥匙交接管理制度、出退乘签到制度。根据原铁道部《关于铁路第六次大面积提速调图有关动车组劳动组织职工培训和工资分配问题的意见》铁劳卫[2007]67 号文件，动车组存放点所需调度人员、地勤机械师由铁路局内部调整解决。

② 存放点的作业管理。

对不进行检修作业的外属停放动车组，由停放地铁路局指定有关单位负责动车组的吸污、防冻、客运整备、保洁等作业及看管，安排乘务人员待乘休息及接送条件；对不进行检修作业的本属动车组管理比照外属动车组执行。

（9）动车组的交接管理。

① 动车组入运用所或存放点，本务司机与地勤司机办理驾驶设备和行车安全设备的状态交接及主控钥匙、司机室门钥匙及列控车载设备柜钥匙交接，并提交动车组运行状态交接单。

地勤司机与调度人员办理主控钥匙、司机室门钥匙及列控车载设备柜钥匙交接，并与行车安全设备检修单位人员办理列控车载设备及 LKJ、CIR 运行技术状态交接。动车组入动车所，随车机械师与调度人员办理动车组技术状态交接及车门集控开关钥匙交接，填写交接记录。动车组入存放点，随车机械师与地勤机械师办理动车组技术状态交接及车门集控开关钥匙交接，填写交接记录；随车机械师持交接记录到调度人员处签到；地勤机械师与调度人员办理车门集控开关钥匙交接。

② 动车组出运用所前，由动车所质检员组织地勤司机、客运人员、随车机械师及列控车载设备、LKJ、CIR 检修单位进行出库联检，填写出库联检记录单。

客运人员负责车厢内服务设施完好状况的检查确认，与质检员办理交接；随车机械师负责动车组技术状态的检查确认，与质检员办理交接；行车安全设备检修单位负责对列控车载设备、LKJ、CIR 设备进行出库检查确认后，填写行车安全设备合格证，地勤司机确认行车安全设备技术状态，与检修单位办理合格证交接；本务司机与地勤司机办理行车安全设备合格证和驾驶设备技术状态的交接。

③ 动车组出存放点前，地勤机械师、随车机械师、地勤司机到调度人员处签到。

地勤司机向调度人员领取主控钥匙、司机室门钥匙及列控车载设备柜钥匙，负责确认行车安全设备技术状态；地勤司机撤除防溜，本务司机签认防溜撤除记录；双方在操纵端驾驶室办理主控钥匙、司机室门钥匙及列控车载设备柜钥匙交接，本务司机负责驾驶设备技术状态的确认，填写交接记录。地勤机械师向调度人员领取车门集控开关钥匙，与随车机械师办理动车组技术状态及钥匙交接，填写交接记录。地勤司机、地勤机械师将交接记录交调度人员。

④ 动车组继乘，由本务司机、随车机械师按规定交接。

⑤ 列控车载设备柜钥匙交接管理。列控车载设备及 LKJ 出入所检测时，由设备检测单位与运用所办理钥匙交接。

（10）动车组本务司机要认真填写《动车组运行技术状态交接单》。

根据动车组专业管理规定，动车组的安全运行需要铁路系统各个部门之间协同作业，所设计的各部门之间的接口管理关系可总结为图 2-2 所示。

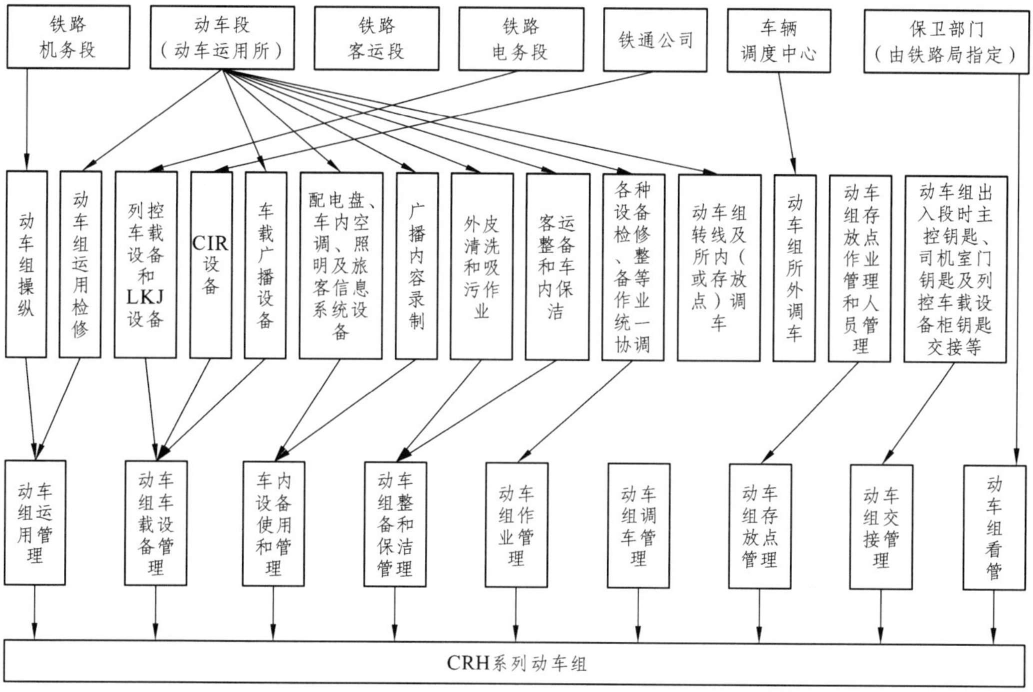

图 2-2　动车组运用维修各部门接口管理关系图

【任务检测】

1. 举例说明动车组编号规则。
2. 动车组本务司机岗位职责是什么？
3. 动车组地勤司机岗位职责是什么？
4. 动车组的交接管理有哪些规定？

任务二　动车组运行安全管理规定

【任务描述】

（1）熟悉动车组安全管理办法。

（2）认知动车组的配属使用及管理分类。

一、安全规则

（1）列车乘务组人员（列车员、保洁员、配餐师、服务员、车辆机械师、乘警）应当接受列车长统一领导，各负其责、各司其职，在确保旅客安全的情况下，质量良好地完成本岗位工作。特殊情况下，按规定也要服从司机统一指挥。

（2）客运乘务组人员上岗前必须通过路局培训，段劳动安全考试合格后，由路局统一颁发上岗证后，方能上岗。

（3）列车长、列车员主要承担服务旅客、查验车票、处理票务、危险品卡控、突发事件应急处理等工作。发生影响旅客安全问题时，客运乘务组应当立即采取有效措施，保护旅客生命和财产安全。

（4）旅客乘降按照“前门下，后门上”分工，特殊情况可通报车站具体变更组织方案。

到达中间站前，列车通过列车广播组织旅客在各车厢运行方向前端车门等候下车。车站开车前提前 5 min 停止检票，始发站提前 20 min 检票放客，列车长提前 20 min（折返站 10 min）按规定通知司机、司机通知机械师开门。到站为低站台时，到站前由列车长组织提前打开车门翻板，并提示附近旅客安全注意事项，开车后及时放平、扣锁翻板；到站为高站台时，车门翻板免开。发车前，由列车长确认旅客乘降完毕后，通知司机关闭车门（始发站为开车前 2 min），用语为“动车××次司机，旅客乘降完毕，请关闭车门”，司机听到后回答“动车××次司机明白”。如自动开关门装置故障时，由司机通知随车机械师和列车长，列车长负责组织手动开关车门，随车机械师负责处理相关故障。动车组到站停稳后，司机负责开启车门。按钮不在司机操作台的，由司机通知机械师开关车门。动车组重联运行时，两列车长同时确认旅客乘降完毕，二组列车长和一组列车长呼应乘降完毕，用语为“××次后部旅客乘降完毕”，由运行前方列车长第一组的列车长负责确认旅客乘降情况并通知司机，呼叫用语同发车呼叫用语。

（5）列车乘务人员应当配备无线对讲机，及时通报各种信息，但不得用对讲机从事与工作无关事情。

动车组列车配备两支长度 1.5 m、杆把为绝缘材料的钩具，定位放置，及时协助旅客捡拾掉入站台下的行李物品。

（6）动车组列车乘务室只能用于放置班组资料和办公用品，不得储物或改作他用。

（7）全列车除指定车厢吸烟处外，其他车厢一律禁止吸烟。列车乘务员要加强宣传，对吸烟的旅客做好解释引导工作。

（8）列车销售的食品、饮品必须为全国名优产品，并实行统一采购、统一进价、统一销售价格，严把食品、饮品进货渠道，防止旅客食物中毒。

（9）列车乘务人员在列车运行中应当注意对列车安全设备的管理，制止旅客搬动、触碰安全设备等不安全行为。严禁任何人在列车运行中打开气密窗。除工作需要列车长或列车长指定的工作人员准许进入司机室外，其他人员一律不得进入司机室。

（10）电气化线路上，接触网的各导线相连部件，通常均带有高压电，禁止直接或间接（通过任何物件如：棒条、导线、水流）与上述设备接触。

为保证人身安全，除专业人员按规定作业外，任何人员所携带的物品（包括长杆、导线等）与接触网设备的带电部分必须保持两米以上距离。动车组需要外皮洗刷作业时，必须在接触网断电区域进行。严禁保洁人员用水冲洗车顶受电弓、高压电缆头连接器，上述部位的清洁应采用湿抹布擦抹方式。同时登高作业要采取安全防护措施。内部保洁严禁用水冲洗地板、墙板和车辆连接处。

（11）全列车门的开启和关闭由司机操控。

列车乘务人员在车门关闭后，不得随意开启车门；遇特殊情况必须开启车门时，须先由列车长确认列车未启动，得到司机同意后方可开启车门；再次关闭后，由列车长逐辆确认车门状态，通知司机已关闭车门，由司机确认车门状态后方可动车。列车运行中如车门发生故障，危及人身安全时，现场发现人员应立即采取临时安全防护措施，并通知机械师处理。列车停车时车门发生故障，列车乘务人员可采取手动开关车门。

（12）列车运行中发生影响列车正常运行时，列车长应向司机询问原因，并应按照晚点处置有关规定向旅客说明情况，做好安全宣传，稳定旅客情绪。防止旅客擅自开启车门。

（13）因接触网临时停电或列车故障造成列车途中停车或中断行车时，列车长应组织列车乘务人员启动动车组发生行车中断应急处置预案，各岗位乘务员要坚守工作岗位，加强车内巡视，照顾好重点旅客，并向旅客做好宣传解释，不得擅自开启车门，防止发生意外。

（14）列车运行中遇有旅客因伤、病必须临时停车抢救时，列车长应通过司机向所在局列车调度员报告情况请求临时停车。

列车长应组织列车乘务人员启动动车组旅客人身伤害或急病事件应急处置预案，及时编制客运记录并做好交接准备。列车长应及时将现场情况报告段调度室及所在车队负责人。列车乘务人员不得下车参与处理。

（15）列车运行中发生火灾爆炸时，列车长应组织列车乘务人员启动动车组发生火灾爆炸事故应急处置预案。列车乘务人员应当立即按动报警按钮和紧急停车按钮，将旅客疏散到安全车厢，有防火隔断门的，应当关闭防火隔断门，及时将情况通报司机及列车长，并及时将现场情况向段调度室报告。

（16）列车运行及途中作业安全：

① 客车运行中工作人员严禁向车下扔、扫垃圾；列车运行中严禁旅客向车下扔东西或杂物；餐车防护栏必须入槽加锁牢固；列车方向牌必须入槽加锁牢固；餐桌、茶桌、空酒水饮料瓶必须及时清理；果皮盘及其他垃圾必须及时清理。

② 运行在提速区段的列车方向牌必须具有锁闭装置，悬挂方向牌前要进行安全状态检查，锁闭装置失灵的严禁悬挂，挂牢方向牌后，必须确认处于锁闭状态。

③ 对列车垃圾处理的管理。客车运行中若工作人员往车下扔、扫垃圾（未造成严重后果的），责任人转岗培训 6 个月，直接责任班组长撤职并转岗培训 6 个月，领导责任班组长转岗培训 3 个月，直接责任干部记过，领导责任干部警告。

二、动车组应急处置及组织机构职责

1. 组织机构及职责

应急处置领导组工作职责是：

（1）根据铁路沿线线桥设备、地质地形、气象水文等条件，确定可能发生的灾害类型，加强危险源的监控，对可能引发事故的重要信息进行汇总并制定相应应急处置的方针、政策、制度、办法。

（2）加强与地方水利、气象、地震、国土资源等相关部门的联系，建立应急联络机制，做好防灾工作。

（3）指挥、指导、监督应急处置指挥组启动应急预案，全面掌握应急预案的实施。

（4）听取应急处置指挥组汇报，对应急处置指挥组的工作提出指导意见。

（5）需要应急处置领导组解决、协调的其他重大事宜。

应急处置指挥组工作职责是：

（1）旅客列车发生火灾、爆炸、灾害、事故危及旅客和职工生命财产安全时，组织启动实施旅客列车安全应急处置预案。

（2）负责制定旅客列车安全应急处置预案，并组织实施。

（3）指挥现场启动安全应急预案，对安全预案在执行中出现的问题，提出指导意见。

（4）需要安全突发事件应急处置指挥组解决、协调的其他问题。

乘务组织突发事件应急处置指挥组工作职责是：

（1）旅客列车发生食物中毒事件及旅客人身伤害或急病、死亡等突发事件时，组织启动旅客列车乘务组织应急处置预案。

（2）负责制定旅客列车乘务组织应急处置预案并组织实施。

（3）针对预案执行中出现的问题，提出指导性意见。

（4）需要乘务组织突发事件应急指挥组解决、协调的其他问题。

现场应急处置组工作职责是：

（1）现场应急处置组组长负责所有应急预案的启动、报告、组织、指挥、实施。

（2）各副组长在列车长的统一指挥下，按照应急处置预案中的职责分工，带领应急处置小组组织实施预案。

（3）应急处置组成员按照预案具体分组的职责，实施预案。

2. 应急处置原则

快速反应、正确处置；先行扑救、统一指挥；站车协同、以站保车；依靠科学、减少损失。

3. 应急处置要求

成立现场处置组；现场反应迅速、信息传递准确、善后处理妥当；分工明确、步调一致、统一指挥；强化培训，提高救治技能。

三、动车组应急处置预案

1. 动车组发生电器初始火灾的应急处置预案

（1）动车组发生电器设备冒烟起火时，最先发现、到达现场的乘务人员应立即关闭电源，使用灭火器灭火。同时应当立即按动报警按钮和紧急停车按钮，并立即使用无线对讲机通知列车长及全体乘务员。列车长应立即组织全体乘务人员参加扑救。

（2）接到通知后的全体乘务人员在列车长、乘警的统一指挥下，各负其责，各司其职，全力以赴进行扑救灭火，动车司机坚守岗位，协同处理。

（3）根据火情启动动车组发生火灾爆炸事故的应急处置预案。全体乘务员到达现场后，在列车长、乘警的统一指挥下集中列车所有的灭火器材，根据火灾现场实际情况，采取有效的灭火方案和扑救措施展开扑救，控制火势，扑灭火源。

（4）车辆机械师根据火情要求司机彻底关闭电源。动车司机应立即停止向车内通风。

2. 动车组发生火灾爆炸事故的应急处置预案

（1）运行途中的处置：

① 动车组发生火灾爆炸事故时，最先发现、到达现场的乘务人员应立即按动报警按钮和紧急停车按钮，并迅速将情况通报司机及列车长，同时使用灭火器灭火或可以灭火的物品迅速扑救。列车长接到通知后应立即使用无线对讲机通告全体乘务员参加扑救，动车司机坚守岗位，立即停止向车内通风，协同处理。

② 在列车长、乘警的统一指挥下，应本着先人员后财产的原则，有序组织人员、灭火器材和可以灭火的其他物品，按预案分工，根据火灾现场实际情况，采取有效的灭火方案和扑救措施迅速展开扑救，控制火势，扑灭火灾。

③ 如衣物、棉絮、地板上的杂物等发生燃烧时，应首先选择用水或就地取材的方式扑救，不得打开车窗通风，如需使用灭火器时应果断使用，以免延误扑救时机；如电源支线处冒烟时，首先将电源关闭或断开保险，使用灭火器向冒烟或烧坏处喷射。

④ 未关闭电源前组织扑救时，应事先确认燃烧物体与接触网带电设备的距离，车厢上部着火处距接触网不足 4 m 时，不得用水灭火，灭火人员所站位置要距离接触网 2 m 以外，用水和一般灭火器灭火必须断电。

⑤ 根据需要动车司机通知就近车站向电力调度员要求切断接触网电源。

⑥ 在扑救火灾的同时，乘务员应迅速有序指挥旅客向车下及相邻安全的车厢疏散，解救被围困的旅客。对已经疏散的旅客，严禁其返回事故车厢。

⑦ 根据旅客伤害程度及是否危及生命情况，有计划地实施抢救，对仍处在危险中的旅客要首先抢救使其脱离危险。组织动员旅客中有医护经验的人员参加抢救伤员。对伤员要根据具体情况采取止血、简易固定、包扎等初期现场救护措施，为医院救治创造条件。

⑧ 要加强宣传，维持好车内秩序，防止旅客跳车和混乱等意外情况发生。火灾处理完毕后，指派专人监护，防止复燃。

⑨ 列车长和机车司机要在最短时间内向事故发生地铁路局客运、行车调度员报告情

况，根据火势情况，提出请求车站、当地消防部门或当地政府、驻军救援的要求。报告内容要简明扼要，主要包括车次、时间、区间、事故概括，火势情况要报告清楚。

（2）停车后的处置：

① 列车停车后动车司机立即打开侧门或由机械师、乘务人员启动侧门紧急开门装置打开侧门，向地面安全地带疏散旅客。车内产生浓烟危及人员生命安全的情况下，应立即使用安全锤击碎侧窗玻璃，必要时可利用侧窗作为紧急出口，向地面疏散旅客。

② 列车在区间停车时，动车司机应立即使用列车无线调度电话通知两端站、追踪列车和列车调度员，并根据需要做好列车防护工作。在区间向地面疏散旅客时，动车司机还应通知过往列车。

③ 须分解列车时，司机、车辆机械师要密切配合，如使用重联车组时，与重联的动车司机、机械师及时沟通、密切配合，按照先摘后、后摘前的方法将着火车组分解分离，即：先将着火车辆与后部车列分离，并将着火车辆尽量转移到线路平坦处，再将前部车列与着火车辆分离，切断火源，防止火势蔓延。

④ 列车分解时，对尾部车厢腰门要加锁，防止意外情况发生。列车分离后，动车司机应迅速做好列车（包括列车分解后区间遗留的车辆）防护工作。

⑤ 乘警长要采取措施，维护现场秩序，防止发生混乱，视情况设置警戒区，禁止实施救援以外的人员进入现场，不得擅自移动现场任何物品，对事故现场痕迹、物证有关证据材料要采取有效措施妥善保护。列车乘务人员在扑救火灾的同时，要配合乘警工作，注意保护好火灾现场，采取多种形式做好宣传工作，稳定旅客情绪，共同维护秩序以免发生混乱。在有条件的情况下，应尽可能地对旅客车票及住址进行登记，以备查证。

⑥ 救援部门到达后，列车长要详细介绍火灾爆炸原因、火势、人员伤亡、疏散情况，协助救援部门灭火。

（3）善后处置：

① 列车长要认真了解伤员人数及伤害程度，登记旅客姓名、性别、年龄、单位、地址、车票、身份证号码、其他证件及随身携带物品，并作详细记录，为车站处置善后事宜提供依据、做好准备。

② 乘警要及时进行调查取证，证据材料要客观、翔实，为现场勘察、认定火灾原因创造有利条件。列车乘务人员要积极帮助公安人员了解情况，提供线索。同时，要积极协助公安机关调查事故情况。

③ 列车长要将掌握的伤亡人员情况和旅客财产损失情况及相关记录，及时移交车站，以便车站尽快处理善后事宜。

3. 动车组发生食物中毒事件应急处置预案

（1）动车组发生疑似旅客食物中毒时，列车长、乘警应立即赶赴现场，及时了解中毒旅客主要症状，掌握中毒旅客人数、发病时间等情况，准确判断毒物根源或确定怀疑导致食物中毒的食物，判明病人基本情况。

（2）列车长要向前方停车站、前方卫生防疫部门、段生产调度室报告。段生产调度室应立即上报铁路局卫生、客运主管部门和列车所在地及本地区铁路疾病防控中心。怀疑投毒导致食物中毒时，还应同时向所在地铁路公安机关报告。报告的内容包括：日期、车次、运行区段、发病时间、地点、病人主要症状、发病人数（包括危重人数及死亡人数）、可能引起中毒的食物等，要求车站组织采取的措施。

（3）由列车救护员利用列车配备的医疗救护药箱，采取应急救治措施，采取催吐导泄等方法和应急救治措施，进行初步救治，积极组织抢救中毒旅客，同时通过广播寻找医生帮助抢救治疗，控制病情进一步发展。按照上级的指示，与有关车站办理交接，对中毒较严重危及生命需立即停车急救的，由列车长立即向所在地路局客调汇报或立即用运转车长电台与调度取得联系，在就近具有抢救条件的停车站临时停车，同时组织急救人员做好与中途车站交接的准备工作，协助车站将病人尽快送往就近医院。

（4）发生 3 人以上具有疑似旅客食物中毒症状时，除按上述要求救治外，列车长立即向前方停车站通报，并汇报所属单位，怀疑投毒导致食物中毒时，还应同时向铁路公安机关报告。并做好相关记载，依据《铁路旅客人身伤害及自带行李损失事故处理办法》（中华人民共和国铁道部令第 12 号）的相关规定处理，需要时编写客运记录交前方停车站处理。作好车站移交的准备工作。必要时列车长与行车调度联系，在前方经过的大站停车抢救。

（5）列车长、乘警长应及时调查发病的原因，搜集证据材料，了解旅客发病症状、进食史并做成记录，形成第一手资料。对中毒病人的基本情况做好登记，以便协助卫生防疫等部门，最终调查确定诊断。

（6）列车长、乘警要组织相关人员认真做好稳定旅客情绪工作，防止造成混乱，追回售出的可疑食物，并在低温下封存可疑食物、原材料，保留造成食物中毒或可能导致食物中毒的包装、器皿，采集呕吐物、排泄物样品，封闭被污染厕所，等待卫生检疫人员查验。如不能排除食物中毒是站车列车供应食品所致，要立即停止食品供应，防止继续食用可疑食物扩大中毒事态。

4. 动车组列车发生行车中断应急处置预案

（1）动车组因故发生行车中断，列车长应与司机或列车停留地车站、铁路局调度联系，掌握情况，做到心中有数。并及时向旅客做出解释，通过广播向旅客表示歉意。

（2）动车组不能继续运行时，列车长应及时与司机或列车停留地车站、调度联系，随时掌握晚点情况，需要时用专用数字通信设备与铁路局客调统一电话联系，掌握晚点时间、原因、预计到达时间等情况，做到心中有数。根据掌握的情况，及时部署下一步应做好的重点工作。列车乘务人员应及时向旅客作出解释，如实说明晚点的时间和原因，并通过广播向旅客表示歉意。

（3）列车晚点通告用语为：旅客们，我是 × × 列车列车长，本次列车因 × × 原因晚点，现在大约晚 × × 小时 × × 分。因列车晚点给您造成不便，我代表铁路部门向您表示诚挚的歉意。晚点或线路中断原因按照以下内容表述：自然灾害（暴雨、大雾、大雪、山体滑坡、泥石流……）、事故影响、设备故障。

（4）线路中断，列车不能继续运行时列车员、乘警要安抚旅客，加强车厢巡视，随时向旅客做好解释和服务工作的同时，稳定车内秩序，保证车内治安秩序良好。

（5）在列车长的统一指挥下，列车乘务人员各负其责，做好安全、服务等各项工作。列车乘务人员必须清楚旅客列车晚点情况，及时向旅客通报预计晚点时间和调整列车运行方案等信息。遇旅客问讯时，应耐心细致回答，不得使用“不知道”“没点”等不负责任语言或有不耐烦表现，以免引起旅客不满而激化矛盾。

（6）如列车停留时间较长时，尽量不要让旅客下车，在车站旅客下车活动时，应将旅客组织到安全地带，确保旅客安全。列车长应组织好对旅客的服务、饮水、饮食供应等工作，尽最大的努力为旅客提供方便，保证旅客生活需要。如饮用水不足时，及时与车站联系上水或补充饮用水，食品不足时应及时与车站或所在地地方政府联系，组织采购，车站应帮助列车解决食品、餐料、饮用水等问题，保证旅客需要或与上级联系，组织供应配餐。

（7）列车停留给旅客生活带来不便或引起旅客不安时，列车乘务人员应主动了解走访旅客，在保证旅客安全的前提下，尽最大的努力为旅客提供方便，尤其是要加强对重点旅客的服务，设法减少因晚点给旅客带来的诸多生活等方面的不便，维护铁路运输企业信誉。

（8）列车必须在中途停留时，应当尽量将旅客列车停留在办理客运较大车站或城镇所在地车站，以方便解决旅客的饮食和急病救治。列车要采取各种措施，保证滞留旅客的生命财产安全。

（9）列车长应积极与铁路局客调联系，汇报车内情况，尽早恢复运行。同时了解掌握继续停留的时间，随时向调度和单位应急领导小组汇报车内旅客、秩序、供应、安全等情况及请求协助解决的问题，让调度随时掌握车内情况，列车长应根据情况积极提出列车迂回、折返运行等建议。

（10）因故中断停运、折返的动车组旅客列车，对中途下车要求退票、换乘、延长有效期及绕道、返回的旅客，列车长应在车票背面注明日期、车次、原因、返回站，加盖名章，作为旅客免费返回、办理退票、换乘或延长有效期的凭证。

5. 发生旅客人身伤害或急病事件应急处置预案

（1）勘察现场，了解伤情、病情，组织抢救、检查车票、采集证言。

① 旅客列车发生旅客人身伤害或急病时，列车长应会同乘警勘察现场，查看旅客受伤程度及发病情况，收集旁证、物证，调查事故发生原因，根据受伤及发病旅客具体情况，积极采取抢救措施。同时检查旅客所持车票的票种、票号、发到站、车次、有效期及加剪情况等；收集不少于两份同行人或见证人的证言和有关证据并保护好证据材料。

② 收集证人证言时，应当记录证人姓名、性别、年龄、地址、联系方式、身份证号码等内容。证言、证据应当准确、真实，并能够证明事故发生的过程和原因（路局补充规定：证人证言，以非铁路工作人员为最有法律效力）。此外事故发生后，要在第一时间取证，如无目击证人，要尽量采集本人的自述材料。采集证言材料后，有条件时，可将证言复写或复印，一份存查，另一份则必须在三日内移交处理站。

③ 旅客在列车上发生急病生命垂危时，当班列车员要立即向列车长报告，列车长要

在第一时间内赶赴现场，并通知广播员利用列车广播找寻医务工作人员到场，在医务人员未到现场或列车上无医务人员时，列车救护员要立即赶赴现场，询问了解旅客病史，根据旅客患病情况，采取措施，做好应急救护工作。

④ 在紧急救护过程中，列车工作人员要将其他旅客疏散到其他席位，维护好车内秩序，确保患病旅客所在位置空气流通，状况良好。

（2）编制客运记录或旅客伤亡事故记录，办理移交。

① 列车上受伤及急病旅客需交车站处理时，必要时应提前通知车站做好救护准备工作，将受伤及急病旅客移交三等以上车站（在区间停车处理时为就近车站）处理，车站不得拒绝受理。发生旅客伤亡人数较多的事故，列车认为必要时，应请求地方政府协助组织抢救。列车向车站办理移交手续时，编制客运记录一式两份（一份存查，一份办理站、车交接），连同车票、旅客随身携带品清单、证据材料一起移交。旅客人身伤害事故系因斗殴等治安或刑事案件所致，列车乘警应在客运记录上签字。

② 因特殊情况来不及编写记录的，列车长必须指派专人下车与车站办理交接，并必须在三日以内向事故处理站补交有关材料。

③ 如受伤人员伤情及病情较严重，需立即下车治疗时，列车长应立即向所在地路局客调报告请示，准备非图定停车站停车移交，并迅速做好移交准备工作，同时向段生产调度室汇报。

（3）报告程序。

① 发生旅客人身伤害或急病时，要在第一时间拍发事故速报，主送责任单位或发生单位（正常意外伤害主送事故处理站、段），抄送路局客运营销处，发生无票人员伤亡时还要抄送路局安全监察室。事故速报内容包括：a. 事故种类；b. 发生日期、时间、车次；c. 发生地点、车站、区间里程（线别、站名、区间、公里、米）；d. 伤亡旅客姓名、性别、国籍、民族、年龄、职业、单位、住址，车票种类、发到站、票号、身份证号码；e. 事故及伤亡简况（描述直观伤害及发病程度）。

② 条件允许时，应当先用电话向段生产调度室报告事故概况。

6. 动车组列车发生重大疫情时的应急处置预案

（1）动车组列车发现疑似新冠、鼠疫、霍乱等重大疫情的病例或接到动车组列车上有疑似病例的通知时，列车长应立即向司机和上级主管部门报告，司机向列车调度员报告，列车调度员立即向值班主任报告，值班主任立即向铁路疾控部门报告。

（2）列车调度员根据铁路局有关部门确定的处置方案，安排动车组在指定地点停车。列车长接司机指定站停车的通知后，做好疾控人员上车和疑似病例交站等相关准备工作，车站及铁路疾控部门做好接车紧急处置准备。

（3）列车长应组织隔离传染病人、疑似病人和密切接触者，紧急疏散其他旅客，并对有关人员进行登记。

（4）列车长应组织封锁已经污染或可能污染的区域，同时做好被隔离人员的交站准备。

（5）列车长在指定停车站将传染病人、疑似病人、密切接触者和其他需要跟踪观察的旅客及相关资料移交车站和铁路疾控部门。

（6）乘警应维护好车内秩序，确保区域封锁、旅客隔离、站车移交等工作正常开展。

（7）铁路疾控部门应上车对已经污染或可能污染的区域进行消毒。铁路疾控部门确认处置完毕后，方可解除区域封锁。

（8）站车应积极配合现场的医疗和疾控部门工作。

7. 动车组列车故障站内换乘热备动车组的应急处置预案

（1）遇车次变动时，车站应收回原票、换发新票，退还票价差额，旅客执电子客票时，应先办理换票。如时间较紧，无法换发新票时，旅客可凭原票直接上车，站车应做好交接工作，旅客执电子客票时，车站应与客票系统提供的售票信息核对确认。

（2）故障车停靠站台时，换乘时应尽可能安排在同一站台的两个站台面进行，不能在同一站台的两个站台面换乘时，车站应组织旅客通过天桥或地道或其他通道换乘，严禁跨越股道换乘；故障车在站内没有停靠站台时，换乘处置程序比照区间换乘热备动车组的处置程序办理。

（3）热备动车组定员少于故障动车组实际人数时，有条件时，使用定员能满足需要的其他动车组组织旅客换乘。如遇车型变动，路局客票管理所应做好票额调整和控制工作。车站要加强与路局客票管理所的联系，及时掌握席位发售情况，制定调整方案，配合列车并做好旅客席位调整和宣传解释工作。

（4）席位调整发生等级差额时，发生席位等级差时，由列车长编制客运记录，到站后退还票价差额。

（5）站、车应加强配合，共同做好旅客的宣传引导、席位安排、服务等工作，尽量满足旅客的合理需求。

（6）换乘时，车站要认真组织验票，严禁持其他车次车票旅客上车。

8. 动车组列车空调失效时应急处置预案

（1）动车组列车全列空调失效超过 20 min 不能恢复，但列车能够正常运行时，列车长可视情况通知司机向列车调度员提出在前方最近客运站停车的请求，列车调度员安排列车在前方最近客运站停车。列车在停车站安装好防护网、打开部分车门后，列车调度员根据司机的报告，向司机（救援时还包括救援司机）及沿途各站发布打开车门限速 60 km/h（通过邻靠高站台的线路时限速 40 km/h）运行的调度命令。

（2）列车因故停车不能维持运行且空调失效超过 20min 不能恢复时，列车长应及时与司机、随车机械师沟通，视情况做出打开车门决定，并通知司机转报列车调度员。

（3）安装防护网、打开车门由列车长组织列车乘务员进行，司机、随车机械师配合。防护网的安装需在列车停车状态下进行，安装位置为运行方向左侧(非会车侧)车门处。防护网安装完毕，列车长确认防护网安装牢固。打开车门后，由列车长组织列车工作人员防护，直到车门关闭。

（4）需要组织旅客下车或换乘其他列车时，应在车站站台进行。必须在站内不邻靠站台的线路或区间组织旅客下车或换乘时，需经铁路局主管运输副局长（总调度长）批准。

【任务检测】

1. 为保证安全，动车组车门的开启和关闭有什么规定？
2. 动车组运行及途中作业安全有哪些要求？
3. 简述动车组应急处置组织机构职责。
4. 动车组应急处置原则是什么？
5. 简述动车组发生电器初始火灾的应急处置预案。
6. 简述动车组发生火灾爆炸事故的应急处置预案。
7. 简述动车组发生食物中毒事件的应急处置预案。
8. 简述动车组列车发生行车中断的应急处置预案。
9. 简述动车组发生旅客人身伤害或急病事件的应急处置预案。
10. 简述动车组列车发生重大疫情时的应急处置预案。
11. 简述动车组列车故障区间换乘热备动车组的应急处置预案。
12. 简述动车组列车空调失效时应急处置预案。

任务三　动车组行车组织

【任务描述】

（1）熟知接发动车组管理办法。

（2）掌握各种行车应急预案的规定。

一、接发动车组

1. 接发动车组“五固定”

为确保动车组列车运行安全、旅客乘降有序，提高动车组行车组织和旅客服务水平，接发动车组列车必须坚持“五固定”。

（1）“五固定”内容：

① 固定进路：接发动车组列车必须固定在基本进路上办理。

② 固定到发线：接发动车组列车必须在固定的到发线上办理。动车组按列控车载设备方式行车时，禁止在未设置 CTCS-2 信息的到发线及进路上接发动车组。

③ 固定站台：接发办理客运业务的动车组列车必须停靠固定站台。

④ 固定停车位置：车站应根据动车组不同车型、不同编组，分别设置动车组停车位置标，固定动车组停车位置。司机对标停车。

⑤ 固定接发车人员：接发动车组人员必须由对动车组相关知识进行专门培训、考试合格的人员担任，并在固定位置接送动车组列车。

（2）接发动车组“五固定”的有关内容应纳入《车站行车工作细则》。接发动车组的固定进路、固定到发线以及动车组变更进路，应列表放置在有关行车调度台、信号楼（行车室）。

（3）调度集中区段，在设备具备条件的情况下，各站接发动车组的固定到发线应纳入基本列车运行图数据。

（4）遇动车组接发不能在基本进路办理时，须经铁路局调度所值班主任准许并发布调度命令。遇办理客运业务的动车组变更到发线接车时，除须经铁路局调度所值班主任准许并发布调度命令外，行车人员应提前通知相关客运人员，做好接车准备。遇接发车人员需临时换班时，应指派经考试合格的胜任人员办理动车组接发作业。

2. 动车组接发车作业办法

（1）动车组发车前，列车长确认旅客上下完毕后，通知司机关闭车门；动车组到站停稳后，司机开启车门。按钮不在司机操作台上的，由列车长确认旅客上下完毕后，通知随车机械师关闭车门；动车组到站停稳后，由随车机械师开启车门。如自动开关门装置故障时，由司机通知列车工作人员手动开关车门。

（2）动车组司机在确认出站（进路）信号机显示或占用区间行车凭证正确，车门已关闭，即可起动列车。出站信号机开放或占用区间行车凭证已交付后，如需取消发车进路，车站值班员应确认列车尚未起动，通知司机，收回行车凭证后，再取消发车进路。

（3）在接发动车组时，车站助理值班员应站在规定地点接送列车。

（4）动车组进站时，在信号机外制动距离内，若进站方向为超过 6‰的下坡道，而接车线末端无隔开设备时，禁止办理相对方向同时接车和同方向同时发接列车（仅运行动车组列车的区段除外）。

（5）动车组进路相对方向不能同时接车时，应先接不适于在站外停车的列车、停车后起动困难的列车或后面有续行列车的列车。遇两列车不能同时接发时，原则上应按列车运行计划顺序接发。

（6）动车组在不满足 5 min 列车追踪间隔的处所，经中国铁路总公司批准，允许在出站信号机显示黄色灯光时，办理动车组由车站通过。

（7）动车组通过车站时，车站须提前停止通过进路上的作业和对列车运行安全有影响的作业。提前时间由铁路局规定。

3. 动车组调车作业的规定

（1）动车组调车作业原则上采用自走行方式，凭地面信号机的显示运行。

（2）禁止通过驼峰、溜放调车、手推调车、连挂其他机车车辆调车（救援、附挂回送过渡车以及动车组无动力调车时的调车机、公铁两用牵引车除外）和跟踪出站调车，禁止向动车组停留线路溜放调车和手推调车。

（3）调车作业时，司机必须在动车组运行方向的前端操作。在不得已情况下必须在动车组运行方向的后端操作时，应指派随车机械师或其他胜任人员站在动车组运行方向的前端指挥，发现危及行车或人身安全时，应立即使用紧急停车按钮（紧急制动装置）或通知司机停车。动车段（动车运用所）设动车组地勤司机，负责动车组在动车段（动车运用所）内调车、试运行等移动动车组作业。

（4）采用机车调车作业时，动车段（动车运用所）人员负责过渡车钩、专用风管和电气连接线的连接和分解并打开车门，调车人员负责车钩摘解、软管摘结。

（5）动车组检修过程中通过检修及检测设备的限速规定：经过踏面诊断设备，通过限速 45 km/h，检测限速 8 ~ 12 km/h；自走行经过洗车机时，通过限速为 3 ~ 5 km/h；牵车机牵引动车组时，通过限速为 1.5 ~ 3 km/h；通过轨道桥时，通过限速为 10 km/h；通过不落轮镟床，转向架更换及落轮设备时，通过限速为 5 km/h。

二、动车组运行

1. 基本要求

（1）动车组设司机、随车机械师、客运乘务组，不设运转车长。

（2）单列动车组为固定编组，运用状态下不得解编；两列同型动车组可重联运行。两列动车组重联时各升 1 架受电弓运行，但不得采用前车升后弓、后车升前弓的模式，采用前后车均升前弓或前后车均升后弓的模式时，工作受电弓间距为 200 ~ 215 m。动车组禁止加挂各型机车车辆；动车组禁止与其他列车混编。超过检修周期的动车组严禁上线运行。

（3）动车组上线运营前，必须达到运用状态，符合动车组运用技术标准要求，运行途中不进行客列检作业。动车组设备故障不能继续运行时，不得拆解、甩车。

（4）两列动车组重联或摘解时，由动车组随车机械师负责引导，司机确认。重联或摘解后的动车组由随车机械师配合司机做相关试验。摘解操作时，主动车组必须一次移动 5 m 以上方可停车。

（5）动车组正常运行中，严禁打开气密窗。

（6）动车组运行遇发生影响行车的设备故障（列车设备故障除外）时，原则上应先处理故障，后组织行车。设备故障暂时无法修复时，确需组织行车时，应根据有关行车限制条件组织行车。

（7）动车组在车站无动力停留时，由车站进行防溜；无停放制动装置的动车组在区间无动力停留时，由动车组司机通知随车机械师进行防溜。防溜时应使用止轮器牢靠固定。在车站站线停留时，应将线路两端的道岔扳向不能进入该线路的位置。

（8）动车组不得通过半径小于 180 m 的曲线，不得侧向通过小于 9 号单开道岔和 6 号对称双开道岔。

（9）动车组通过高度为 1 100 mm 及以上高站台时，速度不得超过 70 km/h。

（10）动车组应能由救援机车连挂运行并实施制动，列车管压力采用 600 kPa。

（11）动车组在 CTCS-2 级区段运行时，禁止在区间与超限货物列车交会。

2. 区间运行

（1）动车组在区间运行，列控车载设备显示停车信号时，列车必须立即停车，司机应使用列车无线调度通信设备通知随车机械师。列车停车等候 2 min，列控车载设备仍未收到允许运行的信号时，司机将列控车载设备转入目视行车模式，列车以遇到阻碍能随时停车的速度继续运行，最高速度不超过 20 km/h，直到列控车载设备收到允许运行的信号，按列控车载设备显示运行。在停车等候的同时，必须与列车调度员、车站值班员联系，如确认前方闭塞分区内有列车时，不得进入。

（2）动车组运行中遇列控车载设备故障并导致列车停车后，司机应使用列车无线调度通信设备报告列车调度员或车站值班员，并通知随车机械师将系统断电 30 s 后重新启动。若设备恢复正常，继续运行；若设备仍不能恢复正常，根据调度命令将列控车载设备转入隔离模式。

（3）动车组在区间被迫停车后须返回后方站时，列车调度员必须确认动车组至后方站间已空闲，方可发布调度命令。司机将列控车载设备转入隔离模式，按调度命令以不超过 20 km/h 的速度人工控制动车组返回。在不得已情况下，列车必须退行时，列车调度员须确认后方区间已空闲，随车机械师或指派的胜任人员应站在列车尾部司机室注视运行前方，发现危及行车或人身安全时，应立即使用列车无线调度通信设备通知司机，使列车停车。列车退行速度不得超过 15 km/h。

（4）动车组在救援、无动力回送连挂机车或回送过渡车时，应进行制动试验。

3. 动车组回送要求

（1）动车组回送按旅客列车办理，原则上采用自走行方式。无动力回送时可根据《回送技术条件》加挂回送过渡车，使用客运机车牵引。高铁线路与既有线并行时，尽可能安排高铁线路回送。两列同型短编动车组可重联回送。

（2）动车组回送运行时，须安排动车组司机及随车机械师值乘。随车机械师由配属局担当，动车组司机由机务部门安排，配属局负责更新 LKJ 数据。自走行回送时，非担当区段应指派带道司机。

（3）动车组回送不进行客列检作业。动车组（回送过渡车）与本务机车车钩摘解、软管摘结按《铁路技术管理规程》有关规定办理。过渡车钩、专用风管和电气连接线的连接和分解由随车机械师负责，动车组司机配合。

（4）动车组安装过渡车钩回送时，限速 120 km/h 运行，尽可能避免实施紧急制动。发生紧急制动后，本务司机必须通知随车机械师，经随车机械师检查过渡车钩状态良好后方可继续运行。

（5）动车组需加挂回送过渡车时，回送过渡车由该动车组使用单位与主机企业协商确定，回送过程必须派员押送，确保回送安全。

动车组回送时，列车调度员应根据相关动车段（动车运用所）提出的限速、回送方式（有、无动力）、可否折角运行等注意事项，发布有关调度命令。

4. 动车组连挂与摘解

（1）单列动车组实行固定编组，运行过程中不解编。

（2）两列型号代码相同的动车组可连挂运行，其连挂与摘解作业由动车组司机和随车机师负责。

（3）两列车连挂时应在站场内进行（尽可能选在直线路），对于需在线路上进行作业时，须按规定进行安全防护。作业过程中须按规定做好动车组的防溜保护。

（4）动车组连挂作业要求如下：

① 车站按规定办理进路，开通信号；司机确认信号正常后，开始连挂作业。

② 移动动车组在距被连挂车组 10 m 处停车，随车机师下车确认连接装置状态良好，向司机显示连挂信号。

③ 连接时，司机分别在连挂端司机室按规定程序操纵，连挂速度为 3 ~ 5 km/h。

④ 连挂后，随车机师确认车下连挂状态良好后通知司机，司机确认车载信息显示正常，并按规定程序进行检测。

⑤ 司机确认动车组连挂作业完成后，转换司机室，进入运行方向前端司机室并检测车载信息，确认显示正常后即向车站报告。

（5）动车组摘解作业要求如下：

① 车站按规定办理进路，开通信号；司机确认信号正常后，开始解编作业。

② 摘解前，随车机师下车检查连接装置状态，确认可以摘解后向司机显示摘解信号。

③ 摘解时，司机分别在连挂端司机室按规定程序操纵，移动其中一列动车组，另一列动车组处于制动状态。动车组移动速度不超过 5 km/h，移动至距停留动车组 10 m 处停车。

④ 停车后，随车机师确认连接装置正常复位，并通知司机。

⑤ 司机接到通知后，按规定程序进行转换司机室作业并检测车载信息，确认显示正常，及时向车站报告。

5. 机车与动车组连挂及摘解

（1）机车与动车组连挂按以下要求作业：

① 连挂前，随车机师在动车组连挂端安装中间过渡车钩及风管、连接线；动车组司机在连挂端司机室按规定程序操作，做好动车组连接前准备，并通知机车司机。

② 机车司机确认符合连挂条件后，方可进行连挂。

③ 连挂时，机车限速 5 km/h。

④ 连挂后，动车组乘务组人员按规定程序进行作业，机车司机组织进行试风及供电状态检查，动车组司机在司机室确认车载信息正常，向机车司机报告。

⑤ 机车司机确认连挂作业完毕，向车站报告。

（2）机车与动车组摘解按以下要求作业：

① 摘解前，动车组处于制动状态，机车停止 DC 110 V 电源供电。动车组随车机师确认动车组制动及停电，摘解机车及动车组间风管、连接线及车钩，并通知司机。

② 机车司机确认具备摘解条件后方可开始摘解作业。

③ 摘解时，机车限速 5 km/h。

6. 动车组救援

（1）动车组在区间被迫停车后，不能继续运行时，司机应立即使用列车无线调度通信设备通知两端站、列车调度员及随车机械师，报告停车原因和停车位置，并迅速请求救援。司机实施停放制动，无停放制动动车组应指派随车机械师做好防溜工作。

（2）列车调度员接到动车组在区间被迫停车的救援请求后，按规定发布调度命令封锁区间，并立即向调度所值班主任报告，按就近最快的原则组织救援机车，开展救援工作，并将救援方案立即通知车站值班员和动车组司机。

（3）已请求救援的动车组，不得再行移动。动车组司机应了解救援列车开来方向，动车组随乘司机（无随乘司机时，由列车长指定人员）协助随车机械师在救援列车来车的一端安装过渡车钩、专用风管。具备升弓条件的，司机升弓前必须与救援机车保持联系，防止发生弓网事故。动车组被救援后，运行途中可关闭司机警惕装置。

（4）如需停电作业，必须按规定办理停电验电手续。

（5）随车机械师在安装完过渡车钩、专用风管后，应到救援机车来车一端不少于 300 m 处设置防护，并指挥救援机车进行连挂作业，确认救援机车与动车组连挂好以及动车组状态正常，将救援运行条件通知救援机车司机。

（6）救援机车司机在救援作业过程中，要严格遵守有关限速等规定，与动车组司机保持联系。救援运行中速度不得超过 120 km/h，并尽可能避免实施紧急制动。

（7）动车组由机车救援返回后方站转入隔离模式，取消机车救援后退出隔离模式，由动车组司机自行转换。

（8）动车组由机车牵引继续运行时，由列车调度员向救援机车司机发布限速 120 km/h 运行的调度命令。

（9）当故障动车组处理后可继续运行时，列车调度员应根据动车组司机的请求，发布取消动车组救援的调度命令。

（10）动车组被迫停在接触网分相无电区，换弓不能正常受流时，应尽量组织内燃机车在列车运行前进方向担当救援。

使用电力机车救援时，动车组司机应查明动车组前方无电区的长度（前方无电区长度的判明方法是动车组前端距“合”电标的距离减去 30 m），前部距离能满足执行救援任务的电力机车在列车前方升弓受流的条件时，动车组司机报告车站值班员或列车调度员“电力机车可以从前部救援”，否则报告“电力机车只能从尾部救援”。从尾部救援时，列车调度员应发布列车救援调度命令，动车组司机应在动车组尾部司机室，并与救援车司机保持联系。动车组拉出无电区后，应在距离分相断电标不少于 800 m 处停车，摘开救援车。动车组司机升弓受流恢复正常运行。列车被迫停于接触网电分相前方，不具备越过电分相条件时，不准退行；动车组司机应立即报告车站值班员或列车调度员，按其指示办理，并按规定指派随车机械师做好防溜、防护工作。

【任务检测】

1. 接发动车组有哪些规定？

2. 动车组进行调车作业时有哪些规定？

3. 动车组运行时有哪些基本要求？

4. 动车组临时限速是如何规定的？

任务四　动车组停放防冻管理办法

【任务描述】

（1）掌握动车组停放防冻管理办法。

（2）熟悉动车组防冻排水作业办法。

一、动车组停放防冻管理办法

动车组在气温低于 0 °C 停放时，为了防止部分设备（重点是高压牵引、空调采暖、供风及制动管系、车体密封、给排水卫生等设施）因存水冻结造成损坏，确保动车组完好，特制订本办法。

（1）气温低于 0 °C 时，动车组应停放于具备防冻保温功能的处所，停放处所应具备下列条件之一：

① 接触网供电。

② 外接单相 AC 400 V 地面电源供电。

③ 暖库。

（2）供电工况下的防冻：

① 确认动车组具备升弓或地面供电条件后，值班人员进行供电操作。

② 值班人员通过 MON 将动车组空调设置在供暖工况，并确认空调、司机室电加热、设备电伴热装置工作正常。

③ 允许间隔供电，当室内温度达到 18 ~ 20 °C 且保持 1 h 方可断电。供电时间间隔，视各地区具体情况由铁路局自行确定。

（3）非供电工况下的防冻执行各型动车组防冻排水作业办法。

（4）动车组防冻工作由车辆部门负责，应成立防冻值班队伍。

（5）动车组进入高级检修前必须进行排空作业，高级检修期间的动车组防冻工作由施修单位负责。

（6）停放前应按照排水操作程序对动车组进行排水、吸污作业，并做好记录。在保持供电工况或暖库停放时动车组可不排水。

（7）供电停放时，值班人员随时掌握供电状态，不得擅自离岗；交接班时办理好动车组钥匙、设备备品交接，认真填写交接记录。

（8）供电期间，值班人员每小时对动车组车内的供电设备运行情况及车内温度进行巡视检查，做好记录。发现问题，及时处理并上报。

（9）停放的动车组，禁止使用坐式卫生间、蹲式卫生间设施。

（10）车辆部门应加强对防冻工作的领导，指定专人负责，定期开展防冻作业的演练，积极探索动车组防冻工作的规律。

二、动车组防冻排水作业办法

当外界环境温度低于 0 °C 时，动车组应供电防冻。动车段不具备防寒防冻条件时，动车组应进行排空作业。中国铁路总公司已颁布了各型动车组防冻排水作业办法，详细规定了各型动车组防水作业的操作规程和操作步骤，以下为 CRH380A 统型动车组防冻排水作业办法：

1. 要　求

时速 350 千米速度级（CRH380A 统型）动车组在气温低于零度环境、非供电工况下停放时，为防止车辆存水结冰导致设备损坏，需提前进行动车组防冻排水作业。

2. 工艺流程

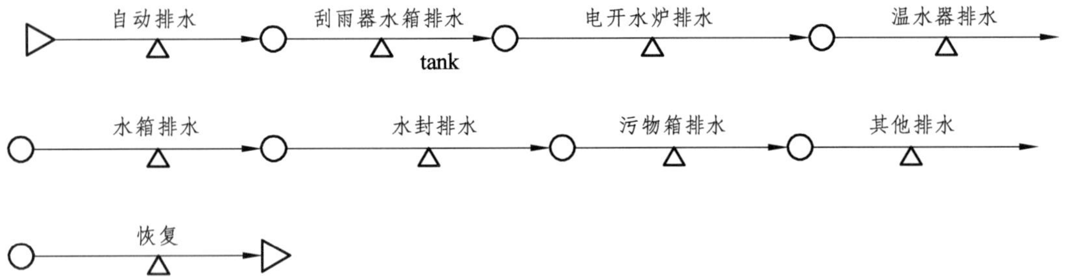

3. 排水办法

1）准备

（1）各车需排水设备布置。

表 2-1　排水设备分布

主要设备分布	车　种							
	T1	M1	M2	M3	M4	M5	M6	T2
水箱分布情况及容量	700 L	车上 400 L	700 L	车上 400 L	700 L	车上 4700 L	700 L	700 L
便器分布（座硬、蹲便）	1 座	1 座 1 蹲	1 座 1 蹲	1 座 1 蹲	—	1 座 1 蹲	1 座 1 蹲	1 座
污物箱分布及容量	450 L	450 L	450 L	450 L	—	450 L	450 L	450 L
电开水炉分布	1 个	1 个	1 个	1 个	1 个	1 个	1 个	1 个
洗脸室	—	有	有	—	—	有	有	—
水封	2 个	2 个	2 个	2 个	1 个	1 个	1 个	1 个
刮雨器水箱	1 个（车下）	—	—	—	—	—	—	1 个（车下）

（2）排水标准。

打开排水阀门，待排水口在 1 min 内无水滴下时，认为设备存水排空，各设备存水排空后方可进行各阀门的恢复。

2）自动排水

（1）自动排水条件：将车辆给水设施整备为正常工作状态，车辆通高压电。

（2）排水范围：设有卫生间车供水主管路、水泵、水增压器及附属管路、便器、排污管路及中转箱；开水炉及餐车水泵及供水管路。

（3）自动排水方式：分为集控防冻排空和单车防冻排空两种，只需选择一种进行操作即可。

（4）集控防冻排空功能：

动车组低压供电（DC 100 V），温水污物配电盘的【集便器控制】（餐车为【给水控制】）和【水泵电源】NFB 设为 ON（见图 2-3，图 2-4），且总风压力不低于 600 kPa 的条件下，右旋打开司机室的【停放】开关或逐车打开 DTC 的【防冻排空】按钮（餐车为【防冻排水】按钮），启动防冻排空功能（见图 2-5，图 2-6）。

图 2-3　温水污物配电盘

图 2-4　餐车温水污物配电盘

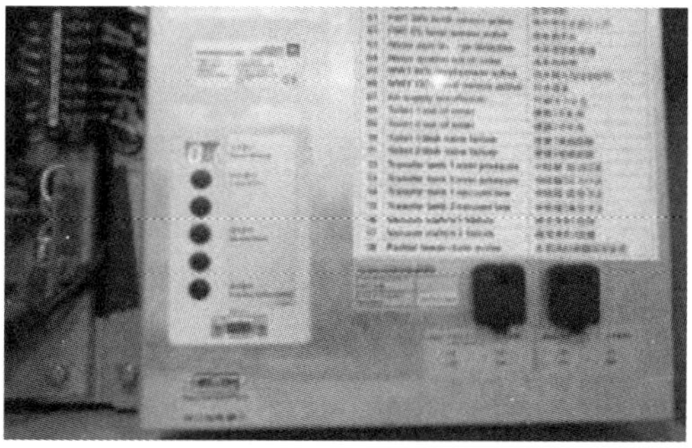

图 2-5 DTC

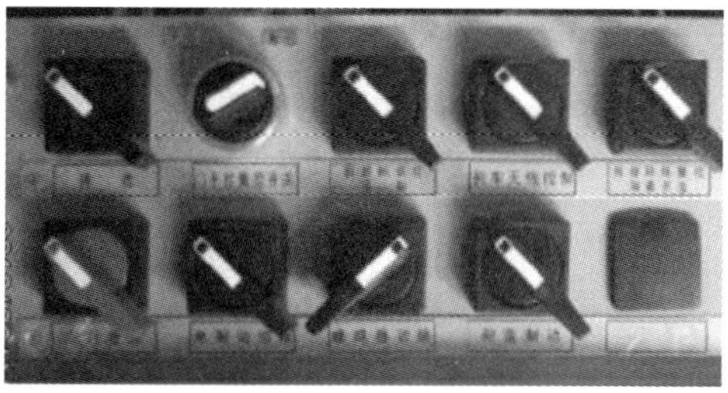

图 2-6 【停放】开关

防冻排空动作过程如下：

a. 给水系统进水电磁阀失电关闭，水泵停止运转；

b. 给水系统排水电磁阀失电打开，排尽供水管路存水；

c. 给水系统供水管路排水 15 min 后，中转箱自动清空 1 次→便器自动冲洗 3 次→中转箱自动清空 3 次，以排尽便器、水增压单元及附属管路、中转箱的存水；

d. 给水卫生系统停止工作，便器禁用。

防冻排空动作完成之后，手动打开水增压单元的电磁阀，确认存水已排尽。

⑤ 单车防冻排空功能。

按动设有卫生间各车【防冻排空】开关，对应本车按设定程序清空供水主管路、水泵、水增压器及附属管路、便器、排污管路及中转箱存水，排空程序与集控防冻排空相同。

排水完毕后，将集控防冻排空用【停放】开关或各车辆单车防冻排空用【防冻排空】开关恢复。

3）车上设备排水

（1）电开水炉排水。

打开电开水炉检查门，将电开水炉产水箱、储水箱、净水器排水塞门全部打开（旋塞与管路平行为开）进行排水，待水排尽后关闭各排水阀（见图 2-7）。

图 2-7　电开水炉储水箱、产水箱排水阀

（2）温水箱排水。

打开温水箱排水阀，卸下热水出水口螺堵和进水口螺堵，手动拔开膨胀水安全阀，待水排尽后恢复螺堵，关闭排水阀。其中因 E28 温水器下无接水盘及地漏，故在温水器排水期间需用干抹布放在两螺堵排水口下端，防止排水漏在地板上，同时在排完水后需将地板上的水迹擦干（见图 2-8，图 2-9）。

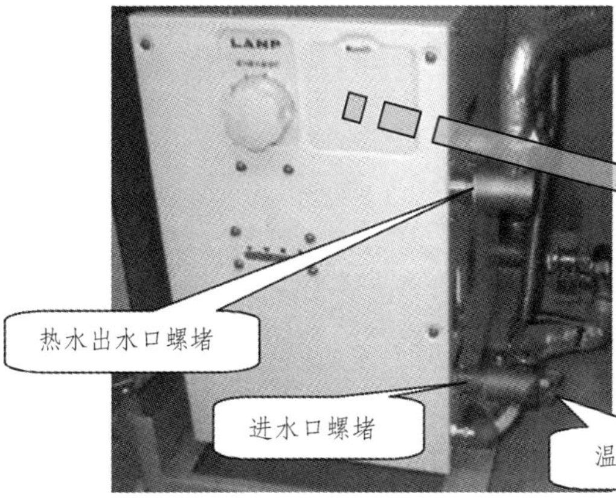

图 2-8　温水箱供水管路

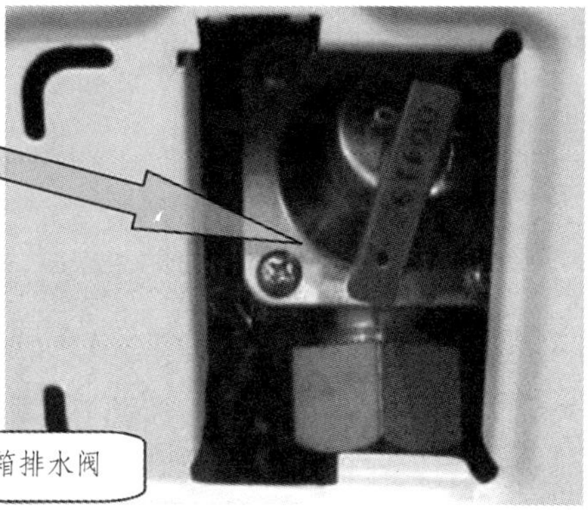

图 2-9　温水箱膨胀水安全阀

（3）水龙头、皂液器排水。

反复按压水龙头和皂液器，直到排尽存水为止（见图 2-10）。

图 2-10　水龙头、皂液器

（4）车上水箱排水。

打开车上水箱的检查门，打开车上水箱和水泵的排水阀（塞门与管路平行为开），进行车上水箱和水泵排水，阀门位置见图 2-11。

图 2-11　车上水箱排水

（5）车上其他排水。

旋转操作黑色手柄将洗水池内存水通过排水阀进行排空（见图 2-12）。同时将洗水池下端两红色阀打开进行排水（见图 2-13）。

图 2-12　车上洗水池排水

图 2-13　车上洗水池下端红色排水阀

4）车下设备排水（无电状态下）

（1）刮雨器水箱排水。

将车下刮雨器水箱排水口打开（见图 2-14 红圈处）对刮雨器水箱进行排水，直至刮雨器水箱液位处于最低处。为防止刮雨器喷水管路有存水，需在通电状态下，进行刮雨器排水动作。直至雨刷无水喷出为止。

图 2-14　刮雨器水箱

（2）车下水箱排水。

打开车下水箱外侧的排水阀和水泵清空阀，进行车下水箱及水泵排水，见图 2-15。

图 2-15　车下水箱排水阀

（3）污物箱排水。

打开污物箱的排污阀排尽污物箱存水（见图 2-16），必要时可采用吸污车进行排空。

图 2-16　污物箱排污阀

（4）水封排水。

卸下水封的排水螺堵，排尽水后恢复螺堵（见图 2-17）。

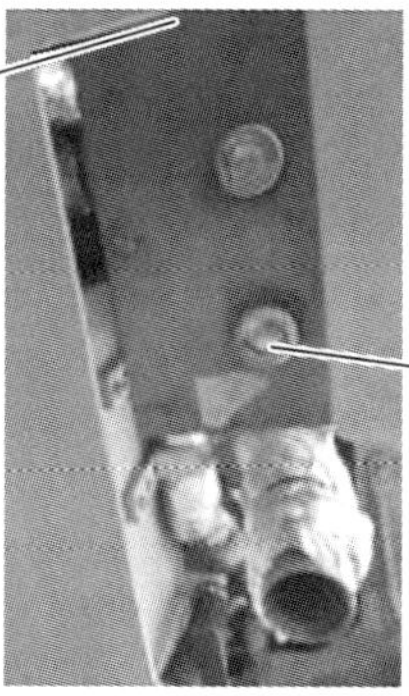

图 2-17　水封排水螺堵

5）制动系统冬季存放

（1）辅助空气压缩机排水。

断电后，打开辅助空气压缩机的油水分离器排水阀和辅助空压机排水阀，排尽存水（见图 2-18，图 2-19）。

图 2-18　油水分离器排水阀

图 2-19　辅助空压机排水阀

（2）制动控制装置排水。

断电后，打开三个风缸（主风缸、供给风缸、控制风缸）的排水旋塞排水（见图 2-20）。

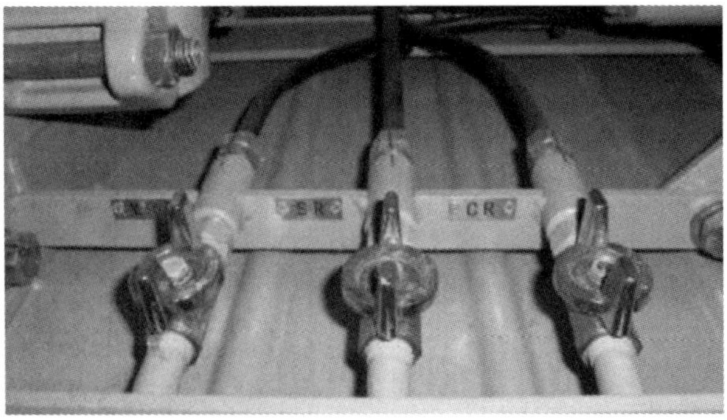

图 2-20　MR、SR、CR 排水阀

6）恢复

各设备均排水完毕后，按次序逐项恢复各水阀、开关、排污阀等，并恢复各设备检查门及罩板。

注意事项：排水完毕，紧固件涂打防松标记，确认各部密封良好。

【任务检测】

1. 动车组在气温低于 0 °C 时停放处所应该具备什么条件？
2. 动车组供电工况下如何防冻？
3. 动车组防冻排水作业的操作流程是什么？

项目三　动车组非正常行车组织

【思政课堂】她的手机号码，就是动车司机的“110”——王晓霞

中国高铁不仅以高速度、高颜值驰名中外更以其高安全性、高准点率，让百姓的出行变得更美好。在高铁安全、快速运行的背后，许多人正为了高铁事业忘我奋斗。中国铁路太原局集团有限公司，太原电务段动车车载设备车间，党支部书记、工程师王晓霞，就是这样一位奋斗在最前沿的铁路科技工作者。

王晓霞所在的动车车载设备车间，肩负着太原局集团公司所属 54 组动车组列控车载设备（ATP）的日常维护和数据分析任务。王晓霞的手机号就是动车司机的“110 服务热线”。多年来，她已习惯了从任何事情、任何状态迅速切换到动车组 ATP 故障处置状态，即使在睡觉、吃饭中也不例外。

“所谓故障，其实就是 ATP 系统中某个模块发出的预警，就像身体通过发烧或疼痛提示我们可能出现健康问题一样。”王晓霞解释，“绝大部分故障都是不危及行车安全的‘小感冒’，越早发现、诊断、处置，对行车安全的影响就越小。

及早发现、准确判断、科学处置……王晓霞所做的一切努力就是不使“小感冒”演化为“大问题”。9 年多来，经她远程指导处置的突发问题超过 300 件，远程处置“零失误”为王晓霞赢得了信任和口碑。

2017 年 11 月 13 日，西安北至太原南的 D2508 次列车，运行途中报警常规处置未果，是继续运行还是更换备用列车，列车调度、动车司机都在紧张地等待着王晓霞的最终决断。王晓霞迅速将车况信息，在大脑中缜密推演，在确定即便是最坏情况，也不会危及旅客和列车安全后，她果断决定让列车继续按图运行，司机不间断观察反馈列车状态，随时做好应急准备。随后，列车准时驶入太原南站。

2015 年 10 月，中国标准动车组 2 辆样车，在原平至太原高铁综合试验段，进行型式试验和运用考核，王晓霞参加了有关 ATP 方面的试验。在全程参与复兴号动车组试验任务的两年中，她根据试验内容提出了多项优化建议，为圆满完成既定试验任务做出了贡献。

2015 年成立的“王晓霞创新工作室”，是她和她的创新团队开展技术攻关的新平台。在她的带领下，工作室已经完成了 200C、200H、300S 三种型号的列控车载设备仿真试验系统，实现了动车组故障在线模拟仿真，填补了全路空白。

【项目描述】

通过本项目的学习，使学生掌握非正常情况下的行车组织办法，掌握动车组灾害天气行车作业办法，学会动车组突发事件的应急处理。

任务一　非正常情况下行车作业

【任务描述】

（1）熟悉非正常情况行车时对动车组司机的要求。

（2）掌握非正常行车组织的相关规定。

一、非正常情况行车时对动车组司机的基本要求

发生非正常情况行车时，动车组司机必须沉着冷静，仔细观察。发生非正常情况后，紧张、图快是大忌。任何的非正常情况，肯定有它最终的正确处理程序和方法，一旦过度地紧张而且盲目求快时，首先对现象的观察就可能有漏项或者错误，对后面的判断处理就会造成毁灭性的作用。如果说，非正常情况行车处理分三步走的话，这第一步的“观察”是至关紧要的，它直接影响第二步的“判断”和最后的“处理”，只要观察出错，判断和处理肯定跟着出错。

二、非正常行车组织

1. 动车组双线区间反方向行车

（1）列车在双线区间，应按左侧单方向运行；只有整理列车运行时，列车可反方向运行。若为旅客列车，仅在正方向区间的线路封锁、发生自然灾害、因事故中断行车，以及正方向设备故障严重影响列车运行秩序而反方向自动站间闭塞设备良好等特殊情况下，经调度所值班主任（值班副主任）准许，可反方向运行。

（2）列车反方向运行时，列车调度员应发布调度命令。列车调度员（车站控制时为车站值班员）确认反方向区间空闲后，发布相应调度命令。

（3）动车组列车在 CTCS-3 级区段反方向运行时，最高允许速度为 300 km/h；在 CTCS-2 级反方向运行时，最高允许速度为 250 km/h；其中在 CTCS-2 级区段，250 km/h 线路上最高允许速度为 200 km/h，200 km/h 线路上最高允许速度为 160 km/h。

2. 列车被迫停车后的处理

（1）列车在区间被迫停车不能继续运行时，司机应立即使用列车无线调度通信设备通知列车调度员（两端站）及随车机械师（车辆乘务员），报告停车原因和停车位置，根据需要迅速请求救援。

① 随车机械师（车辆乘务员）、客运乘务组均应听从司机指挥，处理有关行车、列车防护和事故救援等事宜。

② 列车调度员（车站值班员）接到司机通知后，通知司机区间内列车运行情况，并

立即使用列车无线调度通信设备通知区间内后续列车停车，在停车原因消除前不得再向区间内放行列车。

③ 对已请求救援的列车，不得再行移动，并按规定对列车进行防护。

④ 列车在区间被迫停车后，应保证就地制动，防止列车溜逸。如遇自动制动机故障，动车组以外的旅客列车司机应通知车辆乘务员立即组织列车乘务人员拧紧全列人力制动机；其他列车司机应立即采取安全措施，并向列车调度员报告。

⑤ 需要防护时，列车前方由司机负责，列车后方由随车机械师（车辆乘务员）负责，配备列车防护报警装置的列车应首先使用列车防护报警装置进行防护。

（2）列车被迫停车可能妨碍邻线时，司机应立即使用列车无线调度通信设备通知邻线上运行的列车和列车调度员（两端站），并与随车机械师（车辆乘务员）分别在列车头部或尾部附近对邻线来车方向轨道电路进行短路。配备列车防护报警装置的列车应首先使用列车防护报警装置进行防护。

列车被迫区间停车时，司机应亲自或指派人员沿邻线一侧对列车进行检查，发现妨碍邻线时，应立即报告列车调度员（两端站）。如发现邻线有列车开来时，应鸣示紧急停车信号。列车调度员（车站值班员）接到列车被迫停车可能妨碍邻线的通知后，应立即通知邻线有关列车停车，在停车原因消除前不得向邻线放行列车。

（3）列车在区间被迫停车后，需按规定做好防护。

① 列车已请求救援时，从救援列车开来方向（不明时，从列车前后两方向），距离列车不小于 300 m 处放置响墩防护；在仅运行动车组列车的线路上，列车在区间被迫停车后已请求救援时，由随车机械师在救援列车开来方向，距离列车不小于 300 m 处人工进行防护，不再放置响墩防护。

② 列车分部运行，机车进入区间挂取遗留车辆时，应从车列前方距离不小于 300 m 处放置响墩防护。

③ 防护人员设置的响墩在停车原因消除后，由防护人员撤除。

3. 列车在区间退行、返回

（1）列车特殊情况下必须在区间退行时，列车调度员须扣停后续列车，并确认退行距离内的闭塞分区空闲后，允许退行。随车机械师（车辆乘务员）或指派的胜任人员应站在列车尾部注视运行前方，发现危及行车或人身安全时，应立即使用紧急制动装置（紧急制动阀）或通知司机，使列车停车。列车退行速度不得超过 15 km/h。

（2）列车若需退行至站内，列车调度员还应确认列车至后方站间已空闲。列车调度员（车站控制时为车站值班员）根据线路占用情况，可开放进站信号机或按引导办法将列车接入站内。动车组列车若需退行至站内，列车调度员应发布调度命令。

（3）动车组列车退行时，按隔离模式退行。

（4）在降雾、暴风雨雪及其他不良条件下，难以辨认信号时，列车不准退行。

（5）动车组列车在区间被迫停车后须返回后方站时，列车调度员必须确认动车组列车至后方站间已空闲，方可发布调度命令。司机根据调度命令，在动车组列车运行方向（折返）前端操作，列车按隔离模式返回，运行速度不得超过 40 km/h。

（6）列车在不得已情况下，必须分部运行时，司机应报告列车调度员（车站值班员），并组织做好遗留车辆的防溜和防护工作，车站值班员立即报告列车调度员。司机在记明遗留车辆辆数和停留位置后，方可牵引前部车辆运行至前方站，在运行中仍按信号显示运行。列车调度员应封锁区间，待将遗留车辆拉回车站，确认区间空闲后，方可开通区间。

（7）列车分部运行时，司机必须检查试验列车制动主管的贯通状态，确认具备开车条件后，方可起动列车。但在下列情况列车不准列车分部运行：

① 采取措施后可整列运行时。

② 对遗留车辆未采取防护、防溜措施时。

③ 遗留车辆无人看守时。

④ 司机与列车调度员及车站值班员均联系不上时。

⑤ 遗留车辆停留在超过 6‰坡度的线路上时。

4. 列车冒进信号机

（1）列车冒进信号机后，司机应立即停车报告列车调度员（车站值班员），并不得擅自动车，车站值班员报告列车调度员。列车调度员（车站值班员）接到司机冒进进站（接车进路）信号机报告后，立即通知已进入区间的后续列车停车，不再向该区间放行列车。

（2）列车冒进进站（接车进路）信号机时，列车调度员（车站控制时为车站值班员）在确认接车进路准备妥当和列车运行条件具备后，使用列车无线调度通信设备通知司机进站。

（3）列车冒进出站（发车进路）信号机时，列车调度员（车站控制时为车站值班员）应在具备条件后，布置列车后退。但对出发或通过列车，列车调度员（车站控制时为车站值班员）根据实际情况，可在确认发车进路准备妥当、第一个闭塞分区空闲（自动站间闭塞区段为区间空闲）、列车运行条件具备后，使用列车无线调度通信设备通知司机继续运行。

5. 列车运行晃车

（1）列车运行途中，司机发现晃车时，应立即减速运行并向列车调度员（车站值班员）报告晃车地点及晃车时列车运行速度，待本列无异常状况后恢复常速运行。车站值班员报告列车调度员。

（2）列车晃车并且运行速度为 160 km/h 以下时，列车调度员（车站值班员）立即通知已进入区间的后续列车停车，不再向该区间放行列车，并通知工务部门。列车调度员根据工务部门上道检查的申请，及时发布本线封锁、邻线限速 160 km/h 及以下的调度命令后，准许上道检查。工务检查设备后，根据现场具体情况，确定列车放行条件。

（3）列车晃车并且运行速度为 160 km/h 及以上时，列车调度员应向后续首列发布限速 120 km/h 的调度命令，限速位置按司机汇报的晃车地点前后各 1 km 确定。列车通过晃车地点后，司机应立即向列车调度员报告运行情况。若晃车持续，列车调度员立即通知已进入区间的后续列车停车，不再向该区间放行列车，通知工务部门，根据工务部门上道检查的申请，及时发布本线封锁、邻线限速 160 km/h 及以下的调度命令后，准许上道检查。工务检查设备后，根据现场具体情况，确定列车放行条件。若不再晃车，则按 160 km/h、250 km/h、常速逐级逐列提速。

在逐级逐列提速的过程中，再次发生晃车时，列车调度员应立即通知已进入区间的后续列车停车，不再向该区间放行列车，通知工务部门，根据工务部门上道检查的申请，及时发布本线封锁、邻线限速 160 km/h 及以下的调度命令后，准许上道检查。工务检查设备后，根据现场具体情况，确定列车放行条件。

6. 列车停在接触网分相无电区

（1）动车组列车停在接触网分相无电区不能继续运行时，司机应立即降弓，并报告列车调度员（车站值班员），车站值班员报告列车调度员。列车调度员（车站值班员）立即通知已进入区间的后续列车停车，不再向该区间放行列车。

（2）动车组具备采用换弓、退行闯分相等方式自救时，司机应准确报告动车组停车位置，由列车调度员、供电调度员、动车司机调度员共同根据动车组类型、停车位置、牵引供电设备状况等确定自救方案，组织自救。

（3）动车组不具备自救条件，但可以向中性区远动送电时，可在该分相后方接触网供电臂办理停电后，由列车调度员向供电调度员办理向中性区远动送电手续，通知停在该分相的列车升弓，待该列车驶出分相区后，再通知供电调度员恢复原供电方式并向后方接触网供电臂送电，恢复后续列车正常运行。

（4）动车组不具备自救条件且不能向中性区远动送电时，列车调度员发布邻线限速 160 km/h 及以下的调度命令，司机组织相关人员按规定对列车进行防护，并确认列车前、后方接触网无电区长度，向列车调度员报告。列车调度员根据司机有关前、后方接触网无电区长度的报告，确定救援方案，组织救援。

7. 列车碰撞异物

（1）列车运行中碰撞异物影响行车安全时，司机应立即采取停车措施，并向列车调度员（车站值班员）报告碰撞异物地点、碰撞异物情况及停车地点，动车组列车司机还应通知随车机械师。车站值班员报告列车调度员。列车调度员（车站值班员）立即通知本线已进入区间的后续列车停车，不再向该区间放行列车。需下车检查时，列车调度员根据司机请求及时发布邻线限速 160 km/h 及以下的调度命令，司机在接到列车调度员已发布相关调度命令的口头指示后，下车检查（动车组列车为通知随车机械师下车检查）。

（2）动车组列车经检查可以继续运行时，恢复运行（动车组列车按随车机械师的要求运行），司机向列车调度员报告检查情况。如检查未发现异常情况，列车调度员向本线后续首列发布口头指示限速 160 km/h 运行，限速位置按碰撞异物地点前后各 2 km 确定，列车司机应加强瞭望，确认线路和接触网有无异常状态，在通过限速地点后立即向列车调度员报告，列车调度员在得到司机无异常的报告后，组织本线后续列车恢复正常运行；有影响行车异常情况时，列车调度员根据司机报告，扣停后续列车或组织后续列车限速运行，及时通知有关部门按规定上道检查处理。经下车检查确认不能继续运行时应及时请求救援，并按规定进行防护。

（3）动车组列车碰撞异物，异物侵入邻线影响邻线行车安全时，列车调度员（车站值班员）接到报告后，应立即通知邻线尚未经过该地点的列车停车，不再向邻线该区间放行列车，并通知有关部门按规定上道检查处理。

（4）动车组列车碰撞异物情况不明，不能确定是否影响邻线时，列车调度员接到报告后，应立即向邻线尚未经过该地点的首列发布口头指示限速 160 km/h 运行，限速位置按碰撞异物地点前后各 2 km 确定。

邻线首列列车司机应加强瞭望，确认线路和接触网有无异常状态，在通过限速地点后立即向列车调度员报告，列车调度员在得到司机无异常的报告后，组织邻线后续列车正常运行。有影响行车异常情况时，列车调度员根据司机报告，扣停后续列车或组织后续列车限速运行，及时通知有关部门按规定上道检查处理。

（5）工务、电务、供电部门应利用天窗时间对碰撞异物地点前后 2 km 范围内的设备进行重点检查。

【任务检测】

1. 非正常行车时对动车组司机的基本要求有哪些？
2. 动车组停在接触网分相无电区时如何处置？

任务二　动车组灾害天气行车作业办法

【任务描述】

（1）熟悉灾害天气行车的行车作业办法。

（2）掌握灾害天气行车运用的技术设备。

一、灾害天气行车作业原则

（1）遇发生影响行车的设备故障（列车设备故障除外）时，原则上应先处理故障，后组织行车。设备故障暂时无法修复，确需组织行车时，应根据有关行车限制条件组织行车。

（2）遇有暴风雨雪天气或地震，工务、电务、供电等设备管理单位应加强对重点地段和设备的检查。在天窗时间外，检查人员不得进入路肩和桥面范围内，必要时应封锁或限速，并做好防护后再检查。发现影响行车安全时，须及时通知列车调度员限速运行或封锁线路。

二、灾害天气行车组织

1. 大风天气行车

（1）接到自然灾害及异物侵限监测系统风速监测子系统大风报警信息时的处置。

（2）遇风速监测子系统提示大风报警信息时，列车调度员根据报警提示向相关列车发布限速运行的调度命令。对来不及发布调度命令的列车，立即通知司机限速运行。司机接到调度命令或通知后，应立即采取措施。

（3）遇大风天气，当风速监测子系统发出禁止运行的报警信息时，列车调度员应及时关闭有关信号（车站控制时为通知车站值班员关闭有关信号）并通知司机停车。司机接到通知后，应立即采取停车措施。

（4）列车运行途中，遇大风，司机根据情况控制列车运行速度，并报告列车调度员。列车调度员通知后续首列列车司机在该地段注意运行；列车通过该地段后，司机应及时向列车调度员报告。

（5）遇大风天气，列车调度员按风速监测子系统报警提示发布限速调度命令，遇风速不稳或同一地段多处风速报警时，列车调度员可合并设置，按最低限速值发布限速调度命令。

（6）风速监测子系统限速报警解除后，列车调度员应及时取消前发限速调度命令，恢复正常行车。

（7）动车组列车遇大风行车限速的规定如下：

① 在环境风速不大于 15 m/s 时，可以正常速度运行；环境风速不大于 20 m/s 时，运行速度不大于 300 km/h；环境风速不大于 25 m/s 时，运行速度不大于 200 km/h；环境风速不大于 30 m/s 时，运行速度不大于 120 km/h；环境风速大于 30 m/s 时，严禁动车组列车进入风区。

② 在线路中心线距站台边缘为 1 750 mm 的正线、到发线办理动车组列车通过时，在环境风速不大于 15 m/s 情况下，速度不得超过 80 km/h；当环境风速超过 15 m/s 时，动车组运行速度不得超过 45 km/h，并注意运行。

（8）自然灾害及异物侵限监测系统风速监测子系统故障时的处置。

① 列车调度员发现风速监测子系统故障时，应立即通知设备管理单位，并在《行车设备检查登记簿》内登记；设备管理单位发现风速监测子系统故障时，应立即报告列车调度员，并在调度所《行车设备检查登记簿》内登记。

② 风速监测子系统故障期间，故障区段如遇天气预报 7 级及以上大风天气时，工务部门应及时向列车调度员提交天气预报信息，列车调度员按照天气预报的最大风级向相关列车发布限速调度命令。相关限速规定如下：当最大风速达 7 级时，运行速度不大于 300 km/h；8 级、9 级时，运行速度不大于 200 km/h；10 级时，运行速度不大于 120 km/h；11 级及以上时，禁止列车进入风区。限速里程由工务部门根据故障情况以及天气预报信息确定后，通知列车调度员。

2. 雨天行车

（1）接到自然灾害及异物侵限监测系统雨量监测子系统报警信息时的处置。

遇雨量监测子系统提示雨量监测报警信息时，列车调度员根据报警提示向相关列车发布限速运行的调度命令。对来不及发布调度命令的列车，立即通知司机限速运行。司机接到调度命令或通知后，应立即采取措施。

（2）列车通过防洪重点地段时，司机要加强瞭望，并随时采取必要的安全措施。

动车组列车运行中，司机发现积水高于轨面时，应立即停车，根据现场情况与随车机械师共同确认行车条件或请求救援，并立即报告列车调度员（车站值班员），车站值班员报告列车调度员。列车调度员（车站值班员）立即通知已进入区间的后续列车停车（避免停在隧道内），不再向该区间放行列车。

当洪水漫到路肩时，列车应按规定限速运行；遇有落石、倒树等障碍物危及行车安全时，司机应立即停车，排除障碍并确认安全无误后，方可继续运行。

列车遇到线路塌方、道床冲空等危及行车安全的突发情况时，司机应立即采取应急性安全措施，并立刻通知追踪列车、邻线列车及列车调度员（邻近车站）。配备列车防护报警装置的列车应立即使用列车防护报警。

（3）遇有降雨天气，重点防洪地段 1 h 降雨量达到 45 mm 及以上时，列车限速 120 km/h；1 h 降雨量达到 60 mm 及以上时，列车限速 45 km/h。当 1 h 降雨量降至 20 mm 及以下、且持续 30 min 以上时，可逐步解除限速。

列车调度员在得到工务及其他相关专业调度台检查无异常的报告后，及时取消限速或解除线路封锁。

（4）自然灾害及异物侵限监测系统雨量监测子系统故障时的处置。

列车调度员发现雨量监测子系统故障时，应立即通知设备管理单位，并在《行车设备检查登记簿》内登记；设备管理单位发现雨量监测子系统故障时，应立即报告列车调度员，并在调度所《行车设备检查登记簿》内登记。雨量监测子系统故障期间，由工务部门根据降雨情况在调度所《行车设备检查登记簿》内登记限速或封锁。

3. 冰雪天气行车

1）遇冰雪天气时的处置

（1）自然灾害及异物侵限监测系统雪深监测子系统报警雪深值达到警戒值时，列车调度员应根据报警信息和限速提示及时向相关列车发布限速运行的调度命令。对来不及发布调度命令的列车，应立即通知司机限速运行。

未安装雪深监测子系统的区段或雪深监测子系统故障时，工务、电务部门根据降雪情况和需要，在调度所《行车设备检查登记簿》内登记限速申请，并可根据积雪量变化情况，提出提速或进一步限速的申请，列车调度员要及时发布调度命令。

（2）安装动车组运行故障动态图像检测系统（TEDS）的区段，TEDS 监控中心要加强对动车组转向架结冰、积雪等情况的监测分析，发现动车组转向架结冰需限速运行时，应立即将车次及限速要求等按规定报告动车调度员。动车调度员通知列车调度员进行处置。

列车运行过程中，随车机械师发现动车组车底异响、动车组被击打等异常情况需要列车限速时，应立即通知司机限速。司机根据随车机械师的限速要求运行，并向列车调度员报告被击打地点里程，列车调度员不再发布限速调度命令。列车调度员通知动车调度员，提示后续首列列车司机、随车机械师在该被击打地点注意列车运行状态；动车调度员应立即通知前方 TEDS 监测点进行重点监测。列车通过该被击打地点后，司机、随车机械师应及时上报有关运行情况。

（3）降雪时，应根据线路积雪情况及时启用道岔融雪装置。降雪达到中雪及以上，车站道岔转动困难时，为减少道岔扳动，车站可采取固定接发车进路的方式办理接发列车作业，上下行各固定一条接发车进路。始发、终到列车较多的车站执行有困难时，可选择交叉干扰少、道岔位置改变少的几条线路相对固定办理接发车作业。较大客运站尽量停靠便于上水、吸污的线路。

（4）需人工上道除雪时，上、下道应执行登记签认制度。列车调度员应根据相关单位的申请，停止本线接发列车及调车作业，邻线列车限速 160 km/h 及以下。

（5）道床积雪、接触网结冰受电弓取流不畅时，司机应先采取减速措施，并及时向列车调度员汇报，列车调度员通知有关专业调度，专业调度及时通知有关设备管理单位，设备管理单位及时查明情况，按规定提出限速申请，列车调度员及时发布限速调度命令。

（6）供电部门应掌握接触网导线结冰情况，需要列车限速时，应立即登记《行车设备检查登记簿》，向列车调度员提出限速申请。需要接触网除冰时，供电部门提出除冰申请，列车调度员应及时安排接触网除冰车辆上线运行。

遇接触网导线覆冰时，可取消天窗停电作业，并在天窗时间内开行动车组、单机，进行热滑融冰。

（7）随车机械师在始发、折返站发现动车组转向架结冰、受电弓无法升起、动车组被击打等异常情况需要处理时，应及时通知司机，由司机报告列车调度员，列车调度员通知动车调度员，动车调度员根据随车机械师反映情况和车辆运用情况提出更换车底或限速申请，并组织入库动车组除雪融冰。

（8）降雪结束后,提出限速的设备管理单位应做好对有关行车条件的检查确认，及时恢复常速运行。在具备提速条件或限速情况消除时，应向列车调度员提出申请，列车调度员及时发布相关调度命令。雪后恢复常速运行的具体程序和办法由铁路局规定。

（9）列车调度员发现雪深监测子系统故障时，应立即通知设备管理单位，并在《行车设备检查登记簿》内登记；设备管理单位发现雪深监测子系统故障时，应立即报告列车调度员，并在调度所《行车设备检查登记簿》内登记。

2）冰雪天气限速要求

（1）当运行区段降中雪或积雪覆盖轨枕板或道砟面时，无砟轨道区段限速 250 km/h 及以下，有砟轨道区段限速 200 km/h 及以下；当运行区段降大雪、暴雪时，无砟轨道区段限速 200 km/h 及以下，有砟轨道区段限速 160 km/h 及以下。中雪、大雪、暴雪的界定，以气象部门公布或观测为准。

当无砟轨道区段轨枕板积雪厚度 100 mm 以上时，限速 200 km/h 及以下；有砟轨道区段道砟面积雪厚度 50 mm 以上时，限速 160 km/h 及以下。

（2）接触网导线结冰受电弓取流不畅时，限速 160 km/h 及以下。

（3）动车组转向架结冰需要列车限速时，无砟轨道区段限速 250 km/h 及以下，有砟轨道区段限速 200 km/h 及以下。

4. 异物侵限报警

（1）列车调度员接到异物侵限子系统异物侵限灾害报警信息后，应立即通知区间内已进入报警地点及尚未经过报警地点的列车立即停车，不再向该区间放行列车，同时向调度所值班主任（值班副主任）汇报，值班主任（值班副主任）应立即通知设备管理单位赶赴现场检查处理。

（2）在设备管理单位检查人员到达报警点前，列车调度员通过视频监控系统查看现场情况，有异状或不能确认时，必须经设备管理单位检查处理并具备放行列车条件后，方可组织列车运行。无异状时，按下列规定办理：

① 列车调度员确认报警地点次一个闭塞分区空闲后，对区间内已进入报警地点及尚未经过报警地点的列车，口头通知司机逐列恢复运行，以遇到障碍能随时停车的速度（动

车组列车最高不超过 40 km/h，其他列车最高不超过 20 km/h）越过报警点所在闭塞分区，指示后列恢复运行前必须确认前列已完整越过报警点次一个闭塞分区并得到前列无异状的报告。

② 司机在报警点所在闭塞分区通过信号机（区间信号标志牌）前停车等候 2 min 后，以遇到障碍能随时停车的速度（动车组列车最高不超过 40 km/h，其他列车最高不超过 20 km/h）越过该闭塞分区，按次一通过信号机显示（列控车载设备显示）运行。司机应加强瞭望，发现异状立即停车，并报告列车调度员；如无异状，司机确认列车完全越过报警点次一个闭塞分区后应及时报告列车调度员。司机在停车等候的同时，必须与列车调度员联系，如确认前方闭塞分区内有列车时，不得进入。

③ 区间空闲后，在报警点所在闭塞分区红光带取消前，按站间组织行车。

（3）经设备管理单位现场检查处理，列车调度员根据设备管理单位在《行车设备检查登记簿》内登记的行车限制条件组织列车运行。具备条件时，列车调度员根据设备管理单位允许取消报警点所在闭塞分区红光带的登记，使用临时行车按钮取消异物侵限灾害报警红光带。

（4）在故障未修复前，设备管理单位须派人在现场看守，并及时向列车调度员报告现场情况，在报警点所在闭塞分区红光带取消后，列车调度员应下达限速 120 km/h 及以下注意运行的调度命令，限速位置为报警点所在闭塞分区，司机应加强瞭望。

（5）故障修复后，列车调度员将自然灾害及异物侵限监测系统中复原按钮解锁，使系统恢复到正常状态，恢复正常行车组织。

（6）自然灾害及异物侵限监测系统异物侵限子系统一路电网断线报警时的处置。

当双电网的一路电网断线时，异物侵限子系统发出异物侵限传感器故障报警信息，自然灾害及异物侵限监测系统不向列控系统发送灾害报警信息，不影响正常行车。列车调度员接到异物侵限子系统一路电网断线报警信息后，应按正常组织行车，并立即通知设备管理单位检查处理。

（7）自然灾害及异物侵限监测系统异物侵限子系统故障导致系统不能反映现场情况时的处置。

① 列车调度员发现异物侵限子系统故障导致系统不能反映现场情况时，应立即通知设备管理单位，并在《行车设备检查登记簿》内登记；设备管理单位发现异物侵限子系统故障时，应立即报告列车调度员，并在调度所《行车设备检查登记簿》内登记。

② 异物侵限子系统故障未修复前，设备管理单位须派人在现场看守，并及时向列车调度员报告现场情况，列车调度员应下达限速 120 km/h 及以下注意运行的调度命令，限速位置为监测点所在闭塞分区，司机应加强瞭望。遇有异物侵限时，看守人员应立即通知列车调度员，列车调度员呼叫列车停车。

③ 在看守人员未到达异物侵限监测点前，列车调度员应下达限速 120 km/h 及以下（异

物侵限监测点为隧道口时，限速 40 km/h 及以下）注意运行的调度命令，限速位置为监测点所在闭塞分区，司机在该处注意运行。

5. 地震监测报警

列车调度员接到地震监测子系统地震监控报警信息或接到现场地震报告后，应立即关闭有关信号（车站控制时为通知车站值班员关闭有关信号），通知相关列车停车。列车司机组织列车乘务人员根据现场实际情况，采取应急处置措施。

列车调度员立即报告调度所值班主任（值班副主任），通知工务、电务、供电、通信、房建等设备管理单位检查。设备管理单位检查处理后，根据设备管理单位登记的行车限制条件组织行车。

6. 天气恶劣难以辨认信号行车

（1）接到天气恶劣报告时的处置。

遇天气恶劣，信号机显示距离不足 200 m 时，司机或车站值班员须立即报告列车调度员。列车按地面信号显示运行时，列车调度员应及时发布调度命令，改按天气恶劣难以辨认信号的办法行车。

（2）天气恶劣难以辨认信号行车办法：

① 列车按机车信号的显示运行。当接近地面信号机时，司机应确认地面信号，遇地面信号与机车信号显示不一致时，应立即采取减速或停车措施。

② 当无法辨认出站（进路）信号机显示时，在列车具备发车条件后，司机凭机车信号的显示起动列车，在确认出站（进路）信号机显示正确后，再行加速。

③ 天气转好时，应及时报告列车调度员发布调度命令，恢复正常行车。

【任务检测】

1. 灾害天气行车作业办法？
2. 动车组大风天气限速要求？
3. 灾害天气行车限速规定？
4. 接到地震监测预警时的行车组织办法？
5. 天气恶劣难以辨认信号时的行车办法？

任务三　动车组突发事件的应急处理办法

【任务描述】

（1）掌握动车组发生各种突发事件的处理办法。

（2）熟悉动车组限速运行的条件。

一、动车组故障及处置

（1）动车组运行中出现故障时司机应按车载信息监控装置的提示，按步骤及时处理；需要由随车机械师配合处理时，司机应通知随车机械师。经处置确认无法正常运行时，司机应按车载信息监控装置的提示和随车机械师的要求，选择维持运行或停车等方式，并使用列车无线调度通信设备报告列车调度员或车站值班员。

（2）动车组在区间被迫停车时随车机械师、客运乘务组均应听从动车组司机指挥，处理有关行车、列车防护和事故救援等事宜。

（3）动车组被救援时过渡车钩、专用风管和电气连接线的连接和分解由随车机械师负责，动车组司机配合。具备升弓供电条件的，允许动车组升弓供电。

（4）在 CTCS-2 级区段与 CTCS-0/1 级区段级间自动转换失败时，司机应立即向车站值班员、列车调度员报告，并按下述规定办理：

①若由 CTCS-2 级向 CTCS-0/1 级运行，停车手动转换。

②若由 CTCS-0/1 级向 CTCS-2 级运行，可维持按 LKJ 方式继续运行。

（5）列控车载设备发生故障且动车信号显示不正常时，司机应将列控车载设备转入隔离模式，按照动车信号故障办理。

（6）动车组司机或设备维护单位人员发现应答器故障时应及时报告邻近车站值班员，车站值班员应及时向列车调度员报告。

二、在下列情况下动车组限速运行

（1）动车组制动系统故障切除 25%制动力时，限速 160 km/h 运行；切除 50%制动力时，限速 120 km/h 运行。

（2）空气弹簧故障时，CRH2/CRH380A/AL 型动车组限速 120 km/h，其余车型限速 160 km/h。

（3）车窗玻璃破损导致车厢密封失效时，限速 160 km/h 运行。

三、热备动车组出动

1. 热备动车组的启用时机

动车组故障无法及时修复时，应及时启用热备动车组。启用备用动车组时首先考虑使用热备动车组。无热备动车组或热备动车组定员少于故障动车组实际人数时，应调整在线运行动车组交路，有条件时，利用其他动车组担当救援车底。上述措施无法实现时，就近利用空闲普通客车底担当救援车底。

2. 热备动车组的出动

热备动车组预备司机必须满足担当各线动车组任务配备，在机务段机车调度室出勤时，按照热备动车组担当各线任务办理出勤（包括传达调度命令和 IC 卡）。到动车所调度室报到后，在距动车组停留地点较近的行车公寓或机务段（动车组运用所）候班，充分休息，保证叫班后随时出乘担当任务。热备动车组出动救援跨局动车组时，由铁路总公司调度统一指挥。

（1）铁路总公司运输局调度部调度处动车组调度员应立即报告值班处长、调度处长、调度部主任（副主任），并根据需要通知中国铁路总公司车辆、机务、供电、电务调度；由中国铁路总公司车辆、机务、供电、电务调度分别通知客车处长、机车运用处长、供电处长、信号处长。

（2）铁路总公司运输局调度部调度处值班处长接到应急救援指挥中心领导热备动车组出动的指示后，应立即布置动车组调度台向有关铁路局下达热备动车组出动及开行的调度命令。

（3）热备动车组配属局调度所接到动车组出动命令后，立即（3 min 内）向有关单位下达热备动车组出动的调度命令，有关单位必须在接令后 10 min 内完成热备动车组的调车、整备、司乘人员配备等各项工作，具备发车条件。热备动车组救援出动时本务司机、随车机械师、客运乘务由配属局担当。

（4）热备动车组和预备司机担当非本局动车组担当区段的车次时，由原担当铁路局动车组司机担当，车型不符时，由预备司机担当，原担当任务铁路局司机负责带道，并负责提供动车组司机携带列车时刻表。

（5）对担当换乘任务的动车组列车应优先放行，确保及时到位及返回归位。在站内组织旅客换乘时，应尽量安排在同一站台的两个站台面进行。在区间组织旅客换乘时，列车调度员组织担当换乘任务的动车组列车进入邻线指定位置停车。担当换乘任务的列车到达邻线指定位置停妥后，司机向列车调度员报告。列车调度员通过申请换乘的列车司机通知列车长组织旅客换乘。担当换乘任务的列车长确认旅客换乘完毕后通知司机，司机得到列车长通知，确认车门关闭，具备开车条件后起动列车，并向列车调度员报告。

（6）铁路局应细化热备动车组备用及出动管理办法，明确热备动车组、人员、备品、日常管理和出动各项作业时限标准，确保设备完好和准时出动。

3. 热备动车组运行及返回归位

（1）热备动车组出动在始发站至接续站间运行及返回归位车次在所接续的列车车次前加“R”，行车用语为：“热备动车组××（次）”，行车有关事项按动车组办理。接续后的车次仍使用原车次。

（2）非热备动车组车底出动在始发站至接续站间运行及返回归位车次应根据客车底车型，在所接续的列车车次前加“T”或“K”，行车用语为：“特快动车组××（次）”、“快速动车组××（次）”。

（3）对热备动车组和临时替换故障动车组的客车底应优先放行，确保及时到位及返回归位。

四、动车组故障情况下旅客的组织

1. 动车组因故障组织旅客换乘

（1）使用热备动车组组织旅客换乘时，车站应加强站车组织，按规定做好换乘旅客的饮食供应和后勤服务工作，两列换乘车底应尽量安排在同一站台方便旅客换乘。此时，站段应急领导小组应立即赶赴现场，必要时，铁路局应急领导小组成员应赶赴现场组织指挥。

（2）使用非动车组热备车底替换动车组开行旅客列车时，车次应当相对固定（原则上将原动车组车次改为特快或快速旅客列车车次），开车命令必须在开车 1 h 前下达，跨局旅客列车由中国铁路总公司、局管内由铁路局客运调度下达停运动车组，开行旅客列车的调度命令。客调命令中须明确停运动车组列车车次、车底所属局、开行车次、编组顺位、车种、型号、定员、停车站到开时刻、乘务担当单位等。

（3）车站接到热备车开车命令后，应按票价差备足零款，指定专人到指定地点组织引导旅客收回动车组旅客原票，换发新票并退还票价差额。旅客要求改乘其他列车时，车站应及时办理改签手续，并尽可能地改签为有席位车票。退票、改签不收手续费。

（4）换乘时，站车要认真组织验票，严禁持其他车次车票的旅客上车，持有停运动车组列车车票的旅客，必须换新票后方可上车。

2. 动车组因故障晚点和旅客滞留

（1）铁路局调度所应按规定做好动车组晚点信息的预报和通报工作。

（2）动车组在始发站晚点 30 min 以上时，车站应及时通知旅客，旅客在始发站乘车前要求退票或改签时，车站应及时办理退票或改签；始发站铁路局客运处或客运段须派科长或车队长级干部添乘，组织列车乘务组做好服务、解释和安抚旅客工作。

（3）动车组途中晚点时，列车长要及时联系铁路局客运调度，了解晚点原因等，报告车内情况和请求协助解决的问题，组织乘务员积极主动做好服务。晚点 30 min 以上时，应做好向旅客致歉、解释工作。乘警应与列车长密切配合，经常巡视车厢，维持好车内治安秩序。

（4）接到动车组终到晚点 30 min 及以上的通知后，车站站长、派出所所长须带领客运、公安有关人员到站台接车，组织旅客下车出站，并做好向旅客致歉、解释工作。到站是铁路局所在地的，铁路局客运处、铁路公安局（处）领导要到站台接车，帮助指导车站做好应急处置工作。

（5）发生旅客以滞留列车的方式向铁路要求晚点或空调故障赔偿时，站车工作人员应当以说服劝解、诚恳道歉为主，耐心细致地做好解释和相关法律法规的宣传工作，稳定情绪、化解怨气，力争取得旅客的理解和配合。

（6）公安部门要积极配合客运部门，认真开展滞留旅客的说服劝离工作，争取理解与支持。同时，要向旅客宣讲法律知识，告知旅客可以通过其他合法渠道和方式维护其合法权益，劝说旅客听从车站工作人员的安排到指定地点协商解决，并协助车站工作人员引导旅客下车。公安部门在协助劝离过程中，严禁携带枪支。

客运部门在宣传和说服旅客离开车厢时，现场应有公安人员维持秩序；经反复工作劝离无效时，公安人员应宣布原铁道部、公安部《关于维护铁路运输秩序保证列车正常运行的通告》，并组织足够的公开警力，对拒不下车的人员依法采取措施带离车厢。对煽动旅客滞留车厢和扰乱列车治安、破坏铁路运输秩序、用暴力手段对抗执法的个别人员，要认真调查取证，依法追究其法律责任。劝阻中要依法依规，有理有节，文明执法。

3. 空调故障的应急处理

（1）空调失效超过 20 min 不能恢复但列车能够正常运行时，列车长可视情况通知司机向列车调度员提出在前方最近客运站停车的请求，列车调度员安排列车在前方最近客运站停车。列车在停车站安装好防护网、打开部分车门后，列车调度员根据司机的报告，向司机（救援时还包括救援司机）及沿途各站发布打开车门限速 60 km/h（通过邻靠高站台的线路时限速 40 km/h）运行的调度命令。

（2）列车因故停车不能维持运行且空调失效超过 20 min 不能恢复时，列车长应及时与司机、随车机械师沟通，视情况做出打开车门决定，并通知司机转报列车调度员。

（3）安装防护网、打开车门由列车长组织列车乘务员进行，司机、随车机械师配合。防护网的安装需在列车停车状态下进行，安装位置为运行方向左侧(非会车侧)车门处。防护网安装完毕，打开车门后，由列车长组织列车工作人员值守，直到车门关闭。列车长确认防护网安装牢固、看护到位后报告司机。

（4）需要组织旅客下车或换乘其他列车时，应在车站站台进行。必须在站内不邻靠站台的线路或区间组织旅客下车或换乘时，需经铁路局主管运输副局长（总调度长）批准。

五、动车组设备故障的应急处置

1. 动车组车辆设备发生故障

（1）动车组到站停稳后，遇自动开关门装置故障时，司机应及时通知列车长、随车机械师，改为手动开关门。

（2）遇通风口冒烟时，司机根据情况立即停车或及时报告列车调度员安排在最近前方站停车检查防尘网有无异物。

（3）当轴承温度超过温度报警时，立即停车请求处理，并用列车无线调度通信设备呼叫两端站或列车调度员，报告停车原因和停车位置。随车机械师下车检查故障车轴，根据实测轴温和检查情况向司机报告，司机向列车调度员提出限速运行请求，列车调度员根据司机请求，发布限速运行命令。

（4）根据随车机械师要求，对轮对踏面缺陷停车检查时，司机应及时转报列车调度员，要求前方站停车检查。轮对踏面缺损超出限度时，列车调度员根据司机请求，发布限速运行命令。

（5）当得到轮对因齿轮箱、连接轴卡滞造成抱死运行的报告时，司机应立即停车，并指派随车机械师下车检查处理，无法消除抱死故障时，及时请求救援。

（6）运行中走行部、风挡连接部有异声、异味、异状需要停车检查时，随车机械师根据具体情况向司机报告，并提出停车请求。司机根据随车机械师报告的故障情况立即停车或转报列车调度员，请求前方站停车检查。经停车检查确认无碍或应急处理后方可继续运行。

（7）当得到空气弹簧发生故障的报告时，列车调度员应发布限速 160 km/h 运行的调度命令。

（8）制动系统故障时，列车调度员应按照下列要求发布调度命令：

① 基础制动装置故障抱死车轮不缓解时，司机应立即停车，用列车无线调度通信设备呼叫两端站、追踪列车、列车调度员，报告停车原因和停车位置。随车机械师下车检查处理，切除本车制动运行。

② 动车组制动系统故障切除 25%制动力时，限速 160 km/h 运行；切除 50%制动力时，限速 120 km/h 运行。

（9）当得到车窗玻璃破损导致车厢密封失效报告时，列车调度员应发布限速 160 km/h 运行的调度命令。

2. 接触网停电

（1）动车组运行遇接触网停电时，司机应立即停车并降弓，报告列车调度员（车站值班员）停车原因及停车位置，通知随车机械师（车辆乘务员）、列车长，车站值班员报告列车调度员。供电调度员发现接触网停电时，应立即确认停电范围并通知列车调度员。

（2）列车调度员（车站值班员）接到接触网停电的报告后，应立即扣停未进入停电区域的相关列车，对已进入停电区域的列车应通知司机停车。列车调度员并立即通知供电调度员确认停电范围，通知供电部门检查处理，在 CTC 上设置停电标识。

（3）电力机车牵引的旅客列车因接触网停电在区间停车后，司机应采取保压措施，长时间停车风压不足时，司机通知车辆乘务员组织客运乘务组拧紧全列人力制动机。

（4）接触网跳闸重合或送电成功，原因不明时，供电调度员应立即将接触网跳闸情况、故障标定装置指示地点的里程及限速要求通知列车调度员。列车调度员立即向尚未经过该地点的本线及邻线首列列车发布口头指示限速 80 km/h 注意运行，限速位置原则上按故障标定装置指示地点前后各 2 km 确定。司机应注意观察接触网设备状态，发现影响行车异常情况时应立即停车并向列车调度员报告，列车调度员立即通知尚未经过异常地点的后续列车停车，不得再向该区间放行列车，并立即通知供电部门检查处理，列车调度员按供电部门登记的行车限制条件组织行车；无异常时，司机在通过限速地点后立即向列车调度员报告。列车调度员根据本线司机确认本线无异常的报告，组织本线后续列车正常运行，根据邻线司机确认邻线无异常的报告，组织邻线后续列车正常运行。

（5）供电调度员应立即组织供电人员登乘本线或邻线列车巡视检查设备。供电人员根据需要及时向列车调度员提出利用动车组列车运送人员处理故障的申请，列车调度员应及时安排。

3. 影响动车组运行的信号、联锁、闭塞设备

1）闭塞设备发生故障

（1）在 CTCS-2 级区段，遇基本闭塞法停用按电话闭塞法行车时，列车调度员应布置动车组停车，并向司机发布调度命令将列控车载设备方式控车转入隔离模式，按 LKJ 方式行车。

（2）在按电话闭塞法行车的终止站，列车调度员应布置动车组停车，并向司机发布调度命令将隔离模式退出，转换为列控车载设备方式控车。

（3）若按电话闭塞法行车的终止站且前方交路皆为 CTCS-0 级区段时，动车组不需停车，列车调度员不再发布调度命令。待动车组按图定停车后，司机应及时将列控车载设备主机隔离开关置于“正常”位。

2）区间通过信号机故障

动车组在区间运行，列控车载设备显示停车信号时，列车必须立即停车，司机应使用列车无线调度通信设备通知随车机械师。列车停车等候 2 min，列控车载设备仍未收到允许运行的信号时，司机将列控车载设备转入目视行车模式，列车以遇到阻碍能随时停车的速度继续运行，最高速度不超过 20 km/h，直到列控车载设备收到允许运行信号，按列控车载设备显示运行。在停车等候的同时，必须与列车调度员、车站值班员联系，如确认前方闭塞分区内有列车时，不得进入。

3）出站（发车进路）信号机故障

在 CTCS-2 级区段，出站（发车进路）信号机故障时，动车组的行车凭证为绿色许可证，人工选择列控车载设备目视行车模式运行；当收到允许运行的信号时，按列控车载设备显示运行。

4）进站（接车进路）信号机故障（机械引导）

列控车载设备接收到的轨道电路信息为 HB 码时，越过进站信号机后，自动转入引导

模式运行。

5）车站电码化故障

遇车站电码化故障或其他原因，造成动车组在进站、出站、进路信号机前收不到允许行车的信息时，应立即停车。动车组停车后，司机向车站值班员和列车调度员报告，按调度命令转入目视行车模式运行；当列控车载设备收到允许运行的信号时，按列控车载设备显示运行。

4. 自动过分相地面设备故障

（1）司机发现不能自动过分相时，应立即报告列车调度员（车站值班员），列车调度员（车站值班员）接到报告后，通知后续列车注意运行，通知设备管理单位检查处理；设备管理单位发现自动过分相地面设备故障时，应立即报告列车调度员（车站值班员）。

（2）车载自动过分相装置故障修复前，列车调度员（车站值班员）根据设备管理单位的登记，通知司机采用手动过分相。动车组运行至过分相绝缘区前，司机应提前确认升起受电弓的车号，运行至电分相绝缘区时，要集中精力，加强瞭望，及时切除牵引力并“断电”，确认网压上升并稳定后再“合电”。

（3）车站值班员得到自动过分相“感应器装置”故障通知后，应及时通知临近的动车组（电力机车牵引的列车）并向列车调度员报告。列车调度员应立即使用列车无线调度通信设备向动车组（电力机车牵引的列车）司机、车站按规定发布自动过分相系统停用的调度命令，并向有关设备管理单位和公安机关通报。自动过分相“感应器装置”修复后，列车调度员应及时发布自动过分相系统恢复使用的调度命令，恢复正常行车组织。

5. 运行途中自动降弓

（1）列车在运行途中，因不明原因降弓，司机应立即切断主断路器并停车，同时查看降弓地点公里标，向列车调度员(车站值班员)报告，车站值班员报告列车调度员。列车调度员（车站值班员）应立即通知区间内后续列车停车，不再向该区间放行列车，列车调度员将降弓情况转报供电调度员。动车组列车随车机械师应根据故障信息记录，及时向司机反馈故障发生时间等信息，由司机报告列车调度员，列车调度员及时转报供电调度员。

（2）列车调度员根据司机（动车组列车为随车机械师通过司机提出的）下车检查或登顶作业的请求，发布邻线列车限速 160 km/h 及以下调度命令；需登顶作业时，列车调度员还应通知该供电臂内的列车停车并降弓，与供电调度员办理接触网停电手续，得到供电调度员接触网已停电的通知后，发布准许登顶作业的调度命令。

（3）司机在接到邻线列车限速 160 km/h 及以下调度命令已发布的口头指示后，下车检查（动车组列车为司机通知随车机械师下车检查）。司机根据准许登顶作业的调度命令和邻线列车限速 160 km/h 及以下调度命令已发布的口头指示，方可登顶作业（动车组列车为司机通知随车机械师登顶作业）。

（4）经检查处理，列车恢复运行后，司机应立即报告列车调度员，列车调度员应立即向本线尚未经过该地点的首列列车发布口头指示限速 80 km/h 注意运行，限速位置原则上按司机汇报故障地点前后各 2 km 确定。司机应注意观察接触网设备状态，发现影响行车异常情况时应立即停车并向列车调度员报告，列车调度员立即通知尚未经过异常地点的后续列车停车，不再向该区间放行列车，并立即通知供电部门检查处理，列车调度员按供电部门登记的行车限制条件组织行车。无异常时，司机在通过限速地点后立即向列车调度员报告，列车调度员根据司机确认无异常的报告组织后续列车正常运行。

（5）供电调度员接到报告后，应立即组织供电人员登乘本线或邻线列车巡视检查设备。供电人员根据需要及时向列车调度员提出利用动车组列车运送人员处理故障的申请，列车调度员应及时安排。

【任务检测】

1. 动车组限速运行的条件是什么？
2. 热备动车组出动的规定有哪些？
3. 动车组发生故障情况下如何组织旅客？
4. 动车组车辆设备发生故障时怎么办？
5. 动车组列控车载设备故障时怎么办？
6. 动车组列控地面设备故障时怎么办

项目四　动车组随车机械师作业规程

【思政课堂】与高铁一起奔跑的“动车医生”——董宏涛

当你坐在平稳的列车上观赏沿途的风景时，当你抵达目的地奔向等候已久的亲人时，你是否知道有这样一群人默默守护着这份甜蜜与幸福，他们叫作“动车组机械师”。董宏涛就是其中的一员，26 年磨一剑，一朝试锋芒。不管是上车值乘还是下车检修，他都在和动车疑难杂症死磕！

董宏涛，西安动车段调度科应急台动车组机械师、“宏涛动车难症诊疗组”“董宏涛劳模创新工作室”负责人。入路 26 年来，他先后获得陕西省技术状元、全路技术能手、火车头奖章、全路劳动模范、铁路工匠等荣誉。回顾 26 年铁路生涯，不会“一心二用”的董宏涛用“笨”字调侃自己，但他却用实际行动诠释着动车组安全“守护者”的责任与担当，以强烈的事业心和责任感彰显了一名共产党员的坚定信念，一个动车组机械师的职业追求。

2015 年至 2017 年，董宏涛团队研发的多功能测量尺、动车组救援用 32 芯线电气连接器插头拆装专用工具、受电弓气管圆螺母快速安装扭矩扳手等成果获得 5 项国家专利。作为带头人董宏涛的诊疗组成立以来，先后破解难题 300 余件排查故障近 2000 件。2015 年应急台成立后，处理了 200 余趟动车组运行途中的突发情况，为随车机械师提供了近千次技术支持。一种执着的信念，一名守护者的赤胆忠心，如董宏涛守卫的动车组，只要在路上奔跑唯一的执念，就是奋勇向前、当好先行。

【项目描述】

通过本项目学习动车组随车机械师的岗位职责，熟知动车组随车工具与备品项目和数量；能够按照标准完成随车机械师一次往返作业，并填写有关记录；能够按照车载信息系统提示应急处理动车组突发故障。

任务一　动车组随车机械师作业标准

【任务描述】

（1）熟知动车组随车机械师岗位职责及要求。

（2）能够按照动车组随车机械师一次往返作业标准进行作业。

一、动车组随车机械师岗位职责

作为一名随车机械师主要担负动车组运行(运营、试验、接送等)随车乘务工作，负责保证动车组安全的运行状态，维护正常的车内硬件环境，掌握和传递动车组设备的动态运行信息，应急处理和维修运行中的设备故障，对动车组上部设施进行日常状态检查和质量交接。具体职责如下：

1. 监控动车组运行技术状态

（1）运行中在乘务（监控）室通过车载信息系统监控动车组运行及设备工作状态。

（2）在运行中巡视检查车辆设备时，发现问题正确判断、果断处理。

（3）始发和折返站进行技术检查作业。

（4）及时准确向上级部门反映动车组故障情况和异常环境情况，危及行车安全时可直接向司机提出限速或停车要求。

2. 管理和操作动车组设备

（1）按规定操作动车组设备设施。

（2）配合客运部门，控制车内空调换气装置，设置调节空调及换气装置运行模式；控制车内客室照明，设置调节照明工况；按规定开启旅客信息系统和车次设定信息。

（3）指导客运服务人员正确使用车内设备。

（4）在出乘作业时，按动车组定置管理图对动车组的车载工具、材料、行车备品、安全防护用品存放的位置进行检查，不得私自移动，发现有缺少、损坏、到期（需要校验）的备品及时上报所属车间，车间组织补齐、更换、校验。

3. 应急处理途中突发故障

（1）运行中发生突发故障时，积极进行应急处理。发现或接到车辆设备故障通知后，应及时判明故障，按《动车组途中应急故障处理手册》及有关规定进行处置；非正常运行或停车时，随车机械师立即向故障发生地所在集团公司动车调度员报告。

（2）动车组突发故障分为三类：属司机独立处置的，需加强与司机联系，了解故障处理情况；属与司机协作处置的，在司机指挥下，共同处理；属随车机械师独立处置的，处理完成后及时将情况和运行要求通报司机。

（3）发现危及行车安全的故障或其他紧急情况时，随车机械师可使用紧急制动装置停车或通知司机采取停车措施。动车组发生紧急制动开车后，加强动车组巡视检查，注意监听轮对运行状态。

（4）动车组随车机械师途中故障应急处置，区间超过 20min、站内超过 30min，仍无法判明故障原因或无法处置不能继续运行时，通知司机请求救援。请求救援后，动车组随车机械师须立即向发生地所在集团公司动车调度员报告，服从发生所在地集团公司调度的指挥，按要求做好救援准备或故障应急处置工作。

（5）遇冰雪恶劣天气，列车运行过程中，随车机械师发现动车组车底异响、动车组被击打等情况需要限速时，应立即通知司机限速。

4. 信息报告

（1）动车组列车因动车组故障非正常运行或停车时，随车机械师及时将信息向事发地有调度指挥权的集团公司动车调度报告，并按照规定程序及时向动车段调度汇报。

（2）动车组因故障停车，应认真检查确认动车组各部状态，不能正常运行时应及时处理，需限速运行或请求救援的，立即向司机报告，并按规定汇报。

（3）做好与动车组司机、客运出乘人员信息的沟通。

5. 动车组在外存放出、退乘交接

（1）动车组入外所（存放点）后，到调度室（值班室）交接随车钥匙、CRH 型动车组随车机械师乘务日志、动车组故障交接记录单。

（2）动车组出库前 2 小时，随车机械师到当地车间值班室（存放点值班室）接受酒精含量测试，在《随车机械师出退乘记录表》上登记，并按规定办理交接。

（3）随车机械师在存放点按照接车作业要求对动车组进行检查，重点是过夜作业内容的复查，对存在的问题及时向当地车间值班室（存放点值班室）通报，及时进行处理，并做好记录。

（4）负责检查外地存放动车组的保温、卸污等工作是否进行、作业质量是否合格，存在问题时及时向所在地车间值班室和本属车间值班室报告。

6. 承担部分行车组织职能

（1）动车组在出库前，由随车机械师通知司机通过监控屏远程切除当日不用的受电弓，再升当日所用受电弓。动车组入库后，由随车机械师通知司机通过监控屏远程恢复切除的受电弓。

（2）为保证同一动车组受电弓使用时间均衡，受电弓升弓可按照单日升前弓，双日升后弓的原则（异地过夜动车组在异地出库时应选用前日未使用的受电弓）。

（3）运行中因动车组故障或其他原因在区间被迫停车时，加强与司机联系，掌握情况，及时向所在地集团公司动车调度员报告，并在司机指挥下，做好行车及安全防护相关工作。

（4）动车组被救援时，负责过渡车钩和专用风管的拆装、列车机车与动车组过渡车钩的连结与摘解、软管摘结、电气连接线的连接与摘解，引导救援联挂，联挂状态确认，司机配合。

7. 冬季受电弓操作

（1）当外温低于 -5 °C，在动车所内、存放场、始发站、折返站，动车组均不进行换弓操作，当天运行使用同一受电弓。

（2）动车组出现受电弓不能升起、自动降弓、列车无网压等故障，按照《动车组途中应急故障处理手册》操作，根据情况进行换弓操作。

二、动车组随车机械师岗位管理

因动车组随车机械师在动车运行期间责任重大，为确保其工作规范，动车段设置动车组乘务管理机构对随车机械师的出乘、交接、退乘、作业等工作进行检查、监督、管理。具体要求如下：

（1）动车组随车机械师须持证上岗；工作时须佩戴胸牌（如图 4-1 所示），凭胸牌及工作证拍发铁路电报、在公寓或招待所食宿、进出车站。

图 4-1　动车组随车机械师胸牌样式

（2）动车段要统一规范《CRH 型动车组随车机械师乘务日志》和《动车组故障交接记录单》填写的标准，字迹要工整，项目要完整，内容要具体。动车段要根据实际明确乘务指导、管理乘务工作的主任（所长）、副主任（副所长）检查《CRH 型动车组随车机械师乘务日志》的周期频次并签字。

（3）随车机械师值乘过程中发生的异常信息通过电话及时准确反馈。反馈信息应包含以下内容：

1）动车组非正常停车、晚发晚到信息。

2）影响动车组设备功能和运行安全的设备故障。

3）运行途中车内车外突发、重大事件。

4）动车组运行区段的恶劣天气（风、雪、雨）状态及限速运行信息。

5）总公司、集团公司有关领导上车添乘检查工作情况。

（4）随车机械师乘务工作质量要求

1）严格执行铁路技术管理规程、铁路交通事故调查处理规则、铁路交通事故应急救援规则、铁路动车组运用维修规则、CRH 型动车组途中应急故障处理手册等规章制度的规定和要求。

2）出乘前应充分休息，确保精力充沛。出乘时按规定着装并携带工具，认真听取、记录值班员及各级领导传达部署的工作要求，严格执行作业标准，对值乘动车组进行全面技术检查，确保达到出库质量标准。

3）严格按规定监控动车组运行状态，认真按作业标准巡视车厢，及时准确地反馈运行途中动车组安全和故障信息。

4）对动车组故障能够准确判断、快速处理，确保动车组设备设施正常使用。对动车组运行中出现的突发故障及时正确地进行应急处理，保证动车组运行安全。

5）加强动车组上部设施监管工作，发现损坏和不正确使用动车组设备设施的情况立即制止。

6）各种报表、台账填写应及时、准确、不错、不漏。

7）自觉遵守劳动安全的有关规定，防止自身和他人受到伤害。

8）无责任事故，无违章违纪。

三、动车组随车机械师一次出乘作业标准

1. 出　乘

（1）出乘前，随车机械师应充分休息，严禁饮酒。

（2）出乘时，随车机械师应按规定着装，佩戴胸卡并携带相应证件及随身工具，到动车所调度室（存放点值班室）接受酒精测试，按规定领取动车组固定服务设施状态检查记录、动车组出所质量联检记录单、动车组随车机械师乘务日志、动车组故障交接记录单、随车钥匙、GSM-R 手持终端、无线对讲设备等，听取命令、任务、要求及注意事项，了解动车组检修、故障处理及前次运行情况。

2. 接车作业

（1）作业前，按规定设置安全防护措施。

（2）检查确认动车组头罩锁闭到位、重联端车钩连接状态良好，两侧裙板及盖板锁闭到位、空气弹簧无漏风、车端连接管线无脱落。

（3）作业完毕，撤除安全防护措施。

（4）动车组供电后，开启空调、照明、旅客信息系统等，确认工作状态。

（5）检查随车工具、材料及行车备品。

（6）巡视动车组运转情况，确认非操纵端司机室门窗锁闭，发现异常及时处置。

（7）确认重点故障处置情况。

3. 始发作业

（1）到达车站后，在站台侧检查确认侧门、车外显示器、受电弓状态良好。

（2）到乘务（监控）室，与列车长交接动车组固定服务设施状态检查记录，监视车载信息系统。

（3）始发时，在司机室监控动车组运行情况。

4. 途中作业

（1）发车后，巡视检查车内主要服务设施技术状态，监视列车运行状态。

（2）运行途中，必须按规定巡视，并在乘务（监控）室监控列车运行及设备状况，发

现故障及报警时，按规定程序处置，并做好记录。

（3）动车组司机继乘前，动车组随车机械师应向动车组司机了解运行情况。动车组司机继乘后，与接班司机交接司机室驾驶操纵设备技术状态并在动车组故障交接记录单上签认。

5. 折返站作业

（1）列车到站前，动车组随车机械师到司机室了解运行情况并做好记录。

（2）列车到站后，在站台侧检查确认侧门、车外显示器、受电弓状态良好。

6. 换乘作业

（1）继乘动车组随车机械师提前 15 min 到换乘站接车。

（2）列车到达换乘站前，退乘动车组随车机械师填写 CRH 型动车组随车机械师乘务日志、动车组故障交接记录单，整理交接物品。

① 折返站换乘时，继乘动车组随车机械师在折返始发端立岗接车，监听列车运行声音，检查受电弓等可见部位状态，列车停稳后到乘务（监控）室与退乘动车组随车机械师办理出勤时领取的物品及列车运行状态交接。

② 通过站换乘时，继乘动车组随车机械师立岗接车，继、退乘动车组随车机械师在乘务（监控）室办理出勤时领取的物品及列车运行状态交接。

（3）交接后退乘动车组随车机械师在站台侧立岗送车。

（4）折返站换乘后、始发前，继乘动车组随车机械师到乘务（监控）室监视车载信息系统，等待发车。

（5）折返站换乘作业过程中遇有动车组故障需要应急处理时，退、继乘动车组随车机械师要协同配合，共同处理。

7. 终到作业

（1）列车到站前，向动车组司机了解运行情况并做好记录。

（2）列车到站后，会同列车长巡视车厢，办理车内固定服务设施状态交接并填写动车组固定服务设施状态检查记录，填写 CRH 型动车组随车机械师乘务日志，整理交接物品。

（3）重点故障提前预报动车所，在乘务（监控）室等待随车进入动车所。

（4）进入动车所途中，通过车载信息系统监控动车组运行状态。

（5）进入本动车所后，按规定接受酒精测试，交接随车钥匙及相应记录单。不入本所时，按所在地集团公司有关管理办法执行。

8. 退　勤

（1）入库停稳后与动车组司机做好技术状态交接。

（2）入本所后，随车机械师到动车所调度室报告运行情况，签认交接出乘日志，交接重点故障，交还随车移动电话、动车组相关钥匙、乘务日志等。

四、动车组随车机械师值乘工作用语

1. 工作联系用语

（1）动车组正常运行中，随车机械师需进入主控端司机室时，联系用语如下：

机械师：×××次司机，机械师进行司机室巡视。

（2）因供电、工务、通信、信号等设备故障，动车组在区间或车站站内临时停车后，司机立即报告列车调度员停车原因。使用手持电台通知列车长及随车机械师停车原因，联系用语如下：

司　机：×××次列车长、机械师，因×××故障或原因造成列车区间或站内停车。

列车长：×××次列车长明白。

机械师：×××次机械师明白。

（3）因发生动车组设备故障，在区间或车站站内临时停车后，司机立即报告列车调度员停车原因。并根据车辆状态显示屏报出的故障信息，使用手持电台通知列车长及随车机械师停车原因和故障信息，联系用语如下：

司　机：×××次列车长、机械师，因×××故障造成列车区间（或站内）停车，请机械师查找处理。

列车长：×××次列车长明白。

机械师：×××次机械师明白，立即处置。

（4）设备故障处置完毕或采取非正常行车时，司机报告列车调度员具备开车条件后，司机使用手持电台通知列车长及随车机械师具备开车条件，联系用语如下：

司　机：×××次列车长、机械师，具备开车条件。

列车长：×××次列车长明白。

机械师：×××次机械师明白。

（5）动车组故障处理完毕后，机械师使用手持电台通知司机故障处理完毕（或无法处理请求救援），司机将情况汇报列车调度员，联系用语如下：

机械师：×××次司机，×××故障处理完毕具备开车条件（或故障无法修复请求救援）。

司　机：×××次司机明白。

（6）动车组营业站滞留期间临时开门时，列车长使用手持电台通知机械师和司机。司机并立即报告列车调度员或车站值班员。联系用语如下：

列车长：×××次机械师、司机，需开启×车×位车门。

机械师：×××次机械师明白。

司　机：×××次司机明白。

（7）动车组营业站滞留期间相关作业完毕后，列车长使用手持电台通知机械师和司机。

司机并立即报告列车调度员或车站值班员。联系用语如下：

列车长：×××次机械师、司机，×车×位车门已关闭。

机械师：×××次机械师明白。

司　机：×××次司机明白。

（8）其他情况下的联系用语，由随车机械师与司机根据实际情况进行联系，应力求规范、准确、简洁。

2. 发生行车信息后汇报用语

动车组列车因动车组故障非正常运行或停车时，随车机械师及时将信息向事发地有调度指挥权的集团公司动车调度报告，并按照规定程序及时向动车段调度汇报。报告用语为：

机械师：“我是×××次随车机械师×××，××点××分，××区间，××动车组出现××情况，汇报完毕”。

五、动车组随车工具与备品

动车组随车工具和行车、应急、客运备品应根据车型结构特点随车配备、定置定量存放（见表4-1）。各部门须加强动车组备品的维护管理，定期检查、维护保养，保持技术状态良好。

表4-1　随车工具与备品

类别	序号	名称	数量/列	单位	备注
随车工具	1	钳形电流表	1	支	
	2	红外线测温仪	1	支	
	3	动车组车轮轮缘踏面便携式检查器	1	个	
	4	38件套工具	1	套	
	5	9件套梅花扳手	1	套	
	6	活扣扳手	1	把	
	7	克丝钳	1	把	
	8	卷尺	1	把	
	9	管子钳（12英寸）	1	把	
	10	管子钳（18英寸）	1	把	
	11	圆锉	1	把	
	12	半圆锉	1	把	
	13	组套螺丝刀	1	套	
	14	手锤	1	把	

续表

类别	序号	名称	数量/列	单位	备注
随车工具	15	撬棍	1	根	
	16	扁铲	1	把	
	17	笔记本电脑	1	台	根据车型需要
行车备品	1	响墩	6	个	
	2	火炬	2	支	
	3	短路铜线	2	副	
	4	手信号灯	2	盏	
	5	信号旗	2	套	
	6	防护信号灯	2	盏	
应急备品	1	过渡车钩	2	模块	本车适配模块及机车适配模块各1（前端为AAR车钩的车型仅配本车适配模块1个）
	2	救援风管	2	个	
	3	铁丝	20	m	
	4	接地杆	2	套	
	5	验电杆	1	套	
	6	绝缘靴	1	双	
	7	绝缘手套	1	副	
	8	安全帽	1	顶	
	9	安全带	1	套	
	10	登顶梯	1	架	
	11	铁鞋	根据车型按规定配置	个	
	12	止轮器	根据车型按规定配置	个	
	13	受电弓绑扎用品	根据车型需要	套	

续表

类别	序号	名称	数量/列	单位	备注
客运备品	1	紧急用渡板	2	块	
	2	应急梯	2	架	
	3	车门防护网	根据车型配置	套	单侧全部车门数量配备
	4	应急灯（手电筒）	6	只	
	5	扩音器	1	台	
	6	紧急破窗锤	根据车型配置	个	

【任务检测】

1. 简述动车组随车机械师的岗位职责。

2. 动车组随车机械师需要管理和操作哪些动车组设备?

3. 动车组随车机械师在应急处理途中突发故障时，需要做哪些工作?

4. 动车组随车机械师承担部分行车组织职能是什么?

5. CRH380A 型动车组随车机械师一次往返作业标准中接车作业的内容是什么? 并画出接车作业线路图。

6. 动车组的行车备品及应急备品有哪些?

7. 动车组列车因动车组故障非正常运行或停车时,动车组随车机械师向动车段调度汇报的标准用语是什么?

任务二　动车组随车机械师应急故障处置

【任务描述】

（1）熟知动车组应急故障处置时车上工作人员的职责及分工。

（2）能够按照车载信息系统提示应急处置动车组突发故障。

一、动车组发生故障应急处置原则

动车组故障应急处置基本原则：确保安全、保障运输、统一指挥、科学处置。坚定换车不犹豫思想，杜绝盲目带车；坚定应急处置流程化管理宗旨，杜绝盲目指挥、无序指挥。

（1）动车组列车运行中出现车辆设备故障时，司机应按车载信息监控装置的提示，按规定及时处理；需要由随车机械师处理时，司机应通知随车机械师。随车机械师按照动车组途中故障应急处理手册及有关规定进行处置，动车段调度应急指挥中心负责远程技术支持，根据需要启用应急指挥系统。经处置确认无法正常运行时，司机应按车载信息监控装置的提示和随车机械师的要求，选择维持运行或停车等方式。

（2）动车组发生故障后，应急指挥人员应充分利用地面行车安全监控系统、动车组车载信息无线传输系统、受电弓视频监控装置等安全监控设备配合开展应急处置。动车组发生弓网故障后，随车机械师应立即通过受电弓视频监控装置，确认受电弓状态。

（3）动车组故障停车后，随车机械师故障处置时间，区间停车 20 分钟、站内停车 30 分钟仍无法判明故障原因或无法处置不能继续运行时，通知司机请求救援。当故障造成全列空调失效时，随车机械师应立即通知司机请求救援。动车段调度应急指挥中心应及时提醒随车机械师在规定时间内申请救援。

请求救援后，随车机械师须立即向发生地所在集团公司动车调度报告，并严格服从故障发生地所在集团公司的救援指挥。

（4）救援时应优先采用动车组，其次采用机车。特殊情况下，重联动车组可以采用换端重联方式及动车组解编为单组运行方式进行处置；动车组列车操纵端故障需返回后方站时，必须采取整列换端牵引方式进行处置；若附近无热备动车组时，可启用备用动车组或调整在线运行动车组交路进行救援。采用动车组救援时按照动车组相互救援办法要求办理，采用机车救援时按照动车组回送办法中关于无动力回送操作程序的要求办理。

动车组被救援时，司机应了解和掌握救援列车开来方向，通知随车机械师在救援来车方向做好救援准备工作。

（5）启用热备动车组担当跨集团公司交路时，须经国铁集团调度同意后方可提交换车申请。

（6）动车组无动力停留时，有停放制动装置的动车组，由司机负责将动车组处于停放制动状态；动车组无停放制动装置或在坡度为 20‰以上的区间无动力停留时，由司机通知随车机械师进行防溜，防溜时应使用铁鞋牢固紧靠。

（7）上下车流程及要求：

① 随车机械师下车作业前须按照相关规定办理作业申请。应根据实际需要通过司机向列车调度员提出限速要求及检查条件，作业可能侵入邻线限界时提出封锁要求，司机接到列车调度员已发布邻线列车限速或封锁的调度命令的口头指示后，通知随车机械师，双方互相签认后，随车机械师从非会车侧下车检查、处理故障，客运乘务组做好车门看护，司机、随车机械师保持密切联络。

② 随车机械师作业完毕后，带齐所有的工具备品、材料配件上车。需要限速运行时，通知司机限速要求，司机报告列车调度员（车站值班员）后，按限速要求运行。不能继续运行时，及时请求救援。

（8）放行条件

① 动车组列车运行途中，站车工作人员发现或接到下列情况或信息时，须立即采取停车措施：

a. 车辆下部有拖、拉、击打声、上下振动声、连续摩擦声时；车辆突发剧烈上、下跳动，车体剧烈摆动；连接处明显下垂时。

b. 轴箱轴承、齿轮箱轴承、牵引电机轴承及定子温度报警。

c. 车载信息监控装置提示轴不旋转、抱死故障。

d. 发现制动力不足等异常情况时。

e. 受电弓不明原因自动降弓或挂异物。

f. 运行途中发生外门故障。

g. 重联动车组意外解编、编组间传输不良、重联端车钩故障。

h. 动车组碰撞异物影响行车安全时。

i. 动车组裙板、外掀式盖板开启。

j. TEDS 预报需立即停车检查的故障。

k. 动车组电器设备起火冒烟，动车组其他设备出现明火。

l. 其他影响动车组行车安全时。

② 动车组运行途中发生以下故障时，经应急处置无效须请求救援。

a. 全列制动失效。

b. 全列无牵引。

c. 走行部机械故障无法继续运行。

（9）动车组发生故障后动车段要积极派员进行途中接车或赶赴现场，运行后继续跟踪直至动车组入库作业。

（10）动车组故障非正常运行或停车时，司机立即向故障发生地所在集团公司列车调度员或车站值班员汇报，并通知随车机械师。

（11）随车机械师立即向故障发生局集团公司动车调度报告，然后向本属段调度应急指挥中心进行汇报。动车段调度应急指挥中心接到报告后，应立即启动故障应急处置程序，协助指挥随车机械师进行故障处置，同时须向集团公司动车调度汇报故障信息及处置情况。

（12）动车组故障处置完毕，随车机械师核对无误后，及时通知司机可以开车，并将检查处理结果向故障发生局集团公司动车调度、本属段调度应急指挥中心报告，动车段调度应急指挥中心接到报告后及时向集团公司动车调度报告。

二、动车组随车机械师应急故障处置流程

1. 列车运行途中停车，随车机械师下车检查流程

随车机械师在高速铁路（200 km/h 及以上的铁路和 200 km/h 以下仅运行动车组列车的铁路）需下车检查、处理故障时，下车作业前须按照相关规定办理作业申请，根据实际需要通过司机向列车调度员提出限速要求及检查条件，作业可能侵入邻线限界时提出封锁要求，请求内容包括：停车地点、下车原因、邻线限速值等。随车机械师接到司机邻线列车限速 160 km/h 及以下调度命令已发布的通知后，双方互相签认。随车机械师穿戴好防护用品后，从非会车侧下车检查、处理故障，通知列车长做好车门看护，注意下车时脚下设

施状态，与司机保持密切联络，作业时注意人身安全；在普速铁路（200 km/h 以下的铁路，仅运行动车组列车的铁路除外）需下车检查、处理故障时，随车机械师须征得司机同意后方可从非会车侧下车检查，通知列车长做好车门看护，注意下车时脚下设施状态，与司机保持密切联络，作业时注意人身安全。随车机械师检查处理完毕，带齐所有的工具备品、材料配件上车，通知司机检查处理结果。需要限速运行时，通知司机限速要求，不能继续运行时，及时请求救援。(长大隧道内下车检查时注意携带照明工具)。随车机械师下车检查时，应使用摄录手电筒全程录像。

2. 随车机械师需登顶检查、处理故障流程

（1）随车机械师首先应与司机联系确认动车组停车位置上方接触网是否跨分相，并通过动车组司机向列车调度员提出请求，在得到邻线列车限速 160 km/h 及以下的调度命令、接触网已停电及准许登顶作业的调度命令后（如停车位置跨分相区时，两分相区需同时停电），通知司机切除受损的受电弓后升另一良好受电弓，与司机共同确认无网压，实施放电后（CRH2A/B/C/E/G、CRH380A/AL 型动车组由随车机械师通知司机闭合主断进行放电），随车机械师穿戴好防护用品下车进行作业（随车机械师手动开启车门，下车后加强瞭望，确保人身安全）。

（2）随车机械师首先在本线非会车侧用验电器进行接触网验电，确认接触网已断电。在非会车侧故障部位作业范围内两端邻近接触网腕臂各挂设一根接地杆后方可登车顶检查处理故障（遇多处故障部位时，在最远距离两故障部位外侧邻近接触网腕臂各挂设一根接地杆，如区间或站场非会车侧不具备接触网腕臂挂设接地杆条件时，在动车组两端头部接触网上挂设接地杆），登顶作业严禁超出两端挂设的接地杆之间的接触网范围（如图 4-2 所示）。要将接地线与钢轨连接牢靠，必须除去钢轨接触部位锈斑后方可将接地线与钢轨连接，以确保接地效果良好。挂在操纵端前方的接地线由司机负责看护，挂在其它的接地线由列车长指派列车工作人员负责看护。（看护内容为：接地线脱落或被人撤除时及时通知随车机械师停止作业下车）。

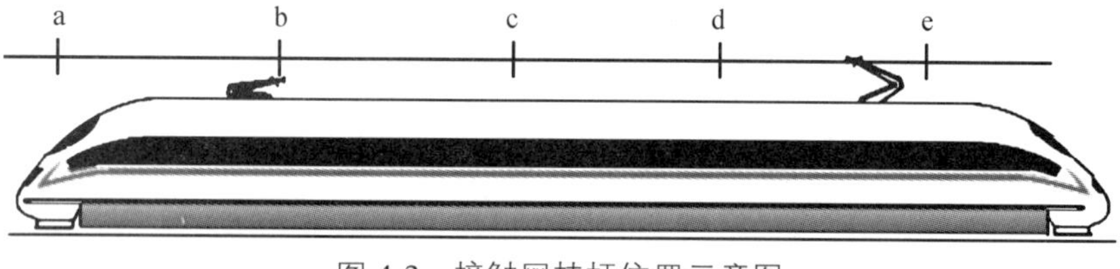

图 4-2　接触网挂杆位置示意图

说明：a、b、c、d、e 分别代表接触网腕臂位置

（1）如上图升起受电弓损坏，接地杆挂在 d、e 两腕臂处。

（2）如上图降下受电弓损坏，接地杆挂在 a、c 两腕臂处。

（3）如上图两受电弓均损坏，接地杆挂在 a、e 两腕臂处。

（3）随车机械师登车顶检查处理（登顶梯要安装稳固，方向正确，在非会车侧），捆扎受损受电弓，确保受损受电弓离开接触网的距离大于 300 mm，无部件脱落危险，且距

离车顶高压器件的距离大于 300 mm；受损受电弓检查完毕后，随车机械师还需要对动车组其他全部受电弓进行检查，确保其他受电弓无部件脱落危险，且距离车顶高压器件的距离大于 300 mm。登顶作业完毕后，随车机械师负责先撤除接触网腕臂端接地线，再撤除与钢轨一端连接的接地线，收集并清点工具无遗落后上车，在司机手账上签认，通知司机使用良好受电弓正常运行。在等待供电期间，随车机械师清点工具并将防护用品和工具收集归位。

（4）随车机械师在挂、撤接地线以及转移、安装、撤除登顶梯和夜间作业辅助照明等工作需协助时，重联编组时由随车机械师负责协助；单编组时由动车组司机负责协助，若单班单司机时，由列车长指派列车工作人员负责协助。

3. 动车组故障需要进行制动切除检查流程

（1）因动车组故障需要进行制动切除操作时：CRH380A(L)型动车组需停车状态下进行操作，CRH380B(L)型、CR400BF 动车组需在速度 200 km/h 以下进行。

（2）因动车组故障空气制动与停放制动同时切除或单独切除停放制动时：涉及停放制动切除操作需要在停车状态下进行，司机、随车机械师按规定对列车采取防溜措施，停放制动及空气制动切除操作完毕后，需要晃动带停放制动缸的制动夹钳，确认各停放制动夹钳已全部缓解。随车机械师通知司机以不高于 5 km/h 速度进行滚动试验，试验过程中随车机械师确认走行部是否出现真正抱死及异常声响等。试验完毕后（对于仅需切除停放制动的动车组，还要恢复空气制动供风），随车机械师要向段安全生产调度指挥中心汇报试验结果（恢复情况），上车后通过显示屏确认停放制动已切除，查看切除制动车辆相关轴温监测数据，确认结果正常，通知司机试验完毕并与司机办理相互签字确认手续。随车机械师未进行滚动试验或滚动试验未通过时，不得开车。

（3）处理完毕后，随车机械师应将切除制动力的情况及限速要求通知司机，并与司机相互签认限速运行要求。

（4）动车组制动切除后恢复运行时，随车机械师要将切除制动的车作为检查巡视重点，除进行必要的检查巡视外，其余时间要在制动切除的车厢进行重点盯控，监控运行中有无异音、异常振动情况，出现异常振动或异音，应立即通知司机停车，下车检查。

（5）动车组制动切除恢复运行后，随车机械师要通过司机向列车调度员申请前方站停车检查，前方站停车后随车机械师按规定下车对切除制动车辆的制动盘、牵引电机、齿轮箱、轴端进行点温，与相邻车进行点温比对，并对制动切除车辆的踏面状态进行重点检查，确认是否存在抱闸现象。检查完毕具备运行条件后，随车机械师通过司机报告列车调度员（车站值班员），司机按照随车机械师要求恢复运行。

4. 动车组运行中受电弓故障处置措施

动车组列车运行途中遇弓网故障时，随车机械师应加强故障判断和处置，原则上不在区间进行登顶作业，必须登顶作业时要严格遵守作业要求。

（1）装有受电弓视频监控装置的动车组，随车机械师应立即通过受电弓视频监控装置确认受电弓外观状态，并及时查看回放视频，如能够确认受电弓状态可见部分无明显异常或不超限、无脱落风险时，通知司机换弓后正常运行。

（2）通过受电弓视频监控装置无法确认受电弓状态或需要下车检查时或未装有受电弓视频监控装置的动车组，按照下车检查流程下车检查。

（3）下车检查。具备条件时，随车机械师在车下可使用望远镜、自拍杆等辅助手段进行进一步检查确认。

① 经初步检查确认受电弓外观可见部分无明显异常或不超限、无脱落风险但未能判明降弓原因时，随车机械师应立即将检查情况及前方站停车的要求报告司机，司机报告列车调度员。司机按随车机械师要求切除已降下的受电弓，换弓运行，限速 160 km/h 运行至前方站进一步检查处置。

如前方站为终点站，随车机械师向司机及集团公司动车调度员申请建议启动热备动车组替换，替换下的故障动车组根据车顶故障状况申请不高于 160 km/h 的限速条件，返回动车所进行处理。

如前方站为非终点站时，随车机械师在停站后使用望远镜或通过受电弓视频监控装置进行进一步检查确认，如确认受电弓外观整体正常或不影响运行安全时，动车组以正常速度维持运行；如不能确认，则必须登顶检查处理。

② 如检查时发现受电弓轻微损坏，且无部件脱落危险时，随车机械师通知司机切除受损的受电弓，并将前方站停车检查的要求报告列车调度员，换弓后以不高于 120 km/h 的速度运行进入前方车站停车，停车后，随车机械师下车进一步确认，检查确认不影响运行时可恢复常速运行；如发现受电弓损坏部位有扩展趋势，则必须登顶检查处理。如受电弓受损严重，但不侵限、无脱落风险、满足与接触网最小间距要求（300 mm），则可切除故障受电弓，换弓以不超过 40 km/h 速度运行至前方站进一步处理。

③ 如检查时发现受电弓刮弓或损坏较严重，有部件脱落危险时，随车机械师应按照登顶检查、处理故障流程进行登顶作业。

（4）随车机械师发现受电弓折断、移位、附挂异物及其他高压配件损伤严重而无法独自处理时，应经司机向列车调度员申请出动供电作业车、接触网检测作业车等，由供电人员协助登顶处理。如经现场登顶确认全部受电弓（包括运用的和非使用的）受损严重，通知司机请求救援，并对受损受电弓捆扎，确认受损受电弓、车顶其它部件离开接触网的距离大于 300 mm。在等待救援时，司机和随车机械师按规定做好列车防溜，同时司机应将制动手柄置于最大制动位，保持客室内应急灯亮，头灯及车尾标志灯亮。随车机械师启动应急通风装置，司机监视蓄电池电压符合规定，低于规定值时关闭蓄电池；无应急通风装置或蓄电池电压低于规定值时，通知列车长组织安装防护网、开启指定车门通风并做好防护，并通知司机转报列车调度员。

5. 受电弓挂有异物处置措施

随车机械师接到受电弓挂有异物通知后立即通过受电弓视频监控装置检查受电弓外观状态，确认是否影响动车组正常运行，如不影响运行，可维持（或限速）运行至前方站检查处理。随车机械师视具体情况提出处置方案和限速要求，遇有长大防尘网缠绕受电弓一时难以快速处置时，应优先考虑启用热备车。

（1）装有受电弓视频监控装置的动车组，随车机械师应立即通过受电弓视频监控装置确认异物及受电弓外观状态，并及时查看回放视频，如能够确认受电弓状态可见部分无明显异常或不超限、无脱落风险不影响运行时，通知司机换弓后正常运行。动车组可在前方（办客）站停车处置时，随车机械师通知司机，司机报告列车调度员，列车调度员组织供电部门在前方（办客）站协助随车机械师登顶清除异物。

发现受电弓异常、影响运行或未装有受电弓视频监控装置的动车组，按照下车检查流程下车检查。随车机械师要控制下车检查时间，加快检查进度，最大程度较少对运输秩序的影响。

（2）随车机械师车下检查，确认受电弓外观整体正常或不影响运行安全时，通知司机换弓后以正常速度维持运行。

（3）随车机械师车下检查，确认发现受电弓滑板及托架有损伤或接触网有异状时，应及时将检查结果汇报司机，报告列车调度员。

（4）需登顶作业时，随车机械师应按照登顶检查、处理故障流程进行登顶作业。

（5）异物处理完毕后，将处置结果汇报司机，恢复正常行车。需限速运行时，随车机械师将限速运行要求通知司机。

6. 车辆设备故障发生火情处置措施

（1）动车组运行途中，随车机械师在得到或发现车厢空调通风口、配电柜、客室内其它设备设施等冒烟、起火、烧焦或有橡胶、塑胶熔化等产生的异味时，应立即通知司机和列车长，要求司机断开主断路器并降弓，并选择安全地点停车。

（2）随车机械师应及时赶到相应车厢关闭空调、通风系统或设备设施电源，并将设备状况通知列车长和司机。

（3）停车后，随车机械师应对车辆设备进行检查，准确判断，果断处理，确认不影响行车安全时，通知司机并签认。

（4）发生火灾时，随车机械师要及时拨打当地“119”请求救援。

7. 车载轴温检测系统检测到轴承温度报警处置措施

（1）动车组运行途中发生走行部轴箱轴承、齿轮箱轴承、牵引电机轴承温度过高响应时，动车组司机应立即停车，报告列车调度员停车原因和停车位置，通知随车机械师处理。

（2）随车机械师机械师将 MON 屏切换至“轴温实时检测”画面，确认故障设备温度并记录。

（3）随车机械师按规定程序下车检查、点温确认，按照由主及次的顺序进行全面检查。重点检查齿轮箱、联轴器、牵引电机、轴箱、制动盘、轮对踏面等部位，要求：齿轮箱无破损、无滴油、齿轮箱油位正常（平直道，如线路存在超高、坡道时，油位会有所变化甚至无法观察到，需检查同一转向架相邻齿轮箱油位加以辅助判断，一侧齿轮箱油位下降甚至无法观察到，另一侧齿轮箱油位上升为正常情况；如无法检查同一转向架相邻齿轮箱油位，需检查相邻两个转向架相同位置齿轮箱油位，如存在坡道或超高，齿轮箱油位均下降甚至无法观察到为正常情况）； 联轴节无破损、无偏斜、无滴油、无变色；牵引电机无破损；轴箱无破损、无变色；电机（轴端）速度传感器无断线、破损，连接器无松脱、无变形。并用红外线点温仪进行“走行部重点部位点温”，与本车邻近相同部位点温温度对比分析，若报警部位点温无异常，需对故障轴其它部位点温确认。根据实测温度和检查情况向司机报告。

必须检查部位：齿轮箱油位、各部温度贴片、橡胶件。

对于下部空间狭小难于目视检查部位，随车机械师需使用自拍杆进行拍照并进行信息反馈，段应急指挥人员要对比照片进行逐项确认。

（4）判断为真报警，确认异常或温升超高时，按规定在司机手账上签认，限速运行。

① 严重机械故障，无法维持运行的严重机械故障，申请救援；

② 齿轮箱、联轴节、牵引电机等异常时，若发现齿轮箱破损、滴油，联轴节破损、偏斜、滴油、变色，牵引电机破损，轴箱破损、变色，轴箱点温超标但可视范围内无其他异常，人工滚动试验后，限速 40 km/h 维持运行，申请前方站救援。

③ 齿轮箱、牵引电机点温超标时，若齿轮箱、牵引电机点温超标但可视范围内无其他异常，人工滚动试验后，限速 140 km/h 维持运行，申请前方站救援。

（5） 检查无异常，确认轴温正常，属误报警时，通知司机恢复正常速度运行，在司机手账上签认。

配属动车组发生走行部轴承温度过高响应时，随车机械师下车检查确认，根据具体情况按应急手册规定采取处置措施，可视范围内无异常且未伴随发生其他故障时按下述限速表（表 4-2）运行。

表 4-2 限速表

级 别	轴箱轴承	齿轮箱轴承	电机轴承
预警级（1 级）	200 km/h	200 km/h	200 km/h
报警级（2 级）	40 km/h	40 km/h	40 km/h

（6）随车机械师在维持运行或恢复正常速度运行途中对故障车辆进行重点监控。 途中密切关注[轴温实时检测]信息。如出现异常振动或异音，应立即通知司机停车，下车确认。本次运营结束或具备换车条件的车站更换车底，故障车组停运回库处理。

8. 动车组列车运行途中发生紧急制动停车时处置措施

（1）若因车辆自身设备故障导致动车组列车紧急制动停车时，随车机械师按照动车组途中应急故障处理手册规定进行处置。随车机械师开车前盯控司机进行简略制动试验，确认制动性能良好后通知司机限速 60 km/h 运行，开车后对全列进行巡视，重点监听走行部是否存在异音、异常振动等现象，无异常后通知司机恢复正常运行。

（2）若因其他异常情况导致动车组列车紧急制动停车时，随车机械师在掌握具体情况后按照相关预案进行处置，开车前盯控司机进行简略制动试验，确认制动性能良好后通知司机限速 60 km/h 运行，开车后对全列进行巡视，重点监听走行部是否存在异音、异常振动等现象，无异常后通知司机恢复正常运行。

（3）若因其他异常情况导致动车组列车紧急制动停车时，随车机械师在掌握具体情况后按照相关预案进行处置，开车前盯控司机进行简略制动试验，确认制动性能良好后通知司机限速 60 km/h 运行，开车后对全列进行巡视，重点监听走行部是否存在异音、异常振动等现象，无异常后通知司机恢复正常运行。

（4）随车机械师全列巡视过程中，若发现走行部有异音或异常振动等现象时，及时通知司机停车，并按规定下车对全列走行部进行检查，根据检查情况向司机提出运行限速条件或申请救援，并及时向事发地有调度指挥权的集团公司动车调度报告。

9. 重联动车组发生异常需要分离运行应急处置措施

重联动车组中一组因故不能继续运行，根据调度命令需要分离运行时，动车组司机、随车机械师按规定做好故障动车组防溜工作（动车组无动力停留时，有停放制动装置的动车组，由司机负责将动车组处于停放制动状态；动车组无停放制动装置或在坡道为 20‰以上的区间无动力停留时，随车机械师根据司机的通知进行防溜），随车机械师配合司机，按动车组摘解操作程序，摘解重联动车组。值乘故障动车组的随车机械师须做好动车组的防护工作，并与故障动车组一起停留原地等待救援，正常动车组按命令单组继续运行。

【任务检测】

1. 自主阅读《CRH380 系列动车组应急故障处理手册》。
2. 简述动车组故障应急处置基本原则。
3. 简述列车运行途中停车，随车机械师下车检查流程。
4. 简述动车组列车运行途中发生紧急制动停车时处置措施。

项目五　动车组的运用维修

【思政课堂】雷打不动的安全理念，铸就28年探伤无缺陷——雷立

“每一次都是第一次，第一次就要无缺陷”是雷立在岗位上坚持的安全理念。1990年10月参加工作以来，雷立潜心钻研、不断创新，填补普速列车探伤工艺空白。创立动车组空心轴超声波探伤“校、洁、全、比、验”五字作业法，探索开发信息化探伤模式，先后发现并排除30多起典型或重大列车轮对故障，实现了28年探伤无缺陷。她把青春奉献给热爱的探伤事业，绽放出巾帼工匠之花的美丽芳华。

工作中，爱岗敬业的雷立多次发现重大裂纹缺陷。在长期的探伤实践中，她勇于创新，认真探索总结普速列车探伤的工艺和方法，提出的“裂有长短、孔是一点、杂波乱动、透锈一片”“十六字”探伤法至今仍被广泛使用。她研发的短前沿K值探头，完全符合生产需要，填补了当时全路盘型制动轮对探伤工艺的一项空白。2010年7月28日，她在对一组CRH1A型动车组进行探伤时发现其中一条空心轴存在3个内部缺陷，并且都比较隐蔽。她通过降低灵敏度、换轴端面探伤、手动检测等多种方法反复探测，用了3个多小时最终判定其中一个缺陷当量已超过3 mm，并作了换轮处理，排除了隐患。

面对近几年高铁动车组技术快速发展的趋势，雷立勇于担当、迎难而上，主动兼任车间技术室副工长。她不仅牵头编制探伤作业指导书和空心车轴探伤缺陷的判定及处置方法，还创新研发信息化探伤新模式，积极组织探伤班生产骨干对配属的5种车型、3种技术平台共130组动车组空心轴和库存34条空心轴履历进行电脑录入，建立数据库，实现了对空心轴健康状况的大数据分析和追踪，有效提高了空心轴运用效率，促使动车探伤更加规范化、科学化、信息化，科学有力地确保探伤质量。

人品铸就精品，正是雷立这种爱岗敬业、持之以恒、精益求精、不断创新的工匠精神，创造了她28年探伤产品，无缺陷零故障的奇迹。这种对工作的极致追求，对产品质量精益求精的执着，是对工匠精神的最好诠释。

【项目描述】

通过本项目学习动车组维修方式、主要维修方法及标准，掌握动车组维修机构的组成和功能；熟知检修基地的功能、布局，了解运用所常用的检修设备；掌握动车组运用级检修作业流程，并能够按照一、二级检修作业标准完成相关内容。

任务一　动车组维修特点

【任务描述】

（1）熟知高速动车组维修特点、维修制度、维修方法及维修范围。

（2）能够根据动车组运行情况判断检修方式。

一、动车组的维修特点

1. 采用大量高新技术设备

以德国汉堡动车段为例，该动车段能在 60 min 内完成 412 m 长整列 ICE 动车组的维修保养和整备工作，就是因为具有先进的维修技术和设备。

（1）车载微机诊断系统，通过远程无线通信技术将运用中检测到的故障信号传输给动车段，提前做好维修准备。

（2）建立三层维修工作面，在下部、内部和顶部同时作业。

（3）具有轨道桥的架空轨道，便于走行部的检查与更换。

（4）具有气垫走行装置的轮对和转向架更换设备。

（5）真空排污处理系统和自动化清洗装置。

（6）自动检测轮对踏面裂纹、磨损和不圆度的诊断设备。

（7）控制和管理整个维修过程的微机信息系统等。

2. 用系统工程观点进行维修

首先，对高速列车寿命周期成本（LCC）进行研究；其次，把技术、财务、管理等各方面的因素综合起来进行全面管理；另外，利用系统工程理论对高速列车可靠性、维修性和可用性进行研究，对高速列车的各环节（草拟，设计，制造，安装，运用，维修和更新等）进行综合分析，此外还要进行信息反馈以便制造部门改进设计。

3. 广泛实施换件修和集中修

在动车组维修过程中广泛实施换件修，即把发现故障或缺陷的部件、模块或零件换以功能完好的相应件（新的或经修复的），而不做现场维修，这样可大大节省在修时间，提高列车利用率。同时这种换修方法也应用于厂修中相应机组的检修，称为大部件换修。对于可修复的主要零部件实行专业化集中修，即将它们送往专业化工厂、车间或工段，实行集中统一修理，则可提高维修质量，节约维修成本。

4. 维修制度更趋合理

高速列车维修制度主要框架仍采用计划预防修制，但是在具体维修中却有着灵活多变的维修体系，状态修占有越来越大的比重。而实施状态修的基础和可靠保证是完备的计算机维修管理信息系统、先进的通信手段和精密可靠的检修诊断设备。

5. 维修停时大为缩短，利用率大大提高

当前世界各国高速列车在大修时均采用整列入库的全新维修模式，例如德国 ICE 列车每年平均运行里程高达 50 万 km，其维修停留时间可不足 3 天，在故障维修时也有良好的设备；再如法国 TGV 列车，更换一根车轴仅需 1 h 左右，更换一个非动力转向架，不超过 1.5 h。

二、基本维修方式及检修方式

1. 基本维修方式

维修方式是指对设备维修时机的控制。也就是对维修时机的掌握是通过采用不同的维修方式来实现的。目前的维修方式有 3 种：定期维修（又称计划修）、视情维修（又称状态修）和事后维修（又称故障修）。

1）定期维修

定期检修又称为计划修，它是以使用时间或运行里程作为维修期限。因此只要设备使用到预先规定的时间或运行的里程，不管其技术状态如何，都要进行规定的检修工作，这是一种带强制性的预防检修方式。

定期维修的实施是由计划修理周期、修理级别和检修范围以及有关的检修工作条例来保证的。动车组的修程和检修周期应根据其构造特点、运用条件、实际技术状态和一定时期的生产水平来确定，以保证动车组安全可靠地运用。

2）视情维修

视情维修又称为状态修，该方式要求动车组按照实际运行状况来确定检修的时间，没有固定的规定限制。通过持续监测动车组以及各个子系统的状态，判断其性能曲线，对系统故障或失效的部件进行定位，并记录、追踪失效的时间和过程。由于故障不是瞬间发生的，总会有时间和机会发觉并采取检修措施。

由此可见该方式针对性强，效率高，但同时成本高，且对检修设备、条件、人员的要求也高，不具有普适性。

3）事后维修。

事后维修方式也称故障维修，它不控制维修时机，在机件发生故障之后才进行修理。实践证明，有些机件即便是发生故障也不会危及安全造成严重后果，采用事后维修则更经济，对于一些采用了冗余技术的机件，如牵引传动系统就适用于事后维修。

2. 动车组主要检修方式

动车组检修采用了高效率的检修方式。其目的是大幅度提高动车组的安全性和可靠性，大幅度提高动车组的使用效率，大幅度压缩休车时分，大幅度提高检修单位的作业效率，实现修车方式制造化。动车组检修方式是建立在部件寿命管理系统的基础上，同时以先进的检修设备和设施及零部件制造工厂的配套检修服务为条件和支撑。其主要形式是换件修、集中修、状态修和均衡修，其主要特点是高度的专业化，高度的集约化，高度的社会化，高度的程序化。

1）换件修

在各级修程中发现部件故障，或在中、高级修程中需要检修或更换部件，都采用换件修的方式，拆下的部件分 3 种情况安排送修。一是对于技术结构比较简单的部件由检修基地检修；二是对于技术结构比较复杂，修程范围较大的部件，在经过经济性分析后，由检修基地提供相应的检修场地和配套设施，委托制造工厂在检修基地内设置的检修单位检修；三是对于大部件，如牵引变流器、牵引变压器等，在高级修程时返回制造工厂检修。

2）集中修

动车组部件的检修主要集中在检修基地，运用所仅承担日常的例行检查和部分临修作业，部件检修集中在相应的制造工厂或其设立的派出机构。

3）状态修

服务性设施一般采取状态修，即随检随修，始终保持技术状态良好；同时部分设备或部件按照使用寿命的界定，在不能适应使用要求，即将发生故障前进行更换，采用监视型的状态修。

4）均衡修

为减少大修休车时分，通过换件的方式将部分部件安排在运用过程中或其他较低级修程中安排检修，减少大修时的工作量，尽可能压缩动车组在修时间。

【任务检测】

1. 结合动车组的维修，阐述维修的定义及其要素。
3. 换件修、专业化集中修各有哪些优缺点？两种维修方式有何联系？
4. 区别高速列车检修方式的不同。

任务二　动车组维修机构

【任务描述】

（1）熟知动车组维修机构的组成及功能。
（2）熟知动车组检修基地的功能及布局。
（3）了解动车组运用所常用的检修设备。

一、动车组维修机构

遵循“集中检修，分散存放”“优势设备相对集中”的基本原则，动车组设置了检修基地和运用所两种不同功能的维修机构，以避免交叉作业和重复投资。检修基地设置在主要的交通枢纽，根据运输组织需要以检修基地为中心设立若干运用所，形成了维修能力的梯次结构；并区分维修任务，科学组织，检修基地承担一级修到五级修（D1~D5）的所有修程，动车组的检修原则上集中在检修基地进行，运用所仅承担一级到二级（D1~D2）修程。

1. 维修机构设置原则

维修机构的设置地点要充分考虑高速铁路客流特点、高速站的分布情况、铁路周围环境条件以及与其相关的既有铁路的情况而确定。考虑因素主要有以下几点：

（1）从始发到终点旅客的输送量。

（2）列车空车回送比较少，动车组利用率高的地方。

（3）离车站比较近的地方。

（4）维修基地所需人员容易得到保证的地方。

所考虑的这些因素主要是为了提高动车组的运用效率，再者也要充分考虑建设用地因素。

2. 维修机构的组成及功能

（1）检修基地。

检修基地配属一定数量动车组，主要功能是动车组的定期维修、故障处理、车辆停留及整备清洗。检修基地承担所有维修级别的修程，负责本基地和外基地动车组的夜间停留和备用车组的长期停放，以及旅客餐饮、车内清洁等整备作业。检修基地既要考虑整列编组的检修，也要考虑列车的到发及夜间作业。检修基地需要具备大修的设备条件。

（2）运用所。

运用所与检修基地相配套，在主要客运站设置若干。设置运用所的原因有以下几点：

① 有利于实现集中检修，分散存放。

② 可以大幅度减少因动车组日常检修需要造成的车体空送，提高动车组的运营能力和使用效率。

③ 可以提高主要客运站的始发能力，有利于安排开行方案。

④ 充分借鉴了国外动车组检修布局设置模式。

运用所配属少量动车组，主要负责高速动车组的 D1~D2 级修程及整备、临修作业，设置存车场以满足动车组夜间停留车需要。

3. 维修机构的布局

（1）我国动车组检修基地、运用所的布局。

参考国外动车组的运营维修经验，为满足我国动车组的检修需求，我国也设置有许多检修机构，按功能等级从高到低依次是动车段（动车检修基地）、动车运用所、动车存车场。

（2）检修基地的管理。

动车组检修基地由国铁集团统一管理，动车组检修基地对外引进和合作工作，统一由中国铁路总公司负责实施。

二、动车组检修基地

1. 检修基地的功能

1）动车组管理功能

动车组检修基地具有管理基地、连接周边、辐射全路的整体管理功能，对动车组的使用、技术整备、检修试验及运行安全进行全面管理。通过信息中心的连接作用对动车组调度、整备、运用、维修、配件及设备进行有效管理。

2）检查整备功能

动车组检查整备功能包括整备作业及一、二级检修作业和临修作业。

整备作业：主要为运用技术整备及客运整备。其作业内容包含上水排水、润滑油脂补充、车厢内部清洁、密闭式厕所系统地面接收及处理设施、车体外皮清洗、车内垃圾收集及转运等。

临修作业：主要是处理动车组临时故障，对动车组主要零部件进行扣车修理及动车组不落轮镟轮和各级修程以外的主要设备、零部件的更换，包括转向架、轮对、受电弓、空调设施、主变流器、主变压器等。

3）检修功能

基地动车组的检修以预防为主、检查为主、换件修为主和组装调试为主；以寿命管理方式对动车组进行管理；尽量减少在修时间，提高效率、可靠性和动车组利用率。动车组换下来的零部件由专业厂商按专业化集中检修方式进行检修。

4）零配件储备及配送功能

基地应设立大型动车组零、配件及备品储存设施，包括材料库、材料棚、备品库等。零配件及材料备品储备采用立体存储方式，其信息管理纳入动车组信息化系统，并能根据维修信息自动进行配送管理。

5）信息化管理功能

信息化管理包括生产调度指挥、动车组运行管理、现场作业监控、车辆配件寿命管理、车辆配件配送支持、入段检测和车载信息地面接收处理。

6）排污处理功能

检修基地设密闭式厕所系统地面接受及处理设施。

真空密闭式厕所系统的地面接收处理设施采用固定式；集便接收作业线应与日检作业

线合并设置于库内。排污的主要设施置于检查库工作平台下，通过管道及快速接头可与车上排污口连接，并设移动式排污车。

2. 检修基地的布局

检修基地结合站型、地形地貌、运输发展、城镇规划等因素，合理布置段内线群、建筑物、通道、各种管线、环保等设施，高速动车检修基地内的设施主要由 3 部分组成：①动车组夜间停留存车场（库或棚）；② 主检修库及修配间（统称综合检修库）；③ 动车组外皮清洗、轮对踏面诊断、不落轮镟、列车排污等设备。

基地内设施的布置力求紧凑、整齐、作业流畅、技术经济指标先进，以体现高速动车组全密封不摘钩整列进段日检、维护保养和定期检修的特点。基地内设施之间不同的形式构成了总体布局的不同方式。

（1）直列式。直列式布局如图 5-1 所示，基地内存车场与检修库成纵向排列布置。在地形狭长、两端均有进出作业的情况下多采用此方案。其特点：

① 布置紧凑，动车组入段作业流畅，段内折角走行次数少，可减少移动转载的次数，走行距离短，提高检修效率。

② 有利于提高检修能力、扩大检修场地。

③ 基地规模及占用面积较大。

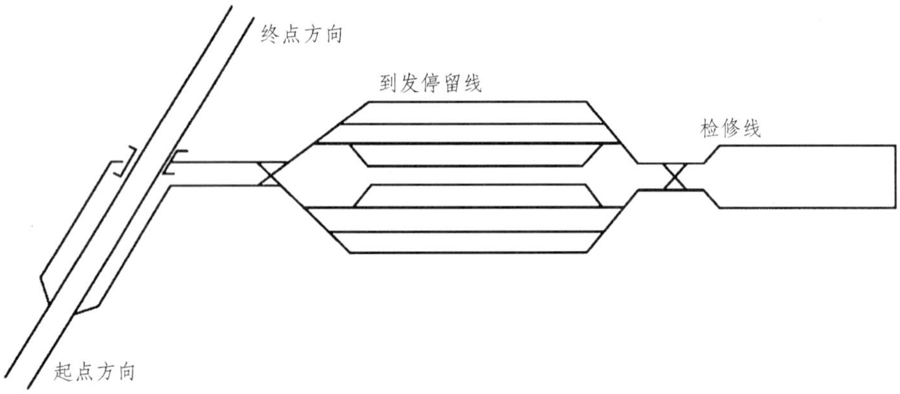

图 5-1 直列式布局

（2）并列式。并列式布局如图 5-2 所示，基地内存车场与检修库成横向并列布置。此方案适应地形条件能力强，占地面积小。其特点：

① 动车组入段作业需多次折角方可进行，动车组段内走行距离长，段内需设专用牵出线，作业效率较低，一般在受场地限制不得已的情况下采用。

② 基地受用地面积制约，列车到发停留线与检修线平行设置，适合于 10 列以下小规模的车辆检修基地。

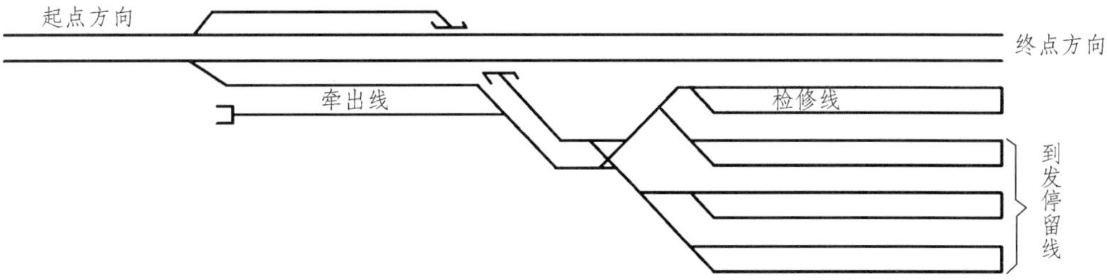

图 5-2　并列式布局

（3）错列式。错列式布局如图 5-3 所示，存车场与检修库部分成横列式布置，部分成纵列式布置或其他受场地控制而形成的总平面布置方案。

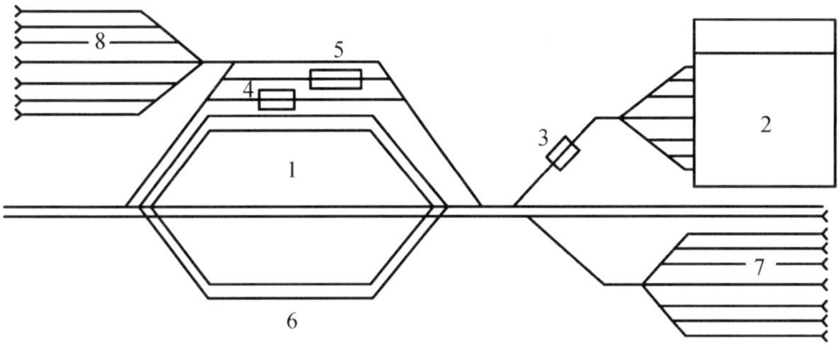

1、7、8—存车场；2—检修库；3—轮对诊断库；4—不落轮轮库；
5—外皮清洗库；6—排污线。

图 5-3　错列式布局

以上 3 种布局中，由于直列式布置方案中动车组入段作业流畅，段内折角走行次数少，走行距离短，条件许可的情况下推荐采用该布置方式。

总平面布置基本类型方案确定后，其他线路和设备的位置根据作业要求和场地条件的不同来确定。一般情况下，到发停留线群和主检修线群以及动车组排污、外皮洗刷、不落轮镟轮、轮对踏面诊断等专用线建成纵列式布置，检修库两端最好分别设两个停车场。

3. 检修库

检修库沿长度方向，每 100 m 设联系库外道路的通道。检修库内可全部或部分股道架设接触网，接触线高度可与库外一致。车顶作业处，接触网必须装设分段绝缘器及带接地的隔离开关，以及与隔离开关联锁的标志灯和作业平台安全锁，以保障作业人员的安全。库内设低压电源和独立风源、水源。

1）库　线

检修基地内根据不同的维修任务（整备、日常检修、更换转向架等），设置不同接入级别的维修库，不同的检修工作在不同的库线进行。

图 5-4 所示为德国动车段内的 1 ~ 3 级维修库。

图 5-5 所示为大修库线，在这些轨道上，可更换大部件，也可将一节车厢解组。

图 5-4　德铁 M1 ~ M3 级维修库

图 5-5　德铁的大修库线

2）设计要求

（1）库线设计要求。

两条检修线的线间距宜为 10 m。库内外侧股道距离检查库侧墙轴线不宜小于 5 m。库内应设置动车组上水、排水及排污设备。检查库净高应考虑作业人员车顶作业的高度要求。底层作业面至库内地坪的纵向运输，应设置坡度不大于 10%的缓坡。修车库净高应根据修车工艺、动车组车辆限界、车顶作业需要、起重机结构尺寸等因素确定。库内起重机走行轨顶高应不小于+8.8 m，如图 5-6 所示。

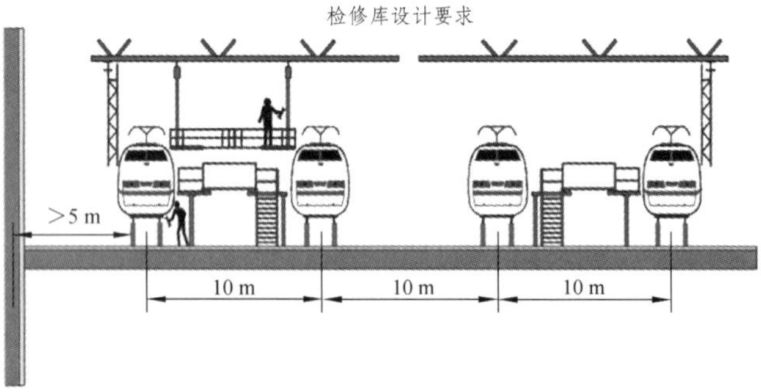

（a）检修线设计要求

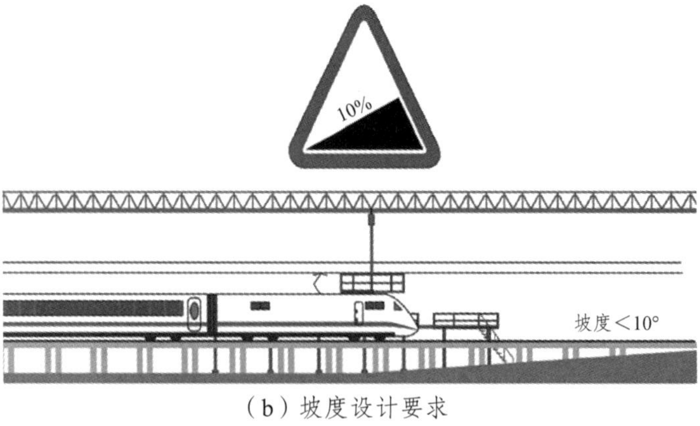

（b）坡度设计要求

图 5-6　库线设计要求

库内应设有更换转向架、轮对、车顶、车下主要部件的设备。转向架和轮对更换，优选采用活动轨道桥及气垫技术进行。

（2）大修库设计要求。

库内股道上方接触网可设置活动式刚性接触网侧移及控制设备。应设安全保护措施以确保作业人员的安全。大修库设三层作业面立体大修线，库线间距为 12 m，库内外侧股道距离修车库侧墙轴线应不小于 6.5 m。大修作业采用整列架车方式，实行部件换件修。设贯通式天车起重设备，如图 5-7 所示。

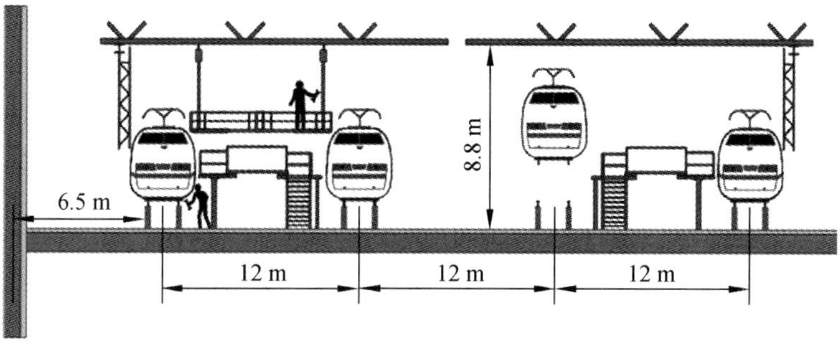

图 5-7　大修库设计要求

4. 作业面

为了进行并行作业，提高检修的效率，检修基地一般设置三层或四层作业面进行高速列车的维修。

（1）三层作业面，如图 5-8 所示。

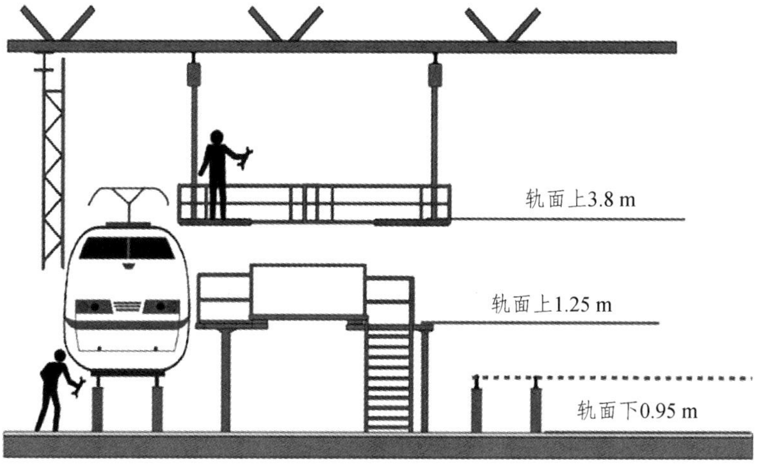

图 5-8　三层作业面

第一层设在轨面以下 0.95 m 标高处，为基本作业平台，用于走行部及下部设施检查、维修和材料运输。

第二层设在轨面以上 1.25 m 标高处，为车内及侧墙作业平台。

第三层设在轨面以上 3.8 m 标高处，为车顶作业平台。无车顶作业平台一侧应设置防止车顶作业人员跌落的防护设施。

（2）四层作业面，如图 5-9 所示。

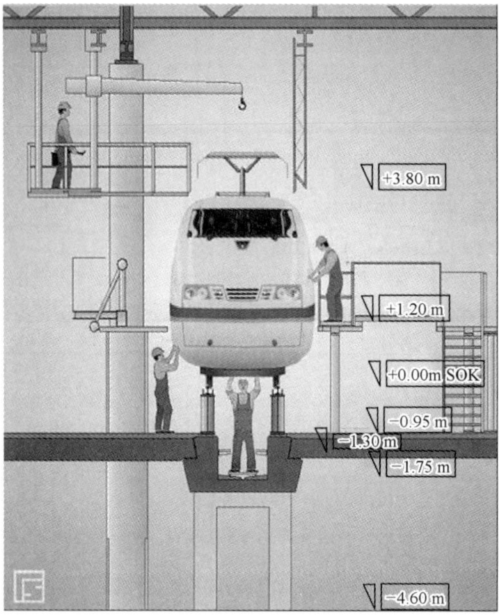

图 5-9　四层作业面

一层作业面（－0.95 m）负责列车底部的检查修理。

二层作业面（+1.2 m）用于车内作业。

三层作业面（+3.8 m）采用移动式空中平台。

四层作业面（－4.6 m）除运输外，安装所有的管线。

5. 主要零、配件辅助检修设施

基地中设置适当场所供主要零部件开展必要的检修工作，主要有转向架间、牵引电机间、变压器间、变流器间、电气及控制设备间、受电弓间、制动设备间、空调设备间、车内设备间。设施能力满足生产需要，布局符合工艺流畅要求。

基地内部检修设施，完成其他配件的检修工作。配件的修配车间应以检修库为主体进行设置。辅助车间主要有：蓄电池间、计量仪表间、材料库等。

6. 组织机构

每个检修基地都设置了若干行政机构，机构间共同协调工作，完成检修任务，其组织机构示例如图 5-10 所示。

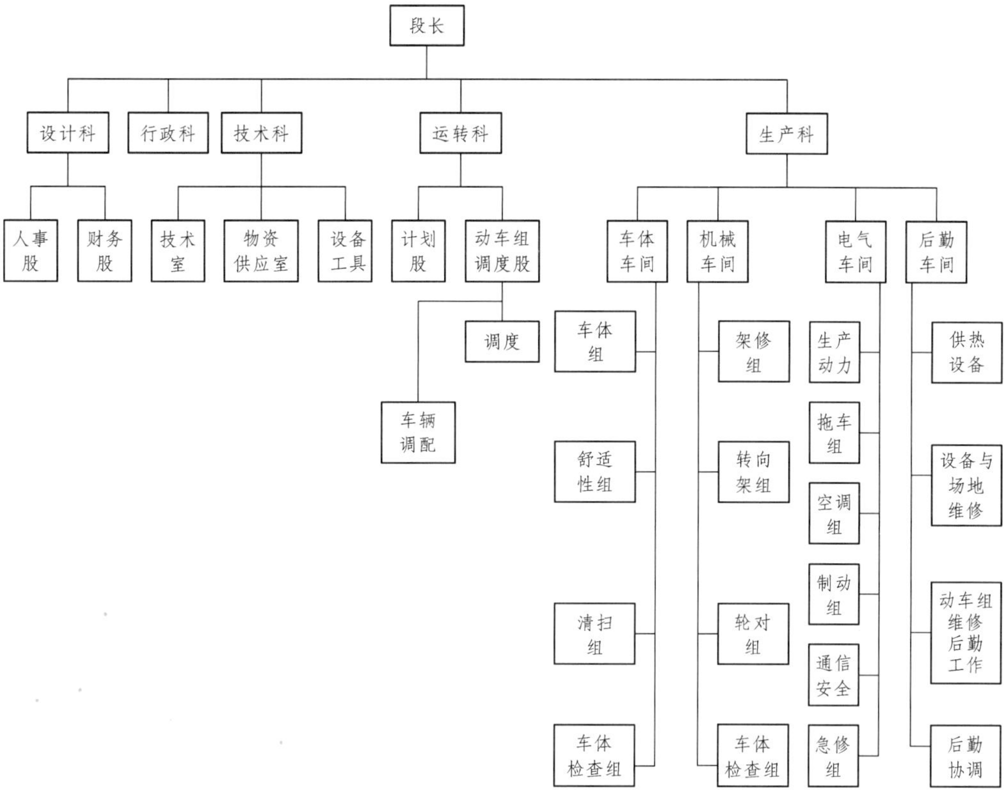

图 5-10　检修基地组织机构示例

三、动车组主要检修设备

动车组的高技术要求催生了动车组检修设备的更新换代，从移动式架车机到地坑式架车机，动车组检修设备有了高速的发展。动车组的整备、维修是保证动车组有效使用和运用质量的前提条件，是高速铁路系统综合保障工程中的重要组成部分。在高速动车组状态监测与故障诊断中，先进技术与智能化、集成化诊断设备的广泛运用，是提升检修质量、提高作业效率的基本要素。

动车组的检修工艺流程见图 5-11，大抵包括入段、外部清洗、踏面诊断、内部修整（库内作业，维修周期作业，修理作业，内部清洗，消毒，物料供给等项目），最后等待、出段。这些流程要求我们检修更加严格精细。

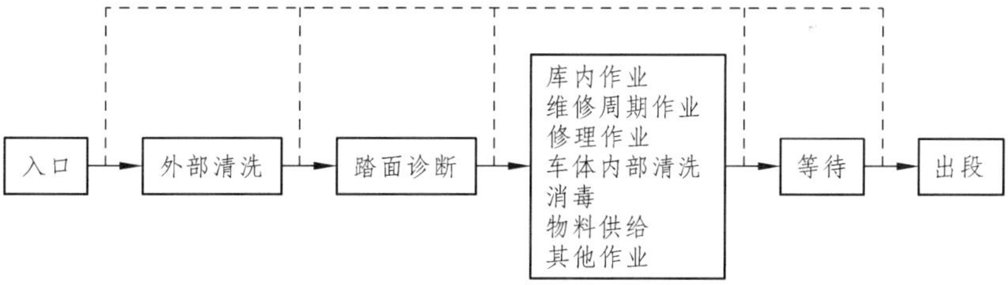

图 5-11　动车组检修工艺流程

1. 动车运用所的基本配置要求

（1）车体自动清洗设备。

（2）地面吸污设施，必要时还要配置移动设备。

（3）不落轮镟装置。

（4）轮对踏面检测设备。

（5）列车监控系统地面接收及信息处理设备。

（6）足够的存放线路。

（7）检修库与临修库。

（8）必要的系统检测设备和机械动力设备。

（9）生产及安全信息管理系统。

2. 动车组检修基地基本配置要求

（1）车体自动清洗设备。

（2）地面吸污设备。

（3）不落轮镟装置。

（4）轮对踏面检测设备。

（5）列车监控系统地面接收及信息处理设备。

（6）足够的存放线路。

（7）车体检修库、油漆库。

（8）转向架检修库（间）及试验设施。

（9）轮对、轴承检修库（间）及检测试验设备。

（10）制动系统检修库（间）及检测试验设备。

（11）牵引系统检修库（间）及检测试验设备。

（12）辅助供电系统检修库（间）及检测试验设备。

（13）车钩及缓冲装置检修库（间）和检修检测设备。

（14）车体气密性试验设备。

（15）其他部件检修场所及检修、检测、试验设备。

（16）单车试验设施。

（17）ATC 试验设施。

（18）必要时在场内设试运行线路。

（19）生产及安全信息管理系统。

3. 主要工具设备介绍

（1）综合检修库内专用设备：

① 带轨道桥的架空轨道系统（或同步架机车）。

② 动力转向架和中间车轮对快速更换设备。

③ 轮对转动设备。

④ 库内列车集便箱真空排污设备。

⑤ 作业升降车。

⑥ 蓄电池充电设备。

⑦ 动力车自动上砂设备。

（2）主要检修试验专用设备：

① ATC 传感器。

② 传感器性能测试台。

③ 真空断路器试验台。

④ 电气回路综合试验台。

⑤ 电气仪表测试台。

⑥ 受电弓磨耗板自动检测装置。

⑦ 转向架、构架、轮对、轴承、牵引机电等主要零部件清洗设备。

⑧ 动力转向架解体及组装设备。

⑨ 盘行制动装置性能试验台。

⑩ 液压减振器性能试验台。

⑪ 各种阀类性能试验台。

⑫ 立体货架及液压提升装置。

⑬ 生产管理计算机控制系统。

⑭ 红外线轴温探测复示设备。

⑮ 自动驾驶模拟装置。

（3）轮对及转向架更换装置。

当高速列车的动车及拖车轮对和转向架出了故障时应进行更换。转向架更换设备是检修基地、运用所必不可少的重要设备，是提高检修效率、提高动车组周转效率的有力保证。从更换方式上来说，可分为两种：活动轨道桥转向架下降方式及同步架车方式。

图 5-12 所示为活动轨道桥方式更换转向架设备，这种方式设备规模小，操作人员效率较高。

图 5-12　活动轨道桥方式更换转向架设备

图 5-13 所示为同步架车转向架更换设备。使用时，每个单元一般应用 4 个架车机，

断开转向架与车体的联结，架车机同时提升，架起车体，推出转向架。由于整列车通过密接式车钩连接，车钩配合间隙很小，所以，对架车机的同步性提出了较高的要求。这种方式设备规模大，一般以 4～8 辆为单位一同起重升起，需要多个操作人员同时工作，容易产生作业损耗。

图 5-13　同步架车转向架更换设备

（4）超声波探伤设备。

图 5-14 给出了几种超声波探伤设备。其中（a）所示为超声探伤台位上检测车轴示例；（b）所示为超声波探伤机探测空心轴，用于检测车轴内部缺陷；（c）所示为踏面超声波检测设备。

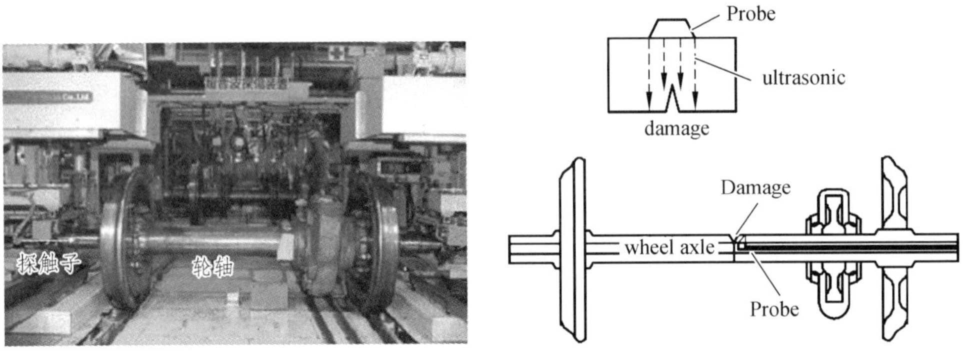

（a）超声探伤台位上检测车轴示例

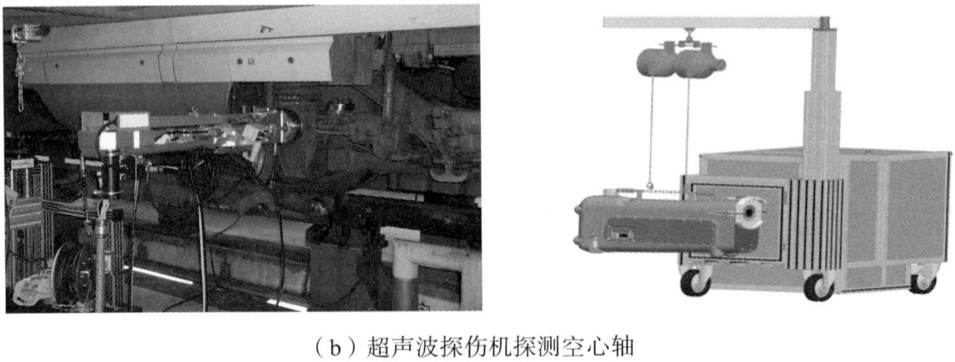

（b）超声波探伤机探测空心轴

（c）踏面超声波检测设备

图 5-14　超声波探伤设备

（5）不落轮镟装置。

当踏面诊断装置诊断出轮对有缺陷（擦伤等）或轮对踏面、轮缘磨耗到限时，应及时进行磨削和检修，以恢复动车组运行的舒适度并确保行车安全。该装置的特点是转向架无需从动车组车体落下分离，动车组直接驶入设备移动轨道上（设备安装于地坑内），通过该设备直接镟修，减少了设备镟修时间及检修人员的工作强度，如图 5-15 所示。

图 5-15　不落轮镟装置

（6）轮对踏面检测设备。

轮对踏面形状直接影响列车的舒适度和行车安全，高速列车尤为如此。轮对踏面诊断装置是检修基地、运用所最重要的检修诊断设备，具有检测踏面裂纹和擦伤、测量踏面形状和几何尺寸、测量踏面擦伤和同心度等功能。该装置同时具备数据的采集和处理功能，并与段内通信计算机联网，完成数据存储、显示、打印、传递等功能。该检测装置的准确度直接影响着整列车的检修效率。图 5-16 所示为线路上的轮对踏面检测设备。

图 5-16　轮对踏面检测设备

（7）车体自动清洗设备。

动车组外皮清洗设备是必不可少的整备设备，用于列车回库、进段时的外皮自动清洗，需用专门的清洗剂。为了满足环保、节能的要求，必须同时建立水循环处理设施（见图 5-17、图 5-18）。

图 5-17　洗车机设备组成示意图

图 5-18　车体自动清洗设备

（8）动车集便箱真空排污设备。

解决高速动车组污物收集及处理，在段内设置一套排污系统。排污作业应尽量与检修整备作业在同一地点进行，以缩短动车组的在段停留时间。排污地面设施主要采用真空抽吸式排污系统，如图 5-19 所示。

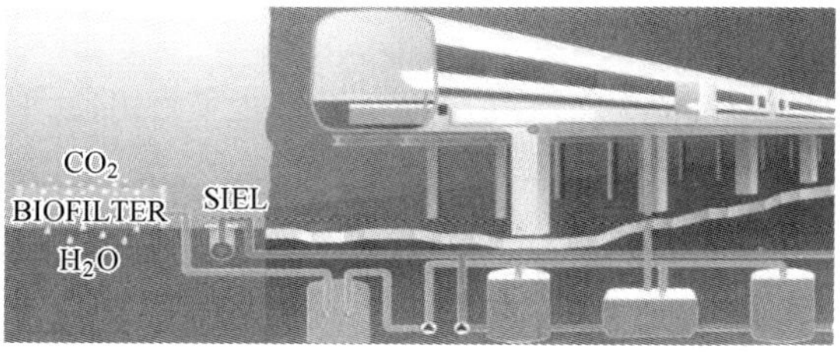

（a）吸污设备原理图

（b）吸污现场

图 5-19　真空排污设备

【任务检测】

1. 我国动车组有哪几种维修机构？各自功能是什么？
2. 简述我国维修基地、运用所的布局。
3. 简述动车组入运用所后的检修流程。
4. 简述检修基地中三层、四层作业面的概念。
5. 检修基地有哪些主要的检修设备？
6. 画出检修基地直列式布局图。

任务三　动车组运用级检修作业流程

【任务描述】

（1）熟知动车组运用级检修作业流程。

（2）能够按照动车组一级检修作业标准完成作业。

CRH 系列各型号动车组的运用级检修（一、二级检修）的作业分工、作业程序、作业步骤、作业流程基本相同，检修范围、检修限度、专项作业内容及方法因车型而异。以下针对动车组一、二级检修内容做详细说明。

一、动车组一级检修

1. 检修周期

（1）动车组一级检修周期执行《中国铁路总公司关于印发<铁路动车组运用维修规则>的通知》（铁总运〔2017〕238 号）规定周期标准。动车组实行以走行公里周期为主、时间周期为辅（先到为准）的计划预防修。（具体检修周期见表 6-1）

（2）临修、二级检修及高级检修动车组修竣后，上线运营前须进行一级检修。

（3）动车组担当热备前须进行一次一级检修作业；动车组累计备用（含热备）时间超过 48h 上线运营前须进行一级检修；上线运营后按运行线路上的动车组一级检修周期规定执行。

2. 检修范围

一级检修是对运用动车组车顶、车下、车体两侧、车内和司机室等部位实施快速例行检查、试验和故障处理的检修作业，须在动车所检查库内实施。

3. 人员配备和分工

（1）短编动车组（8 辆编组）

检修作业小组 1 个（①、②、③、④号共 4 名作业人员），其他辅助人员 2 名（⑤、⑥号），接触网工 2 名。小组①号为该检修小组组长，负责整体工作安排。

①、②号负责车顶设备、司机室设备、车内设备、车载信息系统等设备的检查工作；③、④号负责车体、裙板、底板、转向架、制动、钩缓连接等车体两侧及车下地沟检查，负责止轮器的设置、撤除等工作；2 名接触网工负责入库清道、隔离开关供断电操作；2 名其他辅助人员（⑤、⑥号）协助检查，⑤号具体负责配合技术员进行动车组车载数据下载、配合相关一体化部门作业、动车组相关试验和配合①、②号车顶作业时升降受电弓操作等工作，⑥号协助作业小组处理动车组临修故障、接插外接电源、配件领送等工作。

车顶和司机室故障，由①、②号自检自修，质检进行确认；③、④号检查发现的故障由⑥号进行处理，③、④号进行确认、协助检查；立岗接送车作业原则上由③、④号作业人员负责，作业人员紧张时工长可安排⑤、⑥号作业人员负责，⑤、⑥号应及时将接送车作业情况向③、④号反馈。

注：（1）③、④号在检查各自侧驱动装置齿轮箱时，与齿轮箱连接的牵引电机归齿轮箱检查侧作业人员检查；（2）③、④号车下地沟作业，前后须保持间隔 3 米左右；（3）动车组立岗接送车工作由动车段自行安排实施。

（2）长编（重联）动车组（16 辆）：

检修作业小组 2 个（8 名作业人员），接触网工 2 名，其他辅助人员 2 名。

1）长编动车组。

每个作业小组对长编动车组中的 8 辆车进行检修。主控钥匙、供断电申请等由动车组入库方向作业小组的①号负责，08 ~ 09 车间设备的检查由动车组入库方向作业小组负责。其他作业人员分工由动车段比照短编动车组（8 辆编组）进行明确。

2）重联动车组。

每个作业小组对 1 组动车组进行检修。主控钥匙、供断电申请等由动车组入库方向作业小组的①号负责。重联端钩缓、风管连接等设备的检查由动车组入库方向作业小组负责。其他作业人员分工由动车段比照短编动车组（8 辆编组）进行明确。

（3）专业分工

① 机务司机负责司机室内卫生，终到后对司机室内杂物清除，区域内设备整理归位。

② 客运部门负责动车组客室内卫生间、餐饮设备、旅客服务设施等设施的保洁工作，清除车内杂物，整理归位客室座椅，关闭各冰箱、柜门、抽屉，关闭或断开用电设备电源。

③ 车轮故障在线检测系统、受电弓及车顶状态动态检测系统、动车组运行故障图像检测系统数据的分析和动车组入库后车体外皮清洗、卸污作业、动车检修有关的隔离开关操作和较大故障处理修复等工作由动车段负责。

④ 车载 LKJ、ATP、CIR、EOAS 等电务设备及附属设施的专业维修由电务部门负责。

⑤ 动车组车载接触网检测装置（3C）等供电设备及附属设施的专业维修由供电部门负责。

⑥ 各专业在动车所检修作业完毕后的材料配件整理、工具定置管理、废旧物品清理工作应按照动车所现场管理规定执行。

（4）人员分配

针对短编、长编（重联）动车组检修作业中接触网工、辅助人员的配备及分工，动车段要结合实际不断调整优化。

4. 检修模式

（1）动车组一级检修可采用无电（可接外接电源）-有电或有电-无电-有电作业模式。动车组一级检修主要技术作业时间：检查库内预留 4 h（需融冰除雪时 6 h）。

① 一级检修作业采用无电-有电检修模式。

a. 无电检修项目：车顶、地沟、客室设施及辆动-181 故障处理等。

b. 有电检修项目：车侧检查、各设备供电功能试验、客室设施故障处理复查。电务、通信检测作业，司机室、车内设备设施检查及制动保压试验，车辆设备供电状态检查，辆动-181 故障处理等。

② 一级检修作业采用有电-无电-有电一级检修模式。

a. 有电预检项目：电务、通信检测作业，司机室、车内设备设施检查，车辆设备供电状态检查，车侧检查，辆动-181 故障处理等。

b. 无电检修项目：车顶、地沟检查，客室设施及辆动-181 故障处理等。

c. 有电检修项目：各设备供电功能试验、车侧检查、客室设施故障处理复查等。

（2）动车组车内保洁、外皮清洁、吸污作业、上水作业，由动车段组织一体化相关单位根据《动车组运用检修一体化管理办法》和一级检修作业模式组织实施。

（3）一级检修作业应全面执行动车组检修“必看、必指、必呼、必画”作业要求，具体内容要在一级修作业指导书中明确。

（4）质检员对车内服务设施检修作业质量检查可结合出库联检一并实施。

（5）一级检修完毕后，质检员组织各专业检修作业组进行出库联检作业。

5. 检修作业流程和线路图

1）一级检修流程

① 无电-有电一级检修模式，如图 5-20 所示。

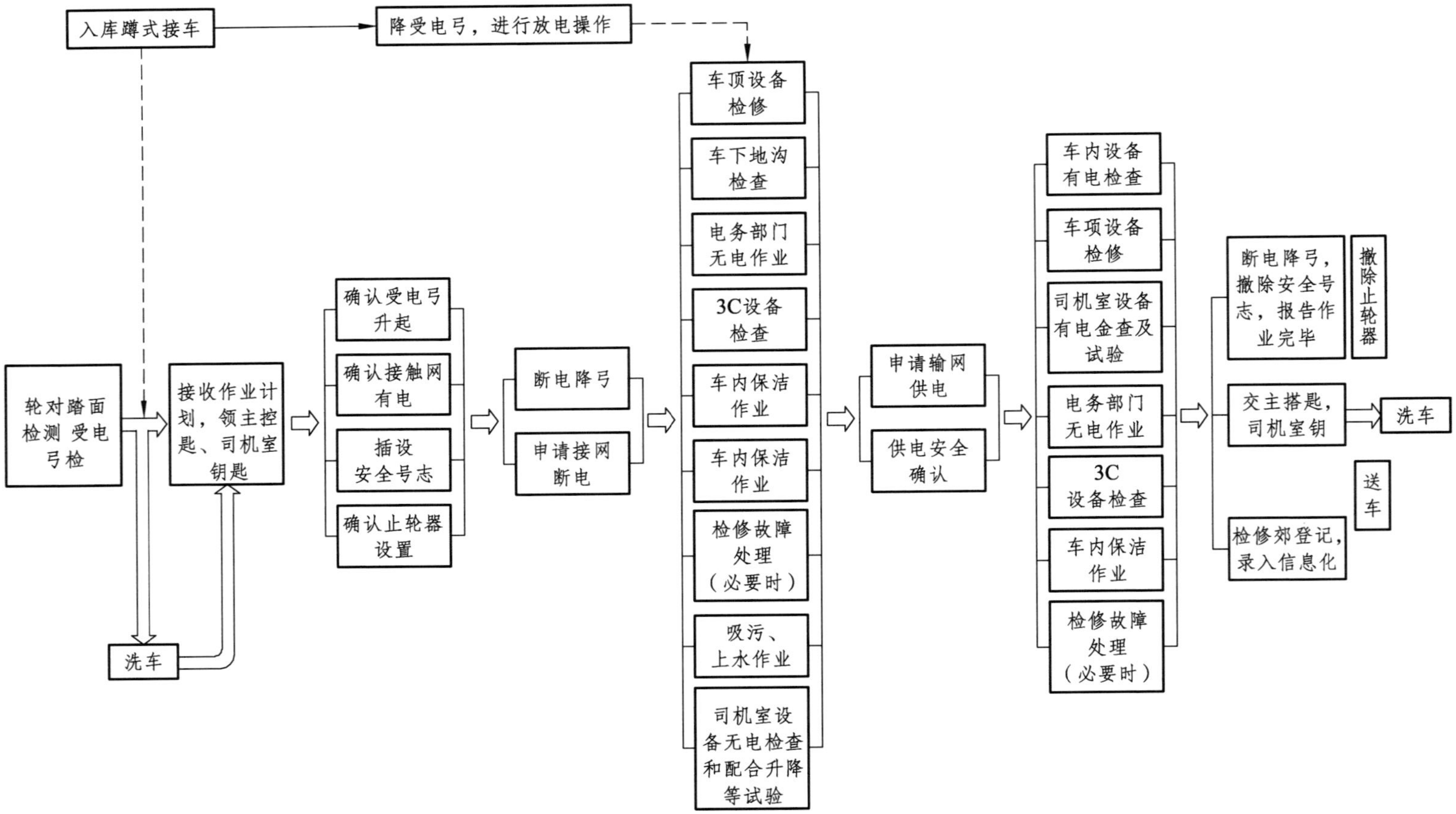

图 5-20　动车组一级检修作业流程

（2）一级检修作业流程时间节点（无电+有电），如图 5-21 所示。

<table>
<tr><td>时间
作业部门</td><td>10</td><td>20</td><td>30</td><td>40</td><td>50</td><td>60</td><td>80</td><td>90</td><td>100</td><td>110</td><td>120</td><td>150</td><td>140</td></tr>
<tr><td>供断电组</td><td colspan="6"></td><td>供电作业</td><td colspan="6"></td></tr>
<tr><td>技术组</td><td colspan="6">数据下载、分析；运行故障检查、故障处理</td><td></td><td colspan="6">故障判定</td></tr>
<tr><td>主机厂售后</td><td colspan="6">无电检查、运行故障检查、故障处理</td><td></td><td colspan="6">有电检查、故障判定</td></tr>
<tr><td>一级修组（①、②、⑤）</td><td colspan="6">车顶设备检查</td><td></td><td colspan="6">车内设施检查、司机室设备功能试验、故障判定试验</td></tr>
<tr><td>一级修组（③、④）</td><td colspan="6">车底设备检查</td><td></td><td colspan="6">车体两侧检查、故障判定试验</td></tr>
<tr><td>电务部门</td><td colspan="6">ATP、CIR无电检查</td><td></td><td colspan="6">ATP、CIR有电检查</td></tr>
<tr><td>供电部门</td><td colspan="6">3C设备无电检查</td><td></td><td colspan="6">3C设备有电检查</td></tr>
<tr><td>外协部门</td><td colspan="6">吸污、上水、外皮清洗、滤网清洁、高压设备擦拭作业</td><td></td><td colspan="6"></td></tr>
<tr><td>客运部门</td><td colspan="13">车内保洁</td></tr>
<tr><td colspan="14">备注：各作业部门要严格按照该时间节点进行作业，动车所值班室要注意时间节点的卡控，确保作业流畅。</td></tr>
</table>

图 5-21　动车组一级检修作业流程（无电+有电）时间节点图

2）CRH380A 型动车组一级检修作业线路

（1）车顶无电作业路线（①、②号无电作业路线），如图 5-22 所示。

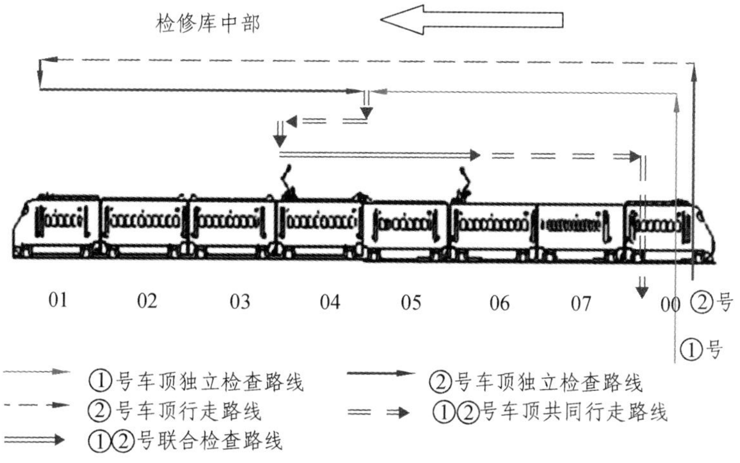

图 5-22　车顶无电作业路线图

（2）车下无电作业路线（③、④号无电作业路线），如图 5-23 所示。

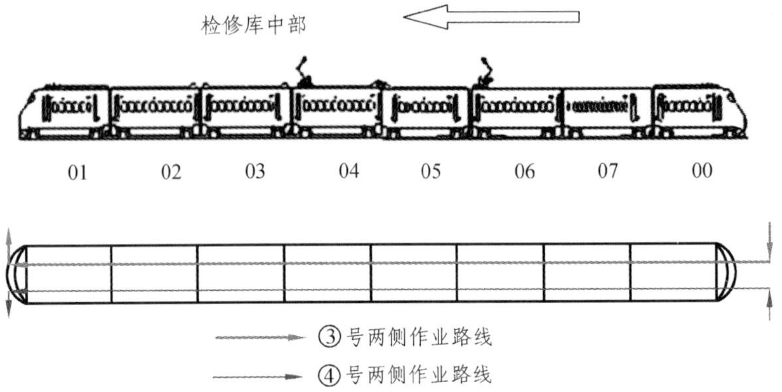

图 5-23　车下无电作业线路图

（3）车内有电作业路线（①、②号有电作业路线），如图 5-24 所示。

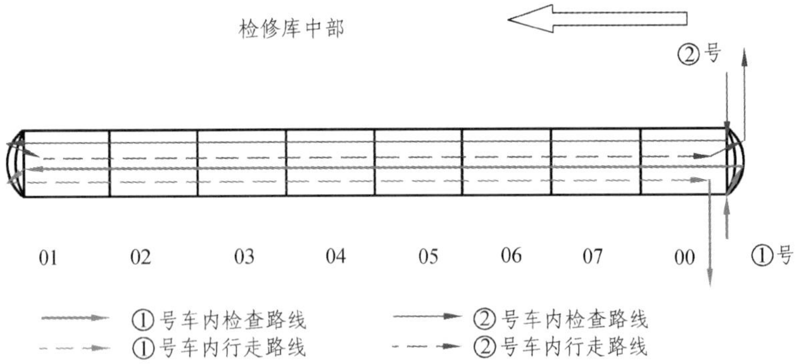

图 5-24　车内有电作业路线图

（4）车下两侧有电作业路线（③、④号有电作业路线），如图 5-25 所示。

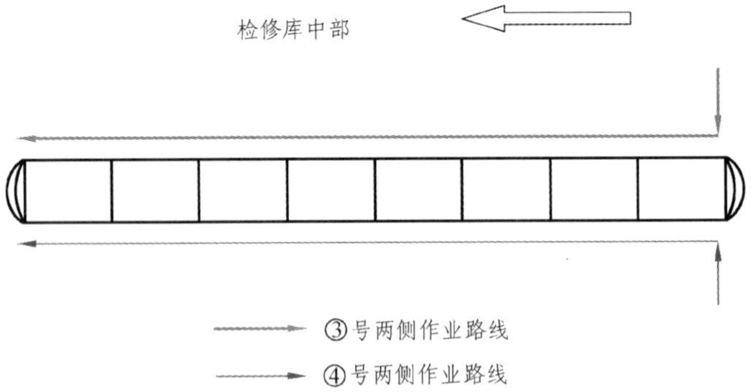

图 5-25　车下两侧有电作业路线图

3）CRH380A（L）型动车组检修作业路线图

（1）车顶无电作业路线（①、②号无电作业路线），如图 5-26 所示。

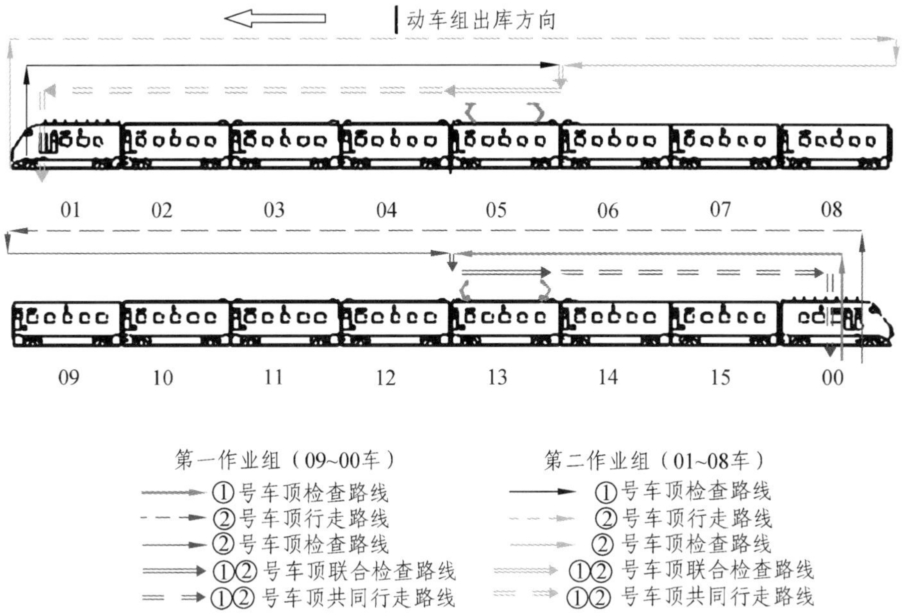

图 5-26　车顶无电作业路线图

（2）车下无电作业路线（③、④号无电作业路线），如图 5-27 示。

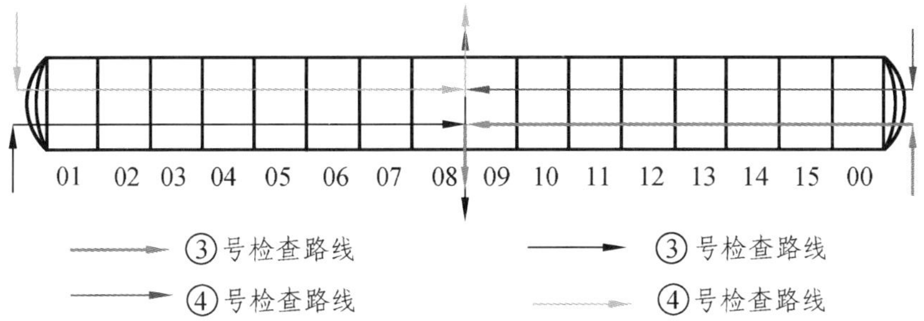

图 5-27　车下无电作业线路图

（3）车内有电作业路线（①、②号有电作业路线），如图 5-28 所示。

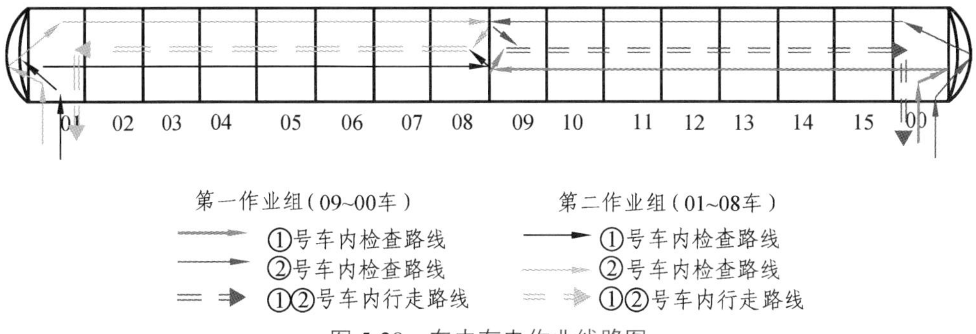

图 5-28　车内有电作业线路图

（4）车下两侧有电作业路线（③、④号有电作业路线），如图 5-29 所示。

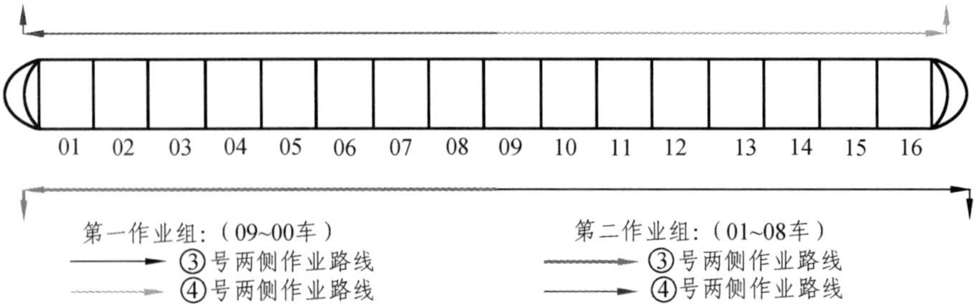

图 5-29　车下两侧有电作业线路图

6. 检修要求

（1）一级检修动车组入库前须使用车轮故障在线检测系统、受电弓及车顶状态动态检测系统等检测设备检测，检测数据须由专人及时进行专题分析。

（2）动车组各车水箱水位在 25%以上、污物箱必须抽空，满足动车组给排水卫生系统具备检修、试验作业条件。

（3）检修作业小组要提前接受作业计划，通过动车组管理信息系统导出待检动车组故障，①号了解动车组运行重点故障，并领取主控钥匙、司机室钥匙，做好作业准备工作。

（4）动车组进库时，接车人员须在动车所入库的指定位置接车，听取转向架及车下设备运转有无异音，检查车号和目的地显示器、侧门关闭及指示灯显示等设备状态。待动车组在库内停妥后，向检修作业小组报告接车情况。动车组在库内停妥并设置止轮器后，按照一级检修流程开始作业，同时按照时间节点做好刷卡确认工作。

二、动车组二级检修

1. 检修周期

（1）动车组二级检修是对动车组各系统、零部件实施的周期性维护保养、检测、试验，不得漏项、超期。

（2）二级检修可采用扣车检修或结合一级检修的方式进行。

（3）动车组检修周期以走行公里为主、时间周期为辅的检修模式，以先到为准。

（4）各项目具体检修周期以集团公司规定周期为准。以走行公里周期实施的二级检修项目允许延后 10%组织实施（有调整检修周期范围的除外）；以时间周期实施的二级检修项目必须在规定时间内完成。

2. 检修范围

二级检修作业项目由预防性检修和更正性检修两部分组成。预防性检修明确了检修项目、检修周期和对应的维修标准；更正性检修是出现故障以后实施的检修，动车段根据运用故障情况，完善更正性检修项目内容及要求，同时固化结合动车组春秋整实施的项目，并及时上报车辆处。

3. 检修作业管理

（1）动车段可根据动车组运用情况，对二级检修实行均衡修或集中修模式。

（2）二级检修以平行作业、立体化作业为基础，突出“专岗、专人、专修”检修，杜绝交叉作业。动车段要加强检修工具、物料管理，全面推行各项目的辆份制配送工作，规范现场作业。

（3）动车段要不断完善动车组状态检测、人员作业监控等工作，建立健全管理制度，配备设备检修和数据分析人员，积极开展数据综合分析运用，不断规范业务流程，改进检修工艺，优化修程修制，保证作业顺畅有序，质量可控。

【任务检测】

1. 简述 CRH380A（L）一级检修作业流程。
2. 简述 CRH380A 动车组检修作业分工情况。
3. 简述 CRH380A（L）动车组检修作业分工情况。
4. 画出 CRH380A（L）型动车组一级检修无电作业线路。
5. 画出 CRH380A（L）型动车组一级检修有电作业线路。

参考文献

[1] 焦凤川，王斌杰. 动车组运用与管理[M]. 北京：北京交通大学出版社，2012.

[2] 王连森，连苏宁. 动车组维护与检修[M]. 成都：西南交通大学出版社，2010.

[3] 王伯铭. 动车组运用与检修[M]. 北京：中国铁道出版社，2011.

[4] 中国铁路总公司.《铁路技术管理规程》(高速铁路部分) [M]. 北京：中国铁道出版社，2017.

[5] 中国铁路总公司. CRH380A 型动车组途中应急故障处理手册[M]. 北京：中国铁道出版社，2019.